THE LONGMAN DICTIONARY OF

FRENCH

GRAMMAR

AND IDIOMS

ANDRÉ HURTGEN

Longman

**The Longman Dictionary of French Grammar
  and Idioms**

Longman, 95 Church Street, White Plains, N.Y. 10601

Associated companies:
Longman Group Ltd., London
Longman Cheshire Pty., Melbourne
Longman Paul Pty., Auckland
Copp Clark Pitman, Toronto

Executive editor: Lyn McLean
Production editor: Dee Amir Josephson
Text design: Dee Amir Josephson
Cover design: Joseph de Pinho

ISBN 0-8013-0547-0 (ppr)
ISBN 0-8013-0560-8 (csd)

1 2 3 4 5 6 7 8 9 10-MA-95 94 93 92 91 90

INTRODUCTION

This is a dictionary, not a textbook or a workbook. Its aim is to provide clear and convenient assistance to students and other users or lovers of the French language who are unsure of, or have completely forgotten, a rule of grammar, an irregular verb, an idiomatic construction, or some other aspect of the tongue.

Language is a complex set of rules, conventions, and idioms, some of them logical, others seemingly flouting common sense. Learning them—or even looking them up—in isolation is no recipe for mastery of a language. It makes no more sense to memorize idioms or grammatical rules out of context than it does to commit to memory lists of vocabulary words. Language must be considered and studied as a whole. This is best done by *living* the language, the way all of us learned our mother tongue.

In practice and of necessity, however, most foreign-language teaching and learning takes place in the artificial context of a classroom. Rules are learned piecemeal, drilled and practiced, and then gradually forgotten as additional material is accumulated. The same is true of vocabulary, much of which the student learns, practices a bit, and then slowly forgets. But here the problem is readily overcome: The forgotten word can be looked up in the dictionary. What to do, though, when a grammar rule has been forgotten? Looking it up in an old first- or second-year textbook (if still on hand) is no simple task. The material there is generally presented in small segments. Conjugations, irregular verbs, rules of syntax, idioms, and the like are scattered all over the book and certainly not listed in alphabetical order.

This dictionary is designed to help solve this problem. It lists alphabetically (French and English combined) the following types of items:

Common French and English abbreviations
Common French and English idioms
Conjugations of regular and irregular verbs
Definitions of grammatical terms
French and English conjunctions and prepositions
Function-related expressions and structures
Letter-writing conventions
Punctuation rules, diacritical marks, and accents
Rules of French grammar and syntax
The metric system and Celsius and Fahrenheit scales

The entries in this work do not pretend to be exhaustive. Rules and common exceptions are stated succinctly and as clearly as possible. Examples in French (with English translations) are provided in every case. Cross references direct the user to all other entries in the dictionary where the same point is discussed.

Suppose, for instance, that the user has forgotten how to say *ago* in French. He may look it up under that word. If the question occurs to him in the form: "What does *Il y a dix minutes* mean?" he will find the answer under the headings **IL YA + TIME EXPRESSION** and **TIME EXPRESSIONS.**

A user who is confused as to the difference between *à cause de and parce que* will find help under **À CAUSE DE vs. PARCE QUE,** where cross-references will direct him also to **BECAUSE vs. BECAUSE OF** and **PUISQUE,** which is a related topic. One who is not sure how to convey *would* in French will find help under the headings **WOULD, IMPERFECT TENSE, HABITUAL ACTIONS,** and **CONDITIONAL MOOD.**

ACKNOWLEDGMENTS

Many people have contributed to this dictionary. First and foremost among them are my students who, by their persistent questions and repeated requests for explanations and clarifications, constantly reminded me that French grammar is hard to learn and easy to forget. They gave me the inspiration to prepare this dictionary. Emily Buxton and Amy Remus in particular should be mentioned for making valuable suggestions and pointing out deficiencies. My colleague Terrence A. Wardrop's indispensable technical assistance, always proffered kindly and with a smile, rescued me on the many occasions when I nudged my word processor beyond its limits. My editor, Lyn McLean, offered enthusiasm and support from the first day to the last. Her wise counsel helped me over many hurdles throughout the past two years. Madeleine Cottenet-Hage and Charles R. Hancock read the manuscript from cover to cover. Their careful and meticulous checking improved the book immeasurably. Any and all remaining errors and omissions are, of course, my own. I ask that readers kindly bring them to my attention so that these failings may be corrected in later editions.

André Hurtgen

A

A, AN
See **ARTICLES, INDEFINITE**

À

(Preposition) (Contracts to *au* with *le* and *aux* with *les*.)
Its meaning depends on the context. It is used to express: (a) destination: "to"; (b) location: "in"; (c) time: "at"; (d) indirect object: "of"; (e) time frequency: "by"; (f) description of a characteristic or feature: "with"; (g) purpose: "for"; etc.

E.g.: (a) *Il va à Paris.*
　　　　He is going to Paris.
　　(b) *Il a mis le vin à la cave.*
　　　　He put the wine in the cellar.
　　(c) *Elles rentreront à onze heures.*
　　　　They will come home at eleven o'clock.
　　(d) *C'est aimable à vous de dire cela.*
　　　　It's kind of you to say that.
　　(e) *Il est payé à la semaine.*
　　　　He is paid by the week.
　　(f) *La fille à lunettes.*
　　　　The girl with the glasses.
　　(g) *Un pot à eau.*
　　　　A water jug.

See **ARTICLES, CONTRACTION OF**

À BIENTÔT

(Idiomatic expression) = "See you soon."
E.g.: *Je m'en vais. À bientôt!*
　　　I am leaving. See you soon!
See *À TOUT À L'HEURE*

À CAUSE DE vs. PARCE QUE

(1) The prepositional expression *À cause de* = "Because of." It introduces a noun or a pronoun.
　　E.g.: *Il n'est pas sorti à cause du froid.*
　　　　　He did not go out because of the cold.
(2) The conjunction *Parce que* = "Because." It introduces a clause.
　　E.g.: *Il n'est pas sorti parce qu'il faisait froid.*
　　　　　He did not go out because it was cold.

À CONDITION DE vs. À CONDITION QUE

"Provided (that)."
(1) The prepositional construction "*À condition de* + infinitive" is used when the subject of the main clause is the same as the subject of the subordinate.
　　E.g.: *J'irai en France à condition d'avoir assez d'argent.*
　　　　　I shall go to France provided I have enough money.
(2) The conjunctional construction "*À condition que* + subjunctive" is used when the subject of the subordinate clause is different from that of the main clause.
　　E.g.: *J'irai en France à condition que tu viennes avec moi.*
　　　　　I shall go to France provided you come with me.

1

À CONTRECŒUR

(Idiomatic expression) = "Unwillingly, against one's wishes."
E.g.: *Ils ont quitté leur pays natal à contrecœur.*
   They left their native land against their wishes.
See **DE BON CŒUR**

À vs. DE

See **ADJECTIVE + PREPOSITION + VERB**
See also **VERBS + PREPOSITION + INFINITIVE**

À FOND

(Idiomatic expression) = "Thoroughly."
E.g.: *Elle connaît à fond l'histoire de France.*
   She knows French history thoroughly.

À FORCE DE

(Prepositional construction) = "By dint of."
E.g.: *Il a réussi à force de travailler.*
   He succeeded by dint of hard work.

À LA LÉGÈRE

(Idiomatic expression) = "Lightly."
E.g.: *Tu traites tes études à la légère.*
   You are taking your studies lightly.

À LA LONGUE

(Idiomatic expression) = "In the long run, in time."
E.g.: *À la longue je me suis habitué à la cuisine chinoise.*
   In the long run I became accustomed to Chinese food.

À L'ÉGARD DE

(Prepositional construction) = "About, concerning."
E.g.: *Je voudrais vous voir à l'égard de cette affaire.*
   I'd like to see you about this business.
See **À PROPOS DE**

À L'ENDROIT

(Adverbial construction) = "Right side out, right way around."
E.g.: *Mettez votre pull-over à l'endroit!*
   Put your sweater on right side out!

À L'ENVERS

(Adverbial construction) = "Inside out" or "Upside down."
E.g.: *Tu as mis ton pull-over à l'envers.*
   You put your sweater on inside out.
   Il tient le journal à l'envers.
   He is holding the newspaper upside down.

A LITTLE

(Adverbial expression) = *Un peu.*
E.g.: *Il lit un peu chaque jour.*
   He reads a little each day.
   Elle est un peu nerveuse.
   She is a little nervous.

A LITTLE + NOUN

(Expression of quantity) = *Un peu de.*
E.g.: *Donnez-moi un peu de vin.*
　　　Give me a little wine.

À MOINS DE vs. À MOINS QUE

(1) The prepositional construction "*À moins de* + infinitive" is used when the subject of the main clause is the same as the subject of the subordinate clause.
　　E.g.: *Il partira demain à moins d'être retardé.*
　　　　　He will leave tomorrow unless he is delayed.
(2) The conjunctional construction "*À moins que* + subjunctive" is used when the subject of the main clause is different from the subject of the subordinate clause.
　　E.g.: *Nous partirons à moins que ta voiture ne soit pas prête.*
　　　　　We shall leave unless your car isn't ready.

À PARTIR DE

(Prepositional construction) = "From, beginning with."
E.g.: *Nous serons libres à partir de dix heures.*
　　　We shall be free from ten o'clock on.

À PEINE

(Adverbial expression) = "Scarcely, hardly, almost not."
E.g.: *Je comprends à peine le français.*
　　　I hardly understand French.
When it is at the beginning of a sentence, it is followed by inversion.
E.g.: *À peine étions-nous arrivés que nous avons dû repartir.*
　　　We had hardly arrived when we had to leave again.

À PEU PRÈS

(Idiomatic expression) = "(Just) about, near enough."
E.g.: *Le travail est à peu près terminé.*
　　　The job is just about finished.
See **ABOUT (meaning APPROXIMATELY)**

À PLUS FORTE RAISON

(Adverbial expression) = "All the more reason."
It comes at the beginning of the sentence and is followed by inversion.
E.g.: *Elle n'a jamais appris à lire. À plus forte raison ne sait-elle pas écrire.*
　　　She never learned to read. All the more reason why she can't write.

À PROPOS DE

(Prepositional construction) = "About, concerning."
E.g.: *Il est venu me voir à propos de son avancement.*
　　　He came to see me about his promotion.

À TORT OU À RAISON

(Idiomatic expression) = "Rightly or wrongly."
E.g.: *À tort ou à raison, il a décidé de quitter son poste.*
　　　Rightly or wrongly, he decided to quit his job.

À TOUT À L'HEURE

(Idiomatic expression) = "See you later."
E.g.: *Je dois m'en aller maintenant. À tout à l'heure.*
　　　I have to leave now. See you later.
See **À BIENTÔT**

À TRAVERS

(Prepositional construction) = "Across, through."
E.g.: *La balle est passée à travers le mur.*
    The bullet went through the wall.
See **ACROSS**

ABBREVIATIONS

(1) SOME COMMON FRENCH ABBREVIATIONS, WITH THEIR ENGLISH EQUIVALENTS
OR MEANINGS:

apr. J.-C.	= *après Jésus-Christ*	= A.D. (Anno domini)
av. J.-C.	= *avant Jésus-Christ*	= B.C. (Before Christ)
c.-à-d.:	= *c'est-à-dire*	= i.e. (that is)
C. C. P.	= *compte chèques postaux*	= Postal checking account
C. E. E.	= *Communauté économique Européenne*	= European Economic Community
CEDEX	= *Courrier d'entreprise à distribution exceptionnelle*	= Special business mail delivery
C. E. S.	= *Collège d'enseignement secondaire*	= four-year high school
C. Q. F. D.	= *Ce qu'il fallait démontrer*	= Q.E.D. (= *Quod erat demonstrandum*)
Dr	= *Docteur*	= Dr.
E	= *est*	= E. (East)
E. D. F.	= *Électricité de France*	= French electric company (public utility)
É.-U.	= *États-Unis*	= U.S.A.
e. v.	= *en ville*	= In town, downtown
F	= *franc(s)*	= Fr.
g	= *gramme(s)*	= gram(s)
G. D. F.	= *Gas de France*	= French natural gas service
hab.	= *habitants*	= inhabitants
H. L. M.	= *habitation à loyer modéré*	= low-income housing
J.-C.	= *Jésus-Christ*	= Jesus Christ
j. f.	= *jeune fille*	= young woman
j. h.	= *jeune homme*	= young man
kg	= *kilogramme(s)*	= kilogram(s)
km/h	= *kilomètres à l'heure*	= kph (kilometers per hour)
l	= *litre*	= liter
M.	= *Monsieur*	= Mr.
Mgr	= *Monseigneur*	= Monsignor
MM.	= *Messieurs*	= Messrs.
Mlle	= *Mademoiselle*	= Miss
Mlles	= *Mesdemoiselles*	= Misses
Mme	= *Madame*	= Mrs.
Mmes	= *Mesdames*	= Mrs. (plural)
N	= *nord*	= N., No. (North)
N.-D.	= *Notre-Dame*	= Our Lady
N. S. J.-C.	= *Notre Seigneur Jésus-Christ*	= Our Lord Jesus Christ
O	= *ouest*	= W (West)
O. N. U.	= *Organisation des Nations unies*	= UN
O. P. E. P.	= *Organisation des pays exportateurs de pétrole*	= OPEC
O. R. T. F.	= *Office de la radiodiffusion et télévision françaises*	= French Radio and Television Corporation

O. T. A. N.	= *Organisation du traité de l'Atlantique nord*	= NATO
P. D. G.	= *Président-directeur général*	= CEO
p. ex.	= *par exemple*	= E.g.
P. J.	= *Police judiciaire*	= FBI (US); CID (GB)
P. M. U.	= *Pari mutuel urbain*	= Official (legal) betting system
p. p.	= *par procuration*	= by proxy
P. et T.	= *Postes et télécommunications*	= Postal and telecommunications service
p.-v.	= *procès-verbal*	= traffic ticket
qqch.	= *quelque chose*	= something
qqn	= *quelqu'un*	= someone
R. A. T. P.	= *Régie autonomes des transports parisiens*	= Paris Public Transport Authority
R. D. A.	= *République démocratique allemande*	= East Germany
R. F. A.	= *République fédérale allemande*	= West Germany
R. E. R.	= *Réseau express régional*	= Express Suburban Network
R. F.	= *République française*	= French Republic
R. N.	= *route nationale*	= national highway
R. S. V. P.	= *répondez, s'il vous plaît*	= RSVP
s.	= *siècle*	= century
S	= *sud*	= S. So. (South)
S^t, S^{te}	= *saint(e)*	= St.
S. A.	= *société anonyme*	= Inc., Corp.
SIDA	= *Syndrome Immuno-Déficitaire Acquis*	= AIDS
S. M.	= *Sa Majesté*	= His Majesty, Her Majesty
S. M. I. C.	= *salaire minimum interprofessionnel de croissance*	= minimum wage
S. M. I. G.	= *salaire minimum interprofessionnel garanti*	= guaranteed minimum wage
S. N. C. F.	= *Société nationale des chemins de fer français*	= French National Railroads Company
S. V. P.	= *s'il vous plaît*	= please
T. G. V.	= *train à grande vitesse*	= high-speed train
T. S. F.	= *télégraphie sans fil*	= (wireless) radio
T. S. V. P.	= *tournez, s'il vous plaît*	= over, PTO (please turn over)
T. T. C.	= *toutes taxes comprises*	= all taxes included
T. V. A.	= *taxe sur la valeur ajoutée*	= VAT (value-added tax)

(2) SOME COMMON ENGLISH ABBREVIATIONS AND THEIR FRENCH EQUIVALENTS:

A.D.	= anno Domini	= *après J.-C.*
AIDS	= acquired immune deficiency syndrome	= *SIDA*
aka	= also known as	= *alias*
A.M.	= ante meridiem (before noon)	= *avant-midi*
ASAP	= as soon as possible	= *aussitôt que possible*
B.C.	= before Christ	= *avant J.-C.*
CEO	= chief executive office	= *P. D. G.*
Co.	= company	= *Cie*
doz.	= dozen	= *douzaine*
Dr.	= Doctor	= *Dr*
e.g.	= exempli gratia	= *p. ex.*
GB	= Great Britain	= *G. B.*

GMT	= Greenwich Mean Time	= *TU (temps universel)*
i.e.	= id est	= *c.-à-d.*
in.	= inch(es)	= *pouce(s)*
Inc.	= Incorporated	= *S. A.*
IOU	= I owe you	= *reconnaissance de dette*
Jr.	= Junior	= *fils*
lb.	= pound(s)	= *livre(s)*
M.D.	= Doctor of Medicine	= *docteur en médecine*
mi.	= mile(s)	= *mille(s)*
mpg	= miles per gallon	= *milles au gallon*
mph	= miles per hour	= *milles à l'heure*
NATO	= North Atlantic Treaty Organization	= *O. T. A. N.*
OPEC	= Organization of Petroleum Exporting Countries	= *O. P. E. P.*
oz.	= ounce(s)	= *once(s)*
Ph.D.	= Doctor of Philosophy	= *docteur en philosophie*
PR	= public relations	= *relations publiques*
psi	= pounds per square inch	= *livres par pouce carré*
pt.	= pint(s)	= *pinte(s)*
Q.E.D.	= quod erat demonstrandum	= *C. Q. F. D.*
qt.	= quart(s)	= *quart(s) (de gallon)*
R.N.	= Registered Nurse	= *infirmière diplômée*
rpm	= revolutions per minute	= *t/m (tours par minute)*
SASE	= self-addressed stamped envelope	= *envelope timbrée et adressée à soi-même*
Sr.	= Senior	= *père*
TBA	= to be announced	= *sera annoncé plus tard*
tbsp.	= tablespoon	= *c. à s. (cuillerée à soupe)*
tsp.	= teaspoon	= *c. à c. (cuillerée à café)*
U.K.	= United Kingdom	= *R.-U.*
UN	= United Nations	= *O. N. U.*
U. S.	= United States	= *É.-U.*
USSR	= Union of Soviet Socialist Republics	= *U. R. S. S. (Union des républiques socialistes soviétiques)*
Xmas	= Christmas	= *Noël*
yd.	= yard(s)	= *yard(s)*

ABLE TO + VERB

"*Pouvoir* + infinitive" or "*Savoir* + infinitive."
(1) *Pouvoir* means "To have the physical or mental ability."
   E.g.: *Est-ce que tu peux conduire?*
      Are you able to drive?
(2) *Savoir* means "To have the knowledge."
   E.g.: *Cet homme sait commander.*
      This man is able to lead.
See **CAN**

ABOUT (HEAR ABOUT, READ ABOUT, WRITE ABOUT, ETC.)

(1) The book is about . . . = *Le livre raconte l'histoire de . . .*
      OR = *Le livre parle de . . .*
   E.g.: Madame Bovary *raconte l'histoire d'une femme qui habite en province.*
      Madame Bovary is about a woman who lives in the countryside.

(2) To ask about . . . = *S'informer de . . .*
                 OR = *Demander des nouvelles de . . .*
    E.g.: *Elle s'est informée du climat.*
        She asked about the climate.
        Elle a demandé des nouvelles de Pierre.
        She asked about Peter.
(3) To hear about . . . = *Entendre dire que* (when followed by a clause)
                 OR = *Entendre parler de* (when followed by a noun or pronoun)
    E.g.: *J'ai entendu dire qu'il est mort.*
        I have heard that he has died.
        J'ai entendu parler de sa mort.
        I have heard about his death.
(4) To talk about . . . = *Parler de . . .*
    E.g.: *Nous parlons de son frère.*
        We are talking about his (or her) brother.
(5) To write about . . . = *Écrire au sujet de . . .* or *Écrire sur . . .*
    E.g.: *Écrivez au sujet de vos vacances.*
     or: *Écrivez sur vos vacances.*
        Write about your vacation.
(6) To tell about . . . = *Raconter.*
    E.g.: *Racontez-moi vos vacances.*
        Tell me about your vacation.
See **to be ABOUT + NOUN**

ABOUT (meaning APPROXIMATELY)

When referring to time, a dimension, or a number: *Environ* or *À peu près.*
    E.g.: *Il était environ trois heures quand il est entré.*
        It was about three o'clock when he came in.
        Il est à peu près six heures et quart.
        It is about a quarter past six.
        C'est à environ dix kilomètres d'ici.
        It is about ten kilometers from here.
        Il y avait à peu près cinquante personnes.
        There were about fifty people.

to be ABOUT + NOUN

(Idiomatic construction)
The construction "This book is about" must be conveyed by the impersonal idiomatic construction *S'agir de* as follows:
    E.g.: *Dans ce livre, il s'agit d'un orphelin.*
        This book is about an orphan.
Do not say *"Le livre s'agit de"*!
See **ABOUT (HEAR ABOUT, READ ABOUT, WRITE ABOUT, etc.)**
See also *AGIR vs. S'AGIR DE*

to be ABOUT TO + VERB

"*Être sur le point de +* infinitive."
    E.g.: *Il était sur le point de partir.*
        He was about to leave.

ABOVE

(1) (Adverb) = *Au-dessus* or *En haut.*
E.g.: *La tour est au-dessus.*
   The tower is above.

   La chambre est en haut
   The room is upstairs.
(2) (Preposition) = *Au-dessus de.*
   E.g.: *L'avion a volé au-dessus des Alpes.*
      The plane flew above the Alps.

ABSOUDRE

(To absolve)
PRÉS.: *absous, absous, absout, absolv-ons, -ez, -ent.*
IMPARF.: *absolv-ais, -ais, -ais, -ait, -ions, -iez, -aient.*
FUT.: *absoudr-ai, -as, -a, -ons, -ez, -ont.*
CONDIT.: *absoudr-ais, -ais, -ait, -ions, -iez, -aient.*
IMPÉR.: *absous, absolvons, absolvez.*
SUBJ. PRÉS.: *absolv-e, -es, -e, -ions, -iez, -ent.*
P. PRÉS.: *absolvant.*
P. PASSÉ.: *absous, absoute.*

ACCENTS

Accents are symbols placed over certain vowels. They frequently (but not always) change the pronunciation of the vowel. There are three accents in French:
(1) Acute accent *(accent aigu)*: (´), which changes the sound of the *e* to a closed *é.*
   E.g.: *Parlé, éléphant.*
(2) Grave accent *(accent grave)*: (`), which changes the sound of the *e* to an open *è.* However, it does not affect the sound of the vowel *a* or *u.*
   E.g.: *Mère, lève, là, où.*
(3) Circumflex accent *(accent circonflexe)*: (ˆ), which changes the sound of the *e* to an open *è* [like the grave accent]. It lengthens the sound of the vowels *a, i, o,* and *u.*
   E.g. *Prêtre, grâce, fît, le nôtre, nous dûmes.*
There is also the diaeresis *(tréma)*: (¨), which indicates that the vowel must be pronounced separately from the vowel preceding it.
E.g.: *Naïf* is pronounced *"na-if"* (not *"nèf"*).
See *DIAERESIS*

ACCENTS ON CAPITAL LETTERS

Accents are normally omitted from capital letters. They are used in textbooks for foreign students of French, and also increasingly in magazines.

ACCUEILLIR

(To welcome, to greet)
Conjugated like *CUEILLIR*

ACHETER

(To buy)
The *e* of the stem changes to *è* in front of a mute syllable. Therefore the following forms are slightly irregular:
PRÉS.: *j'achète, tu achètes, il achète, (nous achetons, vous achetez), ils achètent.*
FUT.: *j'achèterai, tu achèteras, il achètera, nous achèterons, vous achèterez, ils achèteront.*
CONDIT.: *j'achèterais, tu achèterais, il achèterait, nous achèterions, vous achèteriez, ils achèteraient.*
SUBJ. PRES.: *que j'achète, que tu achètes, qu'il achète, (que nous achetions, que vous achetiez), qu'ils achètent.*

ACHEVER

(To finish, to complete)
The *e* of the stem changes to *è* in front of a mute syllable. Therefore the following forms are slightly irregular:
PRÉS.: *j'achève, tu achèves, il achève, (nous achevons, vous achevez), ils achèvent.*
FUT.: *j'achèverai, tu achèveras, il achèvera, nous achèverons, vous achèverez, ils achèveront.*
CONDIT.: *j'achèverais, tu achèverais, il achèverait, nous achèverions vous achèveriez, ils achèveraient.*
SUBJ. PRÉS.: *que j'achève, que tu achèves, qu'il achève, (que nous achevions, que vous acheviez), qu'ils achèvent.*
NOTE:
This verb does not mean "to achieve"! "To achieve" = *accomplir.*

to **ACHIEVE**

(Transitive verb) = *Accomplir.*
E.g.: *Gustave Eiffel a accompli de grandes œuvres.*
Gustave Eiffel achieved great works.
NOTE:
The French verb *Achever* does *not* mean "To achieve" but "To complete, to finish."

ACQUÉRIR

(To acquire)
PRÉS.: *acquiers, acquiers, acquiert, acquérons, acquérez, acquièrent.*
IMPARF.: *acquér-ais, -ais, -ait, -ions, -iez, -aient.*
PASSÉ SIMPLE: *acqu-is, -is, -it, -îmes, -îtes, -irent.*
FUT.: *acquerr-ai, -as, -a, -ons, -ez, -ont.*
CONDIT.: *acquerr-ais, -ais, -ait, -ions, -iez, -aient.*
IMPÉR.: *acquiers, acquérons, acquérez.*
SUBJ. PRÉS.: *acquièr-e, -es, -e, acquér-ions, -iez, acquièrent.*
SUBJ. IMPARF.: *acqu-isse, -isses, -ît, -issions, -issiez, -issent.*
P. PRÉS.: *acquérant.*
P. PASSÉ: *acquis(e).*

ACROSS

(Preposition) = *De l'autre côté, en face, à travers.*
(1) *De l'autre côté.*
  E.g.: *L'église est de l'autre côté de la rue.*
  The church is across (on the other side of) the street.
(2) *En face.*
  E.g.: *L'école est en face de l'église.*
  The school is across the street from the church.
(3) *À travers.*
  E.g.: *Ils sont venus à travers les champs.*
  They came across the fields.
See **À TRAVERS** and **EN FACE (DE)**

ACTIVE VOICE

The active voice *(la voix active)* indicates that the subject performs the action of the verb. It is the voice most frequently used in normal spoken or written language.
E.g.: *L'homme conduit la voiture.*
  The man drives the car.

  Les Alliés ont libéré l'Europe.
  The Allies liberated Europe.

  Il pleuvra la semaine prochaine.
  It will rain next week.

ADJECTIVE

An adjective *(un adjectif)* is a word that qualifies a noun by describing some aspect of that noun. An adjective must agree in number and gender with the noun it qualifies. Some adjectives are placed before the noun, but many go after the noun.

E.g.: *Le grand livre.*   *Une règle difficile.*   *Une femme fatiguée.*
      A big book.   A difficult rule   A tired woman.

See **ADJECTIVES, AGREEMENT OF**
See also **ADJECTIVES, POSITION OF**

ADJECTIVE + ENOUGH + VERB

"*Assez* + adjective + *pour* + infinitive."

E.g.: *Il est assez âgé pour comprendre.*
      He is old enough to understand.

      Tu es assez intelligente pour réussir tes études.
      You are intelligent enough to succeed in your studies

ADJECTIVE + PREPOSITION + INFINITIVE

Adjectives followed by an infinitive take the preposition *à* or *de*.

(1) THE MOST COMMON ADJECTIVES THAT TAKE THE PREPOSITION *à*:

Prêt à
Le premier à
Le dernier à
Le seul à
Prompt à

E.g.: *Je suis prêt à partir.*
      I am ready to leave.

      Tu es le premier invité à arriver.
      You are the first guest to arrive.

      C'est la dernière chose à faire.
      It's the last thing to do.

      Elle est la seule étudiante à comprendre.
      She is the only student to understand.

      Il est prompt à se fâcher.
      He is quick to anger.

Also when the infinitive has a passive meaning:

Aisé à
Facile à
Difficile à
Intéressant à

E.g.: *C'est facile à faire.*
      It's easy to do.

      C'est difficile à comprendre.
      It's hard to understand.

      C'est un film intéressant à voir.
      It's an interesting film to see.

(2) THE MOST COMMON ADJECTIVES THAT TAKE THE PREPOSITION *de*:

Aisé de	*Impatient de*
Avide de	*Malaisé de*
Content de	*Ravi de*
Enchanté de	*Triste de*
Heureux de	

E.g.: *Elle est avide de commencer son travail.*
    She is eager to start her work.

    Je suis enchanté de vous voir.
    I am delighted to see you.

    Il est heureux de vous connaître.
    He is happy to know you

    Je suis impatient de recevoir de tes nouvelles.
    I am longing to hear from you.

    Il est malaisé de voir ce qui va arriver.
    It is difficult to see what will happen.

    Nous serons ravis de vous accompagner.
    We shall be happy to accompany you.

    Elle est triste de partir.
    She is sorry (sad) to leave.

Also with impersonal expressions:

Il est aisé de	*Il est difficile de*
Il est facile de	*Il est intéressant de*

E.g.: *Il est aisé de traduire ce texte.*
    It is easy to translate this text.

    Il est facile de faire cela.
    It is easy to do that.

    Il est difficile de comprendre cela.
    It is difficult to understand that.

    Il est intéressant de voyager à l'étranger.
    It is interesting to travel abroad.

ADJECTIVES, AGREEMENT OF

Adjectives agree in number and gender with the nouns they qualify.

E.g.: *Une grande table.*   *Les nouvelles voitures.*
    A large table.   The new cars.

NOTE:

An adjective referring to several nouns of different genders takes the masculine plural.

E.g.: *Les hommes et les femmes âgés.*
    The old men and women.

ADJECTIVES, COMPARISON OF

(1) Comparisons of equality: ("As . . . as . . .") = *"Aussi + adjective + que."*
    E.g.: *Marie est aussi intelligente que Jacques.*
        Mary is as intelligent as John.

(2) Comparisons of superiority: ("more . . . than . . .") = *"Plus + adjective + que."*
    E.g.: *Les chats sont plus grands que les souris.*
        Cats are bigger than mice.

NOTE:
Before numbers, use *de.*
E.g.: *Il a plus de dix ans.*
   He is more than ten years old.
(3) Comparisons of inferiority; ("Less . . . than . . .") = *"Moins* + adjective + *que."*
   E.g.: *Pierre est moins fort que Maurice.*
      Peter is less strong than Maurice.
NOTE:
Before numbers, use *de*:
E.g.: *Il a moins de cinquante francs.*
   He has less than fifty francs.
SPECIAL CASES:
Comparative form of *bon = meilleur*
            petit = moindre (used only in the abstract sense)
            mauvais = pire
E.g.: *Le café est meilleur que le thé.*
   Coffee is better than tea.

   Ce danger est moindre que la mort.
   This danger is less (fearful) than death.

   La grippe est pire que le rhume.
   The flu is worse than a cold.

ADJECTIVES, COMPOUND

(1) Compound adjectives of color are invariable.
   E.g.: *Des cheveux brun clair.*   *Des yeux bleu vert.*
      Light brown hair.   Blue-green eyes.
(2) Compound adjectives made up of two adjectives: Both parts agree with the noun they refer to.
   E.g. *Des femmes sourdes-muettes.*
      Deaf-mute women.
(3) Compound adjectives made up of a prefix and an adjective: Only the adjective part agrees.
   E.g.: *Les manifestations anti-américaines.*
      The anti-American demonstrations.
SPECIAL CASES:
Demi and *Nu* placed before the noun (and linked to it with a hyphen) are invariable.
E.g.: *Une demi-heure.*   *Il se promène nu-pieds.*
   A half-hour.   He walks around barefoot.
BUT *Demi* and *Nu* placed after the noun agree with the noun.
E.g.: *Deux heures et demie.*
   Two and a half hours. (OR Half past two [o'clock.])

   Il se promène tête nue.
   He walks around bare-headed.

ADJECTIVES, DEMONSTRATIVE

(Les adjectifs démonstratifs) These words point (literally or figuratively) to the noun that follows.
FORMS:
Masc. sing.:   *ce (cet* before a vowel or unaspirated *h)*
Fem. sing.:   *cette*
Masc. and fem. plur.: *ces*
E.g.: *Ce garçon.*   *Cet animal.*   *Cet homme.*
      This boy.   This animal.   This man.
      Cette femme.   *Ces animaux.*   *Ces femmes.*
      This woman.   These animals.   These women.

The suffix *-ci* or *-là* can be used to add specificity to the noun.
E.g.: *Cet homme-ci.*   *Cette-femme-là*
      This man (here).   That woman (there).

ADJECTIVES, DESCRIPTIVE

Descriptive adjectives *(les adjectifs qualificatifs)* merely describe nouns by stating their color, size, type, etc.
E.g.: *La maison blanche.*   *Le grand bateau.*
      The white house.   The big ship.

      Une machine moderne.   *Des jardins magnifiques.*
      A modern machine.   Magnificent gardens.

ADJECTIVES, EXCLAMATORY

For exclamations, use *Quel, quelle, quels, quelles.* No article is used after these adjectives in French (whereas the article *is* used in English).
E.g.: *Quel homme intelligent!*   *Quelle femme intéressante!*
      What an intelligent man!   What an interesting woman!

ADJECTIVES, FEMININE OF

GENERAL RULE: Add an *e.*
E.g.: *La petite fille.*   *La robe bleue.*
      The little girl.   The blue dress.
SPECIAL CASES:
(1) Adjectives ending in *e* do not add another *e.*
      E.g.: *Facile → facile*   Easy
(2) Adjectives ending in *el* or *eil* add *le.*
      E.g.: *Cruel → cruelle*   Cruel
            Pareil → pareille   Similar, alike
(3) Adjectives ending in *en* or *on* and *ne.*
      E.g.: *Bon → bonne*   Good
            Ancien → ancienne   Old, ancient
(4) Adjectives ending in *et* change to *ète.*
      E.g.: *Complet → complète*   Complete
            Concret → concrète   Concret
            Discret → discrète   Discreet
            Inquiet → inquiète   Worried
            Secret → secrète   Secret
EXCEPTIONS:
Muet → muette = Mute
Fluet → fluette = Slender
Simplet → simplette = Simple, ingenuous
(5) Adjectives ending in *x* change the ending to *se.*
      E.g.: *Joyeux → joyeuse*   Merry
(6) Adjectives ending in *er* change to *ère.*
      E.g.: *Fier → fière*   Proud
            Léger → légère   Light
(7) Adjectives ending in *f* change to *ve.*
      E.g.: *Naïf → naïve*   Naive
            Vif → vive   Lively
(8) Adjectives ending in *eur* change to *euse.*
      E.g.: *Menteur → menteuse*   Lying
            Trompeur → trompeuse   Deceitful

SPECIAL CASES:
Bas → *basse*   Low
Chic → *chic*   Stylish
Doux → *douce*   Soft, smooth
Épais → *épaisse*   Thick
Faux → *fausse*   False
Frais → *fraîche*   Fresh
Gros → *grosse*   Fat
Long → *longue*   Long
Roux → *rousse*   Red(-haired)
Sot → *sotte*   Silly

ADJECTIVES, INDEFINITE

(Les adjectifs indéfinis) These are adjectives that indicate a rather vague concept of quantity or quality, identity, resemblance, or difference.
The most frequently used indefinite adjectives are these:
Aucun(e)   = No, not any
Autre   = Other
Chaque   = Each
N'importe quel(le)   = Any
Maint(e)(s)   = Many
Même   = Same
Nul(le)   = No
Plusieurs   = Several
Quelconque   = Some (or other), any
Quelque   = Some
Quelques   = A few
Tout(e)   = All

ADJECTIVES, INTERROGATIVE

(Les adjectifs interrogatifs) These adjectives indicate that the noun they refer to is the topic of a question as to its quality, identity, or rank.
FORMS:
Masc. sing.:   *quel*
Fem. sing.:   *quelle*
Masc. plur.:   *quels*
Fem. plur.:   *quelles*
Like all adjectives, they agree in number and gender with the noun they refer to.
E.g.: *Quelle heure est-il?*   *Quels livres avez-vous?*
   What time is it?   What books do you have?
NOTE:
These same interrogative adjectives can also be used in exclamations.
See **ADJECTIVES, EXCLAMATORY**

ADJECTIVES OF COLOR

Like all adjectives, adjectives of color normally agree with the noun they modify. However:
(1) Compound adjectives of color are invariable.
   E.g.: *Une robe bleu clair.*   *Des souliers noir et blanc.*
      A light blue dress.   Black-and-white shoes.
(2) Nouns used as adjectives are invariable.
   E.g.: *Des jupes orange.*
      Orange skirts.

ADJECTIVES, PLURAL OF

GENERAL RULE: Add *s*.
E.g.: *Petit → petits*   Small
    Intelligent → intelligents   Intelligent
    Secrète → secrètes   Secret
BUT:
(1) Adjectives ending in *s* or *x* do not change.
    E.g.: *Gris → gris*   Gray
        Heureux → heureux   Happy
(2) Adjectives ending in *al* change to *aux*.
    E.g.: *Général → généraux*   General
EXCEPTIONS:
Banal → banals   Banal
Fatal → fatals   Fatal
Final → finals   Final
Naval → navals   Naval
SPECIAL CASES:
Beau → beaux   Beautiful
Nouveau → nouveaux   New
Jumeau → jumeaux   Twin
Hébreu → hébreux   Hebrew

ADJECTIVES, POSITION OF

The following rules are general and allow some exceptions.
(1) A few adjectives go before the noun:
    (a) Short, one- or two-syllable adjectives describing beauty, age, and size.
        E.g.: *Une belle fille.*   *Un vieux livre.*
            A beautiful girl.   An old book.

            Une petite maison.   *Une mauvaise note.*
            A little house.   A bad grade (mark).
    (b) Ordinal numbers.
        E.g.: *Le seizième siècle.*   *Le deuxième sexe.*
            The sixteenth century.   The second sex.
(2) Most adjectives go after the noun:
    (a) Adjectives containing two or more syllables.
        E.g.: *Un repas délicieux.*   *Un accident mortel.*   *Une guerre catastrophique.*
            A delicious meal.   A fatal accident.   A catastrophic war.
    (b) Adjectives describing color or shape.
        E.g.: *Une fleur rose.*   *Un bâtiment rond.*
            A pink flower.   A round building.
    (c) Adjectives of nationality, religion, or race (remember that they are not capitalized in French).
        E.g.: *Un général russe.*   *Un prêtre catholique.*   *Le peuple juif.*
            A Russian general.   A catholic priest.   The Jewish people.
NOTE:
Some adjectives have a different meaning depending on their position:
E.g.: *Mon ancien professur*   BUT   *Une ville ancienne*
      My former teacher   An ancient city

      Un homme brave   BUT   *Un brave homme*
      A brave man   A worthy man

      Mon cher ami   BUT   *Une voiture chère*
      My dear friend   An expensive car

      Le dernier mois   BUT   *Le mois dernier*
      The last month   Last month

Un homme grand A tall man	BUT	*Un grand homme* A great man
Le même jour The same day	BUT	*Le jour même* The very day
Une nouvelle voiture A new car	BUT	*Une voiture nouvelle* A new (design) car
Un homme pauvre A poor man	BUT	*Un pauvre homme* A miserable man
Ses propres paroles His own words	BUT	*Une serviette propre* A clean towel (or napkin)
Un homme seul A man alone (solitary)	BUT	*Un seul homme* Only one man
Certains résultats Certain results	BUT	*Des résultats certains* Results that are certain
Les différentes opinions The various opinions	BUT	*Les opinions différentes* Opinions that are different

ADJECTIVES, POSSESSIVE

(Les adjectifs possessifs) These adjectives indicate the possessor of the noun they refer to.
FORMS:
Referring to a masculine singular noun: *mon, ton, son , notre, votre, leur*
               a feminine singular noun: *ma, ta, sa, notre, votre, leur*
               a masculine or feminine plural noun: *mes, tes, ses, nos, vos, leurs*

NOTES:
(1) Unlike English, possessive adjectives agree in number and gender with the noun they modify.
    E.g.: *Mon* frère = My brother
          Ma sœur = My sister
(2) French possessive adjectives do not indicate the gender of the possessor.
    E.g.: *Il aime son père.*   *Elle aime son père.*
          He loves his father.   She loves her father.
(3) *Ma, ta*, and *sa* are replaced by *mon, ton,* and *son* in front of any noun or adjective that begins with a vowel or an unaspirate *h*.
    E.g.: *Mon ancienne école.*   *Son habitude.*
          My old (former) school.   His (or her) habit.
(4) Do *not* use the possessive adjective for parts of the body when the context makes clear who the possessor is. Use the definite article instead.
    E.g.: *J'ai mal à la tête.*   *Elle s'est coupé les cheveux.*
          I have a headache.   She cut her hair.

ADJECTIVES, SUPERLATIVE OF

"Le plus (la plus, les plus) + adjective + *de."*
E.g.: *Charlotte est la plus jeune de la classe.*
      Charlotte is the youngest in the class.
      C'est le meilleur film de l'année.
      It is the best film of the year.

NOTES:
(1) If the adjective is placed after the noun, the definite article must be repeated: "Article + noun + *le (la, les) plus* + adjective."
    E.g.: *La femme la plus généreuse.*
          The most generous woman.

(2) The English "in" or "of" is conveyed by *de*.
    E.g. "In the class" = *De la classe*

ADJECTIVES used as NOUNS

Certain adjectives can be used as nouns, in which case they are preceded by an article.
E.g.: *Un riche.*   *Les riches.*   *Un pauvre.*
      A rich man.   The rich.   A poor person.

ADVERB

An adverb *(un adverbe)* is an invariable word that modifies the meaning of a verb, an adjective, or another adverb.
E.g.: *Elle mange rapidement.*   *Il est très gros.*   *Tu écris trop vite.*
      She eats fast.   He is very fat.   You write too fast.
FORMATION OF ADVERBS:
GENERAL RULES:
(1) Add *-ment* to the feminine form of the adjective.
    E.g.: *Actuel → actuelle → actuellement*   At present
          Doux → douce → doucement   Gently
          Joyeux → joyeuse → joyeusement   Joyfully
(2) If the masculine form of the adjective ends with a vowel, simply add *-ment* to the masculine form of the adjective.
    E.g.: *Joli → joliment*   Attractively
          Vrai → vraiment   Really
          Facile → facilement   Easily
(3) If the adjective ends in *nt*, replace *nt* by *m* before adding *-ment*.
    E.g.: *Élégant → élégamment*   Elegantly
          Fréquent → fréquemment   Frequently
IRREGULAR ADVERBS:
Bon → bien   Good → well
Mauvais → mal   Bad → badly
Énorme → énormément Enormous → enormously
Précis → précisément Precise → precisely
Profond → profondément Deep → deeply
Gentil → gentiment   Kind → kindly
REMEMBER: *Vite* (= "Quickly, fast, rapidly") is an adverb. Do not say *"vitement"*!
POSITION OF ADVERBS IN THE SENTENCE:
(1) The adverb comes after the verb it modifies.
    E.g.: *Les Français mangent bien.*   *Je parle aussi français.*
          The French eat well.   I also speak French.
When the verb is in a compound tense, the adverb comes after the past participle.
E.g.: *Elle a parlé doucement.*
      She spoke softly.
EXCEPTIONS:
The short and frequently used adverbs come after the auxiliary verb. They are *assez, aussi, beaucoup, bien, bientôt, déjà, encore, mal, peu, souvent, tant, tellement, toujours, trop, vite, vraiment.*
E.g.: *J'ai assez mangé.*   *Elle a déjà fini.*
      I have eaten enough.   She has already finished.
      Il a beaucoup voyagé.   *J'ai aussi appris le russe.*
      He has travelled a lot.   I also learned Russian.
(2) The adverb comes before the adjective or adverb it modifies.
    E.g.: *Elle est très grande.*   *Il est extrêmement fatigué.*
          She is very tall.   He is extremely tired.

ADVERBS, COMPARATIVE AND SUPERLATIVE OF

GENERAL RULES:
(1) COMPARATIVE: *"Plus (moins, aussi) + adverb + que."*
    E.g.: *Elle parle plus (moins, aussi) rapidement que moi.*
        She speaks faster than (less fast than, as fast as) I.
(2) SUPERLATIVE: *"Le plus (le moins) + adverb."*
    E.g.: *Elle parle le plus (le moins) rapidement.*
        She speaks the fastest (the least fast).

NOTE:
If a context is given for the superlative, use the preposition *de* (corresponding to the English "in" or "of").
E.g.: *C'est elle qui parle le plus rapidement de toutes.*
      She is the one who speaks the fastest of all.

IRREGULAR FORMS:
(1) *Bien → mieux → le mieux*
    Well → better → the best
    E.g.: *Elle parle mieux que moi.*
        She speaks better than I.

        Elle parle le mieux <u>de</u> toute la classe.
        She speaks the best in the class.
(2) *Mal → pire → le pire*
    Badly → worse → the worst
    E.g.: *La situation est pire qu'avant.*
        The situation is worse than before.

ADVERBS, POSITION OF

(1) Adverbs modifying a verb go after the verb.
    E.g.: *Elle parle vite*   *Les Français mangent bien.*
        She speaks fast.   The French eat well.
When the verb is in a compound tense, the adverb goes after the past participle.
E.g.: *Elle a parlé doucement.*
      She spoke softly.

EXCEPTIONS:
Short and frequently used adverbs, such as *assez, beaucoup, bien, bientôt, déjà, encore, mal, peu, souvent, tant, tellement, toujours, trop, vite*, and *vraiment* go after the auxiliary verb.
E.g.: *J'ai assez étudié.*   *Elle est déjà partie.*
      I have studied enough.   She has already left.

      Ils ont beaucoup voyagé.   *Il a toujours faim.*
      They have traveled a lot.   He is always hungry.
(2) Adverbs modifying adjectives or other adverbs go before the adjective or adverb.
    E.g.: *Elle est très douée.*   *Je suis extrêmement surpris.*
        She is very gifted.   I am extremely surprised.

ADVERBS, SUPERLATIVE OF
See **ADVERBS, COMPARATIVE AND SUPERLATIVE OF**

ADVISING

Several expressions can be used to give advice.
(1) *"Conseiller (à qqn) de + infinitive."*
    E.g.: *Je te conseille de rester au lit.*
        I advise you to stay in bed.
(2) *"Recommander (à qqn) de + infinitive."*
    E.g. *Le médecin lui a recommandé de ne pas manger de viande.*
        The doctor advised him not to eat any meat.

(3) "*Engager (qqn) à* + infinitive."

E.g.: *Elle m'a engagé à tenter ma chance.*

She advised me to try my luck.

AFIN DE vs. AFIN QUE

(1) The prepositional construction "*Afin de* + infinitive" is used when the subject of the subordinate clause is the same as the subject of the main clause.

E.g.: *Il ira en France afin d'étudier la langue.*

He will go to France in order to study the language.

(2) The conjunctional construction "*Afin que* + subjunctive" is used when the subject of the subordinate clause is different from that of the main clause.

E.g.: *Je te téléphonerai afin que tu saches la nouvelle.*

I shall call you so that you may know the news.

See **IN ORDER TO**

AFRAID OF

See **AVOIR PEUR DE**

AFTER + VERB (AFTER + -ING)

"*Après* + past infinitive."

E.g.: *Après avoir mangé.*   *Après être arrivé.*

After eating (having eaten).   After arriving (having arrived).

NOTES:

Don't forget to make the past participle agree, if necessary.

E.g.: *Après être arri<u>vées</u>, elles ont mangé.*

After arriving, they ate.

This construction is used *only* if the subjects of the two verbs are the same. For guidance when the subjects are different, see **APRÈS, APRÈS QUE**

AGE

Age is expressed with the idiomatic construction *"avoir . . . ans."*

E.g.: *Elle a dix-sept ans.*

She is seventeen (years old).

But when the age is stated as an adjective, use the construction *De . . . ans.*

E.g.: *Un homme de 45 ans.*

A 45-year-old man.

AGENT

The agent *(l'agent)* is the person or thing performing the action of the verb. It is preceded by the preposition *par* (sometimes by *de* with verbs expressing like or dislike).

E.g.: *Le voleur a été arrêté par la police.*

The thief was arrested by the police.

La princesse est aimée de tout le monde.

The princess is beloved of everyone.

AGIR vs. S'AGIR DE

(1) *Agir* = "To behave, to act."

E.g.: *Elle a agi avec courage.*

She acted with courage.

(2) "*S'agir de* + infinitive or noun or pronoun" = "To be a matter or question of, to be about."

NOTE:

This is an impersonal verb; it must have *il* for its subject.

E.g.: *Dans ce livre il s'agit d'un crime bizarre.*

This book is about a strange crime.

(It is not correct to say *"Ce livre s'agit d'un crime. . . ."*)

AGO

"*Il y a* + time expression."
E.g.: *Il y a dix minutes.*
   Ten minutes ago.
Do not confuse this construction with "For + duration of time."
See **IL Y A + TIME EXPRESSION + QUE**

to AGREE (WITH)

Être d'accord (avec).
E.g.: *Je suis d'accord avec vous.*
   I agree with you.

AGREEMENT OF ADJECTIVES

See **ADJECTIVES, AGREEMENT OF**

AGREEMENT OF PAST PARTICIPLES

See **PAST PARTICIPLES, AGREEMENT OF**

AGREEMENT OF TENSES

See **APRÈS vs. APRÈS QUE; QUAND, TENSES WITH; SI CLAUSES;** and **SUBJUNCTIVE MOOD**

AINSI

(Adverb) = "In this way, in this manner, thus."
E.g.: *Tu ne devrais pas agir ainsi.*
   You should not act in this way.
When it is at the beginning of a sentence, it is sometimes followed by inversion.
E.g.: *Ainsi sont-ils arrivés à leurs fins.*
   Thus did they reach their goal.

ALL (meaning EVERYTHING)

(Pronoun) = *Tout.*
E.g.: *Tout va bien.*   *Tout est bien qui finit bien.*
   Everything is going well.   All is well that ends well.
See **TOUT, TOUTE, TOUS, TOUTES**

ALL (OF) THE + NOUN

(Adjective) = *Tout le, toute la, tous les, toutes les.*
E.g.: *Tout le pays.*   *Tous les enfants.*
   All (of) the country, the whole country.   All (of) the children.

   Toute la ville.   *Toutes les femmes.*
   All (of) the town, the whole town.   All (of) the women.

ALLER

(To go) (Conjugated with *être*)
PRÉS.: *vais, vas, va, allons, allez, vont.*
IMPARF.: *all-ais, -ais, -ait, -ions, -iez, -aient.*
PASSÉ SIMPLE: *all-ai, -as -a, -âmes, -âtes, -èrent.*
FUT.: *ir-ai, -as, -a, -ons, -ez, -ont.*
CONDIT.: *ir-ais, -ais, -ait, -ions, -iez, -aient.*
IMPÉR.: *va,* allons, allez.*
SUBJ. PRÉS.: *aille, ailles, aille, allions, alliez, aillent.*
SUBJ. IMPARF.: *all-asse, -asses, ât, -assions, -assiez, -assent.*
P. PRÉS.: *allant.*
P. PASSÉ; *allé(e).*
*The imperative *va* takes an *s* before *y* and *en* if they are not followed by an infinitive.
E.g.: *Vas-y!*　　　BUT　　*Va y mettre ordre!*
　　Go ahead!　　　　　　Go to put it in order!
NOTE:
"*Aller* + infinitive" = Going to + verb."
E.g.: *Qu'est-ce que tu vas faire?*
　　What are you going to do?

ALMOST + VERB (IN PAST TENSE)

(Idiomatic construction) There are two ways of expressing this in French.
(1) The adverb *Presque* with the verb.
　　E.g.: *Je suis presque tombé.*　　*Nous avons presque terminé.*
　　　　I almost fell.　　　　　　We have almost finished.
(2) Another construction is frequently used when the context means "To escape narrowly:"
　　"*Faillir* (in the *passé composé*) + infinitive."
　　E.g.: *J'ai failli tomber.*　　*Nous avons failli ne pas terminer à temps.*
　　　　I almost fell.　　　　We almost didn't finish in time.
See **FAILLIR**

ALORS QUE

(Conjunctional construction) = "When, while, whereas."
(1) To express simultaneity:
　　E.g.: *Le téléphone a sonné alors que je faisais la sieste.*
　　　　The telephone rang while I was taking a nap.
(2) To express contrast or opposition:
　　E.g.: *Sa mère habite Paris alors que son père habite New York.*
　　　　His mother lives in Paris, whereas his father lives in New York.
See **AS**

ALPHABET

The French alphabet *(l'alphabet)* is identical to the English alphabet. The letters are pronounced as follows: *a, bé, cé, dé, e, effe, gé, ache, i, ji, ka, elle, emme, enne, o, pé, ku, erre, esse, té, u, vé, double vé, ikse, i grec, zède.*
NOTE:
The grave accent (`), the circumflex accent (ˆ) and the acute accent (´) change the pronunciation of the letter e to "è," "è," and "é," respectively. The cedilla under the letter c *(ç)* changes its pronunciation to "s."

ALSO

(1) Adverb meaning "Too" = *Aussi.*
　　E.g.: *Ils ont aussi visité l'Espagne.*
　　　　They also visited Spain.

(2) Adverbial expression meaning "Moreover" = *En outre.*
E.g.: *Je suis fatigué, et en outre je me sens malade.*
I am tired and also, I feel sick.

ALTHOUGH

(Conjunction) = "*Bien que* + subjunctive" or "*Quoique* + subjunctive."
E.g.: *Bien qu'elle ait la grippe, elle va en classe.*
Although she has the flu, she is going to class.

Quoiqu'il soit malade, il est allé travailler.
Although he was ill, he went to work.
See **BIEN QUE** and **QUOIQUE**
See also **SUBJUNCTIVE MOOD**

AMENER

(To take, to bring along)
Conjugated like **MENER**
This verb is used for people. For things, use *apporter.*
E.g.: *Nous l'avons amenée à l'aéroport.*   *As-tu apporté ta valise?*
We took her to the airport.   Did you bring your suitcase?

AMONG

(Preposition) = *Parmi.*
E.g.: *Il s'est perdu parmi les arbres.*
He got lost among the trees.
See **PARMI**

AN vs. ANNÉE

(1) *An* (masculine) is generally used to express time and age.
E.g.: *L'an 1986.*   *Julien a dix-neuf ans.*
The year 1986.   Julien is nineteen years old.
(2) *Année* (feminine) is generally used to stress duration.
E.g.: *Il a fait froid pendant toute l'année.*
It was cold during the entire year.
One may use either form in such expressions as these:
L'an dernier   or   *L'année dernière.*
Last year.
L'an prochain   or   *L'année prochaine.*
Next year.

ANOTHER

(Adjective)
(1) Meaning "One more" = *Encore un(e).*
E.g.: *Apportez-moi encore un café, s'il vous plaît.*
Bring me another (cup of) coffee, please.
(2) Meaning "Different" = *Un(e) autre.*
E.g.: *C'est une autre histoire.*
That is another story.

ANTECEDENT

An antecedent *(un antécédent)* is the word (noun or pronoun) that a pronoun replaces.
E.g.: *Le livre que je lis.*
The book that I am reading.
(Le livre [The book] is the antecedent of the relative pronoun *que.*)

ANY

(Indefinite adjective)

(1) With a negation or an implied negation = "Not any" = *Pas de.*

    E.g.: *Elle n'a pas de frères.*

          She doesn't have any brothers.

See **ARTICLES, PARTITIVE**

(2) In an interrogative sentence = (partitive): *Du, de la, de l', des.*

    E.g.: *Avez-vous du beurre?*

          Do you have any butter?

See **ARTICLES, PARTITIVE**

(3) In an affirmative sentence = "No matter which" = *N'importe quel.*

    E.g.: *Apportez n'importe quel livre.*

          Bring any book (no matter which one).

See ***N'IMPORTE QUEL (QUELLE, QUELS, QUELLES)***

ANYHOW, ANYWAY

(Adverb)

(1) Meaning "In any way whatever, any old way" = *N'importe comment.*

    E.g.: *Elle fait son travail n'importe comment.*

          She does her work any old way.

(2) Meaning "In any event" = *De toute façon.*

    E.g.: *Ils partiront demain de toute façon.*

          They will leave tomorrow anyhow.

ANYONE, ANYBODY

(Pronoun)

(1) In an affirmative sentence = *N'importe qui.*

    E.g.: *N'importe qui peut faire cela.*

          Anyone can do that.

See ***N'IMPORTE QUI***

(2) In a negative sentence = "Not anybody, nobody" = *Ne . . . personne* or *Personne . . . ne.*

    E.g.: *Il n'y a personne ici.*   *Personne n'a appelé.*

          There is nobody here.   Nobody called.

See ***NE . . . PERSONNE***

(3) In an interrogative sentence = *Quelqu'un.*

    E.g.: *Y a-t-il quelqu'un ici?*

          Is there anybody here?

See ***QUELQU'UN***

ANYTHING

(Pronoun) = *N'importe quoi.*

E.g.: *Vous pouvez écrire sur n'importe quoi.*

      You may write on anything.

NOTE:

"Not . . . anything" = *Rien.*

E.g.: *Il n'y a rien dans la boîte.*

      There isn't anything in the box.

See ***N'IMPORTE QUOI***

ANYTIME

(Adverb) = *N'importe quand.*

E.g.: *Venez me voir n'importe quand.*

      Come see me anytime.

See ***N'IMPORTE QUAND***

ANYWHERE

(Adverb)

(1) In an affirmative sentence = *N'importe où.*

E.g.: *On peut voir cela n'importe où.*

One can see that anywhere.

See **N'IMPORTE OÙ**

(2) In a negative sentence = "Not anywhere, nowhere" = *Nulle part.*

E.g.: *Ils ne vont jamais nulle part.*

They never go anywhere.

See **NULLE PART**

APERCEVOIR

(To see, to notice, to catch a glimpse of)

PRÉS.: *aperçois, aperçois, aperçoit, apercevons, apercevez, aperçoivent.*

IMPARF.: *apercev-ais, -ais, -ait, -ions, -iez, -aient.*

PASSÉ SIMPLE: *aperç-us, -us, -ut, -ûmes, -ûtes, -urent.*

FUT.: *apercevr-ai, -as, -a, -ons, -ez, -ont.*

CONDIT.: *apercevr-ais, -ais, -ait, -ions, -iez, -aient.*

IMPÉR.: *aperçois, apercevons, apercevez.*

SUBJ. PRÉS.: *aperçoiv-e, -es, -e, apercevions, aperceviez, aperçoivent.*

SUBJ. IMPARF.: *aperç-usse, -usses, -ût, -ussions, -ussiez, -ussent.*

P. PRÉS.: *apercevant.*

P. PASSÉ: *aperçu(e).*

APOLOGIZING

Apologies are conveyed by the following expressions:

(1) *S'excuser (de qqch. auprès de qqn).*

E.g.: *Je me suis excusé auprès du professeur pour avoir fait tant de fautes.*

I apologized to the teacher for making so many mistakes.

(2) *Présenter ses excuses (à qqn pour qqch.).*

E.g.: *Tu devras présenter tes excuses à la voisine pour avoir fait tant de bruit.*

You must apologize to the neighbor for making so much noise.

APOSTROPHE

The apostrophe (') *(l'apostrophe)* indicates the dropping ("elision") of a letter. Such elision occurs in such words as *Ce, de, la, le, lorsque, me, ne, que, se, si,* and *te* when they are followed by a vowel or an unaspirated *h.*

E.g.: *C'est, d'un, lorsqu'elle, quelqu'un, s'il.*

NOTE:

There is elision after *si* only when it is followed by *il* or *ils*

E.g.: *S'il vient.*   *S'ils arrivent.*

   If he comes.   If they arrive.

APPARAÎTRE

(Intransitive verb): "To appear."

E.g.: *Un fantôme est apparu au milieu de la scène.*

A ghost appeared in the middle of the stage.

Conjugated like **PARAÎTRE**

APPARTENIR

(To belong)

Conjugated like **TENIR**

APPELER

(To call)
PRÉS.: *appelle, -es, -e, appelons, appelez, appellent.*
IMPARF.: *appel-ais, -ais, -ait, -ions, -iez, -aient.*
PASSÉ SIMPLE: *appel-ai, -as, -a, -âmes, -âtes, -èrent.*
FUT.: *appeller-ai, -as, -a, -ons, -ez, -ont.*
CONDIT.: *appeller-ais, -ais, -ait, -ions, -iez, -aient.*
IMPÉR.: *appelle, appelons, appelez.*
SUBJ. PRÉS.: *appell-e, -es, -e, appelions, appeliez, appellent.*
SUBJ. IMPARF.: *appel-asse, -asses, -ât, -assions, -assiez, -assent.*
P. PRÉS.: *appelant.*
P. PASSÉ: *appelé(e).*
NOTE:
"S'appeler" = "To be called."
E.g.: *Il s'appelle Pierre.*
     His name is Peter.

APPOSITIVES

Appositives are nouns or pronouns placed beside other nouns or pronouns to explain or identify them. Appositives do not take the article in French.
E.g.: *Monsieur Durand, président de la compagnie.*
    Mr. Durand, the president of the company.

APRÈS vs. APRÈS QUE

(1) The preposition *après* is followed by (a) a noun, (b) a pronoun, or (c) a verb in the past infinitive.
    E.g.: (a) *Après la victoire.*
          After the victory.
        (b) *Après moi.*
          After me.
        (c) *Aprè avoir mangé.*   *Après être arrivées*
          After eating (having eaten).   After arriving (have arrived).
(2) The conjunction *après que* takes the indicative.
    E.g.: *Nous partirons après qu'elle aura fini.*
        We shall leave after she has (will have) finished.
REMEMBER THE RULES for the agreement of tenses:
The auxiliary verb is in the same tense as the main verb; that is, the tense of the subordinate clause is "once removed" from that of the main clause.
E.g.: *J'irai chez moi après que j'aurai fini mes examens.*
    (futur)   *(futur antérieur)*

    I shall go home after I have finished my exams.
    Nous allions au cinéma après que nous avions fini notre travail.
    (imparfait)   *(plus-que-parfait)*

    We used to go to the movies after we had finished our work.
    Elles se reposent après qu'elles ont travaillé.
      (présent)   *(passé composé)*

    They rest after they have worked.
(3) The adverb *après* is used to modify verbs.
    E.g.: *Maintenant, on travaille; le repos vient après.*
        Now we work; rest comes after (ward).

ARITHMETIC OPERATIONS

The terminology for arithmetic operations is as follows:
(1) Addition *(une addition):*
E.g.: *Deux et deux font quatre.*
Two plus two makes four.
(2) Subtraction *(une soustraction):*
E.g.: *Sept moins cinq font deux.*
Seven minus five leaves two.
(3) Multiplication *(une multiplication):*
E.g.: *Trois fois huit font vingt-quatre.*
Three times eight is twenty-four.
(4) Division *(une division):*
E.g.: *Dix divisé par deux fait cinq.*
Ten divided by two is five.

AROUND

(1) (Preposition) Meaning ''all the way around'' = *Autour de.*
E.g.: *Il y a un jardin autour de la maison.*
There is a garden (all the way) around the house.
See ***AUTOUR (DE)***
(2) (Preposition) Meaning ''in,'' use the appropriate preposition.
E.g.: *Ils ont fait le tour de l'Europe.*   *On a voyagé au Japon.*
They traveled around Europe.   We traveled around Japan.
(3) (Adverb) Meaning ''approximately'' = *Environ.*
E.g.: *Il y a environ cinquante personnes.*
There are around fifty people.

ARTICLE

An article *(un article)* is a word placed before a noun to give it definiteness or indefiniteness. In French the article also indicates the number and the gender of the noun. Articles are (a) definite, (b) indefinite, or (c) partitive.

E.g.: (a) *Le cahier.*   *La voiture.*   *Les enfants.*
The notebook.   The car.   The children.
(b) *Un cahier.*   *Une voiture.*   *Des enfants.*
A notebook.   A car.   (Some) children.
(c) *Du pain.*   *De l'eau.*   *De la bière.*   *Des gâteaux.*
Some bread.   Some water.   Some beer.   Some cakes.

ARTICLES, CONTRACTION OF

The definite article *(le, l', la, les)* preceded by the prepositions *à* and *de* contracts as follows:
(1) *à + le = au*
à + les = aux
à + la   does not contract.
à + l'   does not contract.
(2) *de + le = du*
de + les = des
de + la   does not contract.
de + l'   does not contract.

ARTICLES, DEFINITE

(Les articles définis) Words that come before nouns to give them specificity (''the'' in English).
FORMS:
Masc. sing.:   *le (l'* before a vowel or an unaspirated *h)*
Fem. sing.:   *la*
Masc. and fem. plur.:   *les*

USAGE:

The definite article is used:

(1) Before a noun taken in the general sense.

E.g.: *J'aime le sport.*   *Les voitures coûtent cher.*
I like sports.   Cars are expensive.

(2) Before names of countries and languages (EXCEPT after *Parler*).

E.g.: *La Belgique.*   *Le Japon.*   *Le latin est difficile.*
Belgium.   Japan.   Latin is difficult

BUT: *Je parle français.*   *Elle parlait chinois à la maison.*
I speak French.   She spoke Chinese at home.

(3) Before a title.

E.g.: *Le général de Gaulle.*   *Le professeur Dupont.*
General de Gaulle.   Professor Dupont.

(4) Instead of the possessive adjective, with parts of the body.

E.g.: *Elle a les yeux bleus.*
She has blue eyes.

(5) Before exact dates.

E.g.: *Le premier juillet.*
July 1 (The first of July).

Le 23 janvier.
January 23.

(6) Before days of the week and parts of the day, but only in the sense of repeated or habitual times.

E.g.: *Il va au cinéma le samedi (= tous les samedis).*
He goes to the movies on Saturdays.

Nous sortons l'après-midi (= tous les après-midi).
We go out in the afternoon.

BUT: *J'irai au cinéma samedi.*
I shall go to the movies on Saturday.

(7) Before a day of the week modified by *précédent* or *suivant*.

E.g.: *Elle est allée en ville le samedi suivant.*
She went to town the following Saturday.

Ils sont arrivés le mardi précédent.
They arrived on the previous Tuesday.

(8) Before weights and measures, when talking about price.

E.g.: *Cela coûte 25 francs le kilo.*
That costs 25 francs a kilogram.

C'est quatre francs le litre.
That's four francs a liter.

OMISSION OF THE DEFINITE ARTICLE:

The definite article is not used:

(1) Before a title when one is addressing the person.

E.g.: *Bonjour, docteur.*
Hello, Doctor.

(2) After the verb *parler* before the name of a language.

E.g.: *Tu parles chinois?*   *Vous parlez russe.*
Do you speak Chinese?   You speak Russian.

(3) After the verb *être* before the name of a profession or nationality.

E.g.: *Il est ingénieur.*   *Elle est américaine.*
He is an engineer.   She is an American.

(4) Before nouns placed in apposition.

E.g.: *Paris, capitale de France.*   *M. Dupont, directeur de la compagnie.*
Paris, the capital of France.   Mr. Dupont, the president of the company.

(5) Before the number following the name of a monarch or a pope.

E.g.: *Louis XIV (read "Louis quatorze").*   *Jean XXIII ("Jean vingt-trois").*
Louis XIV (read "Louis the fourteenth").   John XXIII ("John the twenty-third").

ARTICLES, INDEFINITE

(Les articles indéfinis) Words that come before nouns to indicate that they are taken in an unidentified or unidentifiable sense ("A, some" in English).

FORMS:

Masc. sing.:   *un*

Fem. sing.:   *une*

Masc. and fem. plur.:   *des*

E.g.: *Un homme.*   *Une femme.*   *Des amis.*
      A man.   A woman.   (Some) friends.

NOTES:

(1) The singular forms *un* and *une* also mean the numeral "one."

    E.g.: *Cela coûte un franc.*

       That costs one franc.

(2) The plural form *des* also has the meaning of the partitive article "some."

    E.g.: *J'ai des amis français.*

       I have some French friends.

(3) Before an adjective in the plural form, *des* changes to *de* (with no article).

    E.g.: *Voici des roses.*   *Elles ont des projets.*
       Here are some roses.   They have (some) plans.

    BUT: *Voici de belles roses.*   BUT: *Elles ont d'autres projets.*
       Here are some beautiful roses.   They have other plans.

(4) Do not use the indefinite article with *ni . . . ni.*

    E.g.: *Je n'ai ni frère ni sœur.*

       I have neither brother nor sister.

(5) Do not use the indefinite article with *sans* or *avec.*

    E.g.: *Il a fait cela sans difficulté.*

       He does that without (any) difficulty.

       Elle l'a fait avec soin.

       She did it with care.

OMMISSION OF THE INDEFINITE ARTICLE:

The indefinite article *(un, une, des)* is omitted after the verb *être* + an unmodified noun of nationality, profession, or religion.

E.g.: *Il est espagnol.*   *Elle est actrice.*   *Je suis catholique.*
      He is a Spaniard.   She is an actress.   I am a Catholic.

NOTE:

The indefinite article is used if the noun is modified (and in this case *c'est* or *ce sont* is used rather than *il est, elle est, ils sont, elles sont*).

E.g.: *C'est un Espagnol célèbre.*

       He is a famous Spaniard.

       C'est une actrice de cinéma.

       She is a movie actress.

       C'est un catholique pratiquant.

       He is a practicing Catholic.

ARTICLES, OMISSION OF

See **ARTICLES, DEFINITE** and **ARTICLES, INDEFINITE**

ARTICLES, PARTITIVE

(Les articles partitifs) Words placed before nouns of objects that cannot be counted, to indicate that only a part or a certain quantity is meant ("some" in English).

FORMS:

Masc. sing.:   *du (de l'* before a vowel or an unaspirated *h)*

Fem. sing.:   *de la (de l'* before a vowel or an unaspirated *h)*

Masc. and fem. plur.: *des*

E.g.: *J'ai du travail.*   *Nous avons de l'argent.*   *Il a des problèmes.*
      I have (some) work.   We have (some) money.   He has (some) problems.

NEGATIVE PARTITIVE:

In a negative sentence, the partitive is simply *de*, without any article (''no, not any'' in English).

E.g.: *Je n'ai pas de travail.*

    I have no work.

    Nous n'envoyons pas d'argent.

    We send no money.

    Il ne cause pas de problèmes.

    He does not cause any problems.

This construction also applies with the negative constructions *plus de, jamais de, guère de*, etc.

E.g.: *Je n'ai plus de travail.*

    I have no more work.

    Il ne cause jamais de problèmes.

    He never causes any problems.

    Nous n'écrivons guère de lettres.

    We scarcely write any letters.

EXCEPTION:

Ne . . . que takes the normal affirmative partitive.

E.g.: *Je n'ai que du vin.*

    I have only wine.

NOTES:

The particle *de*, without any article, is always used after any expression of quantity (*assez de, beaucoup de, peu de, trop de, deux kilos de*, etc.).

E.g.: *Vous avez assez de temps.*

    You have enough time.

    J'ai acheté deux kilos de pommes.

    I bought two kilograms of apples.

    Nous gagnons peu d'argent.

    We earn little money.

    Il nous donne trop de travail.

    He gives us too much work.

AS

(1) (Conjunction) Meaning ''When, while'' = *Comme* or *Alors que* or *Tandis que* or *Pendant que*.

    E.g.: *J'ai vu Marie comme elle sortait de chez toi.*

        I saw Mary as she was leaving your house.

See ***ALORS QUE***

See also ***COMME*** and ***TANDIS QUE***

(2) (Conjunction) Meaning ''Since'' = *Puisque*.

    E.g.: *Elle n'a pas répondu puisqu'elle ne parle pas anglais.*

        She didn't answer as (since) she doesn't speak English.

See ***PUISQUE***

(3) (Preposition) Meaning ''In the capacity of'' = *En tant que*.

    E.g.: *Il a agi en tant que chef.*

        He acted as a leader.

See ***EN TANT QUE***

(4) (Conjunction) Indicating manner = *Comme*.

    E.g.: *Faites comme vous voudrez.*

        Do as you wish.

See ***COMME***

(5) (Adverb) In comparisons of equality.

See ***AS + ADJECTIVE or ADVERB + AS***

AS + ADJECTIVE or ADVERB + AS

"Aussi . . . que."

E.g.: *Elle est aussi grande que Pierre.*   *Il court aussi vite que moi.*
      She is as tall as Peter.   He runs as fast as I.

See **ADJECTIVES, COMPARISON OF** and **ADVERBS, COMPARATIVE AND SUPERLATIVE OF**

AS IF, AS THOUGH

(Idiomatic construction) = "*Comme si* + imperfect or pluperfect indicative."

E.g.: *Il agit comme s'il avait peur de toi.*
      He acts as if he were afraid of you.

      Ils dépensent comme s'ils avaient gagné un million.
      They spend as if they had won a million.

See **COMME SI** and **SI CLAUSES**

AS IS

See **TEL(S) QUEL(S), TELLE(S) QUELLE(S)**

AS LONG AS + VERB

(1) "*Tant que* + indicative."

   E.g.: *Tant que tu vas en ville, achète-moi des bonbons.*
         As long as you're going downtown, buy me some candy.

(2) "*Aussi longtemps que* + indicative."

   E.g.: *Il n'y a pas de solution aussi longtemps qu'il refuse de nous aider.*
         There is no solution as long as he refuses to help us.

AS MUCH AS

(Adverb) = *Autant que.*

E.g.: *Elle travaille autant que Pierre.*
      She works as much as Peter.

See **AUTANT DE, AUTANT QUE**

AS MUCH + NOUN + AS

"*Autant de* + noun + *que.*"

E.g.: *Il a autant d'argent que moi.*
      He has as much money as I.

See **AUTANT DE, AUTANT QUE**

to ASK vs. to ASK FOR vs. to ASK ABOUT

(1) "To ask a question" = *Poser une question.*

   E.g.: *Les étudiants américains posent beaucoup de questions.*
         American students ask a lot of questions.

(2) "To ask for something" = "*Demander* + direct object."

   E.g.: *J'ai demandé une augmentation de salaire.*
         I asked for a salary raise.

(3) "To ask about something or someone" = *S'informer de* or *Demander des nouvelles de.*

   E.g.: *Je me suis informé de ma cousine qui est malade.*
         I inquired about my cousin, who is ill.

         J'ai demandé des nouvelles de ma cousine qui est malade.
         I inquired about my cousin, who is ill.

ASSAILLIR

(To assail, to attack)
PRÉS.: *assaill-e, -es, -e, -ons, -ez, -ent.*
IMPARF.: *assaill-ais, -ais, -ait, -ions, -iez, -aient.*
PASSÉ SIMPLE: *assaill-is, -is, -it, -îmes, -îtes, -irent.*
FUT.: *assailler-ai, -as, -a, -ons, -ez, -ont.*
CONDIT.: *assailler-ais, -ais, -ait, -ions, -iez, -aient.*
IMPÉR.: *assaille, assaillons, assaillez.*
SUBJ. PRÉS.: *assaill-e, -es, -e, -ions, -iez, -ent.*
SUBJ. IMPARF.: *assaill-isse, -isses, -ît, -issions, -issiez, -issent.*
P. PRÉS.: *assaillant.*
P. PASSÉ: *assailli(e).*

ASSEZ

(Adverb) = "Enough, rather, fairly."
E.g.: *J'ai assez mangé.*   *Ils sont assez riches.*   *Il fait assez froid aujourd'hui.*
   I have eaten enough.   They are fairly rich.   It's rather cold today.
NOTE:
In compound tense, *assez* goes immediately after the auxiliary verb.
See **ASSEZ + ADJECTIVE + *POUR* + INFINITIVE** and **ASSEZ DE + NOUN**

ASSEZ + ADJECTIVE + *POUR* + INFINITIVE

This construction corresponds to the English "Adjective + enough to + verb."
E.g.: *Elle est assez intelligente pour comprendre.*
   She is intelligent enough to understand.

ASSEZ DE + NOUN

(Adverb) = "Enough + noun."
E.g.: *Nous avons assez de temps.*
   We have enough time.

ASSISTER À + NOUN

(Idiomatic construction) = "To attend."
E.g.: *Nous avons assisté au concert hier soir.*
   We attended the concert last night.
NOTE:
It does not mean "To assist, to help." "To help" = *Aider.*

AT

(Preposition) Indicating (a) place or position: *à, chez*; (b) direction: *vers*; (c) time: *à*; (d) cause: *de.*
E.g.: (a) *Elle est à l'école.*   *Le dîner aura lieu chez moi.*
      She is at school.   The dinner will take place at my house.
   (b) *Le télescope est pointé vers Mars.*
      The telescope is pointing at Mars.
   (c) *Le magasin ferme à six heures.*
      The store closes at six o'clock.
   (d) *Il a été furieux d'apprendre la nouvelle.*
      He was mad at learning the news.

AT THAT TIME

(Idiomatic expression)
(1) Meaning "At that moment" = *À ce moment-là.*
E.g.: *À ce moment-là la police est arrivée.*
At that time (moment) the police arrived.
(2) Meaning "In those days" = *À cette époque.*
E.g.: *Il y avait beaucoup de guerres à cette époque.*
There were many wars in those days.

AT THE SAME TIME

(Idiomatic expression)
(1) Meaning "At the same instant" = *Au même moment.*
E.g.: *Elle est arrivée au même moment que moi.*
She arrived at the same time as I.
(2) Meaning "Simultaneously" = *En même temps.*
E.g.: *Elle étudie et elle mange en même temps.*
She studies and eats at the same time.

ATTEINDRE

(To attain, to reach)
PRÉS.: *atteins, atteins, atteint, atteign-ons, -ez, -ent.*
IMPARF.: *atteign-ais, -ais, -ait, -ions, -iez, -aient.*
PASSÉ SIMPLE: *atteign-is, -is-, -it, -îmes, -îtes, irent.*
FUT.: *atteindr-ai, -as, -a, -ons, -ez, -ont.*
CONDIT.: *atteindr-ais, -ais, -ait, -ions, -iez, -aient.*
IMPÉR.: *atteins, atteignons, atteignez.*
SUBJ. PRÉS.: *atteign-e, -es, -e, -ions, -iez, -ent.*
SUBJ. IMPART.: *atteign-is, -is, -ît, -issions, -issiez, -issent.*
P. PRÉS.: *atteignant.*
P. PASSÉ: *atteint(e).*

ATTENDRE

(Transitive verb) = "To wait for, to await."
E.g.: *Elles attendent leurs parents à l'aéroport.*
They are waiting for their parents at the airport.
NOTES:
(1) This is a transitive verb; i.e., it takes a direct object, unlike the English equivalent, which requires the preposition "For."
(2) Do not confuse this verb with the English "to attend," which is *Assister à.*
See ***ASSISTER À*** + **NOUN** and ***S'ATTENDRE À***

ATTENDRE À(S')

See ***S'ATTENDRE À***

ATTRIBUT

L'attribut (the predicate) is the part of a sentence that expresses what is said of the subject. It must be linked to the subject by means of the verb *être* or a verb such as *devenir, paraître,* or *sembler.*
E.g.: *Elle veut devenir <u>la plus grande artiste de son époque</u>.*
She wants to become <u>the greatest artist of her time</u>.

AU, AUX

Contractions of the preposition *à* and the definite article *le, les*.
See **ARTICLES, CONTRACTION OF**

AU BESOIN

(Idiomatic expression) = "If need be."
E.g.: *Au besoin, je t'aiderai.*
    If need be, I'll help you.

AU + **COUNTRIES**

The preposition *au* means "to" or "in" and is used before names of masculine countries, states, and provinces.
E.g.: *Elle est au Brésil.*   *Il va au Poitou.*
    She is in Brazil.   He is going to Poitou.
See **GEOGRAPHICAL NAMES, PREPOSITIONS WITH**

AU COURANT (DE)

(Idiomatic expression) = "Informed (about)."
E.g.: *Êtes-vous au courant de ce qui se passe en Afrique?*
    Are you informed about what is going on in Africa?

AU FOND

(Idiomatic expression) = "Basically, fundamentally."
E.g.: *Au fond, ça ne me concerne pas.*
    Basically, it doesn't concern me.

AU MOINS

(Adverbial expression) = "At least."
E.g.: *Il a au moins cinquante ans.*
    He is at least fifty years old.
NOTE:
Do not confuse with *À moins (de* or *que)* (= "Unless").

AU SUJET DE

(Prepositional construction) = "About, concerning."
E.g.: *Elle m'a parlé au sujet de son frère.*
    She talked to me about her brother.

AUCUN(E)

(Indefinite adjective or pronoun) = "No, not any, none."
E.g.: *Je n'ai aucun problème.*
    I have no problem.
NOTE:
When used without a verb the *ne* is omitted.
E.g.: *Avez-vous des problèmes? Non, aucun.*
    Do you have any problems? No, none.

AUSSI

(1) (Adverb) Meaning "also, too, as."

E.g.: *Elle est fatiguée et moi aussi.*

She is tired and I am too.

Elle est aussi fatiguée que moi.

She is as tired as I am.

See **ADJECTIVES, COMPARISON OF** and **ADVERBS, COMPARATIVE AND SUPERLATIVE OF**

NOTE:

Do not place *aussi* at the beginning of a clause. In the sense of "moreover," use *En outre* or *de plus.*

E.g.: *En outre, je dois dire que j'ai eu peur.*

Also, I must admit that I was afraid.

(2) (Conjunction) Meaning "Therefore." When it comes at the beginning of a clause, this conjunction requires inversion.

E.g.: *Il avait faim, aussi a-t-il mangé.*

He was hungry; therefore, he ate.

AUSSI BIEN

(Adverbial expression) = "Just as well, just as easily."

E.g.: *Cette toile peut aussi bien être un fantôme qu'une tempête de neige.*

This painting could just as well be a ghost as a snowstorm.

AUSSITÔT QUE, TENSES WITH

(Conjunctional expression) "*Aussitôt que* + indicative."

The agreement of the verb tenses is important.

(1) If the two actions are simultaneous, both verbs are in the same tense.

E.g.: *Aussitôt qu'il est entré, nous nous sommes levés.*

As soon as he entered, we stood up.

(2) If the action of the subordinate clause takes place before that of the main verb, the auxiliary verb of the subordinate clause is in the same tense as the main verb; that is, the subordinate verb is "once removed" from the main verb.

E.g.: *Aussitôt qu'elle aura fini le livre, elle se présentera à l'examen.*

(futur antérieur)   (futur)

As soon as she has finished the book, she will take the exam.

E.g.: *Aussitôt que nous avions fini les examens, nous partions pour la plage.*

(plus-que-parfait)   (imparfait)

As soon as we had finished the exams, we used to leave for the beach.

NOTE:

When the main clause is in the future, you must use the future tense in French. This contrasts with English, where the present tense is used.

E.g.: *Nous commencerons à manger aussitôt qu'elle arrivera.*

We shall start to eat as soon as she arrives.

See **DÈS QUE, TENSES WITH**

AUTANT DE, AUTANT QUE

(Adverb) = "As much as, as many as."

E.g.: *Elle a autant d'amis et autant d'argent que toi.*

She has as many friends and as much money as you.

See **AS MUCH AS** and **AS MUCH + NOUN + AS**

AUTOUR (DE)

(Preposition) = "Around, all the way around."
E.g.: *Il y a un jardin autour de la maison.*
There is a garden (all the way) around the house.

AUTRE

(Indefinite adjective) = "Other, different."
The feminine form is the same as the masculine.
E.g.: *Un autre jour.*   *C'est une autre histoire.*
Another day.   That's another story.

AUTREFOIS

(Adverb) = "In the past, in bygone days."
E.g.: *Autrefois il n'y avait pas de chauffage central.*
In bygone days there was no central heating.

AUTREMENT DIT

(Idiomatic expression) = "In other words."
E.g.: *Il est très occupé. Autrement dit, ne le dérangez pas.*
He is very busy. In other words, don't disturb him.

AUTRUI

(Indefinite pronoun) = "Other people, others."
E.g.: *Il ne fait rien pour autrui.*
He does nothing for others.

AUXILIARY VERBS

(Les verbes auxiliaires) They are used to form the compound tenses of other verbs. The two main auxiliary verbs are *avoir* and *être*. Of course, both verbs can be used alone, in which case they retain their own meaning.
USAGE:
AVOIR
(1) *Avoir* is used to form the compound tenses of:
    (a) *Avoir* and *être.*
        E.g.: *Nous avons eu un accident.*
           We have had an accident.
           Nous avons été surpris d'apprendre la nouvelle.
           We were surprised to learn the news.
    (b) All transitive verbs.
        E.g.: *Ils ont mangé la salade.*
           They ate (have eaten) the salad.
    (c) All impersonal verbs.
        E.g.: *Il a plu hier soir.*
           It rained last night.
ÊTRE
(2) *Être* is used to form the compound tenses of:
    (a) Certain intransitive verbs.
        E.g.: *Je suis arrivé hier.*
           I arrived yesterday.
    (b) All reflexive (or reciprocal) verbs.
        E.g.: *Elle s'est levée très tôt.*
           She got up early.
    (c) All tenses of the passive voice.
        E.g.: *Il est accusé de meurtre.*
           He is accused of murder.

NOTE:

The principal intransitive verbs conjugated with *être* are:

aller = to go	*monter* = to go up	*rester* = to stay
arriver = to arrive	*mourir* = to die	*retourner* = to return
demeurer = to stay, to remain	*naître* = to be born	*sortir* = to go out
descendre – to go down	*partir* = to leave	*tomber* = to fall
devenir = to become	*repartir* = to leave again	*venir* = to come
entrer = to enter	*rentrer* = to go home	

As an AID TO MEMORY these are sometimes called the
"DR & MRS VANDERTRAMP" verbs:

Descendre	**V**enir	**T**omber
Rentrer	**A**ller	**R**etourner
Monter	**N**aître	**A**rriver
Repartir	**D**evenir and **D**emeurer	**M**ourir
Sortir	**E**ntrer	**P**artir
	Rester	

REMEMBER that certain verbs can be intransitive or transitive, depending on their meaning.

A. *Descendre* =
  (1) to go down: *Ils <u>sont</u> descendus à la cave.*
  They went down to the cellar.
  (2) to take (something) down: *Ils <u>ont</u> descendu les valises.*
  They took the suitcases down(stairs.)
  (3) to go down the stairs: *Ils <u>ont</u> descendu l'escalier.*
  They went down the stairs.

B. *Monter* =
  (1) to go up: *Elle <u>est</u> montée dans sa chambre.*
  She went up to her room.
  (2) to take (something) up: *Elle <u>a</u> monté les valises dans sa chambre.*
  She took the suitcases up to her room.
  (3) to go up the stairs: *Elle <u>a</u> monté l'escalier.*
  She went up the stairs.

C. *Passer* =
  (1) to pass by or through: *Nous <u>sommes</u> passés par Bordeaux.*
  We passed through Bordeaux.
  (2) to pass something to someone: *Elle ne m'<u>a</u> pas passé le sel.*
  She did not pass me the salt.

D. *Rentrer* =
  (1) to go (back) in, go home: *Elles <u>sont</u> rentrées tard.*
  They came home very late.
  (2) to take (something) in: *Elles <u>ont</u> rentré les chaises de jardin.*
  They brought in the garden chairs.

E. *Sortir* =
  (1) to go out: *Nous <u>sommes</u> sortis hier soir.*
  We went out last night.
  (2) to take (something) out: *Nous <u>avons</u> sorti le chien.*
  We took the dog out.

NOTES:

Aller, devoir, and *venir* are sometimes used as auxiliary verbs.
(1) "*Aller* + infinitive" expresses the immediate future.
  E.g.: *Je vais lire la lettre.*
    I am going to read the letter.

(2) *Devoir* is used to form the future of the subjunctive when it is necessary to distinguish between the future and the present.

> E.g.: *Est-il possible qu'ils doivent partir demain?*
> Is it possible that they will have to leave tomorrow?

(3) "*Venir de* + infinitive" expresses the immediate past ("Have just + past participle").

> E.g.: *Je viens de lire la lettre.*
> I have just read the letter.

See **RECENT PAST**
See also ***VENIR DE* + INFINITIVE**

AVANT vs. *AVANT DE* vs. *AVANT QUE*

(1) The adverb *avant* modifies verbs.

> E.g.: *Comme le film est très long, mangez avant.*
> As the movie is very long, eat first.

(2) The preposition *avant* is used (a) before a noun, (b) before a pronoun.

> E.g.: (a) *Avant la classe.*
> Before the class.
>
> (b) *Avant nous.*
> Before us.

(3) The prepositional construction *avant de* is used before an infinitive.

> E.g.: *Il pense avant de parler.*
> He thinks before speaking.

(4) The conjunction *avant que* is used before a cause in the subjunctive.

> E.g.: *Il finira avant que tu (ne) viennes.*
> He will finish before you come.

NOTE:
Remember not to use the subjunctive if the two verbs have the same subject.

> E.g.: *Il finira avant de venir.*
> He will finish before coming.

AVANT vs. *DEVANT*

(prepositions)
(1) *Avant* is used for time.
(2) *Devant* is used for space.

> E.g.: (a) *Il est parti avant moi.*
> He left before me.
>
> (b) *Elle est devant la maison.*
> She is in front of the house.

AVOIR

(To have)
PRÉS.: *ai, as, a, avons, avez, ont.*
IMPARF.: *avais, avais, avait, avions, aviez, avaient.*
PASSÉ SIMPLE: *eus, eus, eut, eûmes, eûtes, eurent.*
FUT.: *aur-ai, -as, -a, -ons, -ez, -ont.*
CONDIT.: *aur-ais, -ais, -ait, -ions, -iez, -aient.*
IMPÉR.: *aie, ayons, ayez.*
SUBJ. PRÉS.: *aie, aies, ait, ayons, ayez, aient.*
SUBJ. IMPARF.: *eusse, eusses, eût, eussions, eussiez, eussent.*
P. PRÉS.: *ayant.*
P. PASSÉ: *eu.*
NOTE:
"*Avoir* + noun + *à* + infinitive" = "To have + noun + verb."

> E.g.: *J'ai du travail à faire.*
> I have work to do.

AVOIR BEAU + INFINITIVE

(Idiomatic construction) = "To (do something) in vain."
E.g.: *J'ai beau crier, personne ne m'entend.*
    No matter how much I shout (= I shout in vain), nobody hears me.

AVOIR BESOIN DE

(Idiomatic construction) = "To need."
E.g.: *J'ai besoin de nouvelles lunettes.*
    I need new eyeglasses.

AVOIR CHAUD

(Idiomatic construction) = "To be hot" (used only of persons).
E.g.: *J'ai chaud; je vais enlever mon pull-over.*
    I'm hot; I'm going to remove my sweater.

AVOIR ENVIE DE

(Idiomatic construction) = "To want, to feel like."
E.g.: *Elle a envie d'aller se coucher.*
    She feels like going to bed.

AVOIR FAIM

(Idiomatic construction) = "To be hungry."
E.g.: *J'ai faim parce que je n'ai pas déjeuné aujourd'hui.*
    I am hungry because I didn't have lunch today.

AVOIR FROID

(Idiomatic construction) = "To be cold" (used only of persons).
E.g.: *J'ai froid; je vais mettre un manteau.*
    I am cold; I'm going to put on a coat.

AVOIR L'AIR (DE)

(1) "*Avoir l'air* + adjective" = "To seem."
    E.g.: *Vous avez l'air fatigué.*
        You seem tired.
(2) "*Avoir l'air de* + infinitive" = "To seem to."
    E.g.: *Vous avez l'air d'avoir peur.*
        You seem to be afraid.

AVOIR LIEU

(Idiomatic construction) = "To take place."
E.g.: *La conférence aura lieu demain soir.*
    The lecture will take place tomorrow evening.

AVOIR + MEASUREMENT or SIZE
See SIZES AND MEASUREMENTS

AVOIR + NUMBER + ANS

(Idiomatic construction) used to express age.
E.g.: *Elle a dix-sept ans.*
    She is seventeen years old.
See **AGE**

AVOIR PEUR DE

(Idiomatic construction) = "To be afraid."
E.g.: *Qui a peur du grand méchant loup?*
    Who's afraid of the big bad wolf?

AVOIR RAISON

(Idiomatic construction) = "To be right"
E.g.: *Ils ont raison de partir tout de suite.*
    They are right to leave right away.
NOTE:
This expression can be used only when talking about people. When talking about things or situations, use *être* + an adjective such as *Correct, équitable, juste.*
E.g.: *Cette réponse n'est pas juste.*
    This answer is not right.

AVOIR SOIF

(Idiomatic construction) = "To be thirsty."
E.g.: *Il a soif mais il n'y a rien à boire.*
    He is thirsty but there is nothing to drink.

AVOIR TORT

(Idiomatic construction) = "To be wrong" (used only of persons).
E.g.: *Vous avez tort de boire tant d'alcool.*
    You are wrong to drink so much alcohol.

AVOIR vs. ÊTRE AS AUXILIARY VERB
See **AUXILIARY VERBS**

B

BACK

(1) (Noun) = *le dos.*
    E.g.: *Je me suis fait mal au dos.*
        I hurt my back.
(2) (Idiomatic expressions):
    (a) "To be back" = *Être de retour.*
        E.g.: *Nous serons de retour vers huit heures.*
            We'll be back around eight o'clock.
    (b) "To go back" = *Retourner.*
        E.g.: *Elle retournera chez elle demain matin.*
            She will go back home tomorrow morning.
    (c) "To send back" = *Renvoyer.*
        E.g.: *J'ai renvoyé le colis.*
            I sent the package back.

BATTRE

(To beat)
PRÉS.: bats, bats, bat, battons, battez, battent.
IMPARF.: batt-ais, -ais, -ait, -ions, -iez, -aient.
PASSÉ SIMPLE: batt-is, -is, -it, -îmes, -îtes, -irent.
FUT: battr-ai, -as, -a, -ons, -ez, -ont.
CONDIT.: battr-ais, -ais, -ait, -ions, -iez, -aient.
IMPÉR.: bats, battons, battez.
SUBJ. PRÉS.: batt-e, -es, -e, -ions, -iez, -ent.
SUBJ. IMPARF.: batt-isse, -isses, -ît, -issions, -issiez, -issent.
P. PRÉS.: battant.
P. PASSÉ: battu(e).

BEAU, BEL, BELLE

(Adjective) *Beau* changes to *Bel* in front of a vowel or an unaspirated *h*.
E.g.: *Un beau livre.*
    A beautiful book.
BUT: *Un bel enfant.*   *Un bel homme.*
    A beautiful child.   A handsome man.
The feminine form is *Belle*.
E.g.: *Une belle femme.*
    A beautiful woman.
NOTE:
This adjective always comes before the noun.

BEAU (AVOIR + INFINITIVE)

See **AVOIR BEAU + INFINITIVE**

BEAUCOUP (DE + NOUN)

(Adverb) = "A lot, many, much."
E.g.: *Elle étudie beaucoup.*   *Ils ont beaucoup d'argent.*   *Elles ont beaucoup d'amis.*
    She studies a lot.   They have much money.   They have many friends.

BECAUSE vs. BECAUSE OF

(1) The conjunctional construction *Parce que* takes the indicative.
    E.g.: *Il est furieux parce qu'il a perdu son emploi.*
        He is mad because he lost his job.
NOTE:
Avoid *Parce que* at the beginning of a sentence. Use *Puisque* instead.
E.g.: *Puisqu'il est malade, il restera au lit.*
    Because he is ill, he will stay in bed.
(2) The prepositional construction *À cause de* introduces a noun or a pronoun, never a clause.
    E.g.: *Il est fatigué à cause de l'effort qu'il a fait.*
        He is tired because of the effort he made.
See **À CAUSE DE vs. PARCE QUE**
See also **PUISQUE**

BEFORE + VERB (BEFORE + -ING)

(1) If the subject of the subordinate clause is the same as the subject of the main clause, use the prepositional construction "*Avant de* + infinitive."
    E.g.: *Il s'habille avant de sortir.*
        He gets dressed before going out.

(2) If the subject of the subordinate clause is different from that of the main clause, use the conjunctional construction "*Avant que* + subjunctive."
E.g.: *Il s'habille avant que ses amis (ne) viennent.*
He gets dressed before his friends come.
See **AVANT vs. AVANT DE vs. AVANT QUE**

to BE HAVING . . . + PAST PARTICIPLE

E.g.: *Je fais réparer ma voiture.*
I am having my car repaired.
See **FAIRE + INFINITIVE**

to BELONG TO

(1) Indicating possession = "*Appartenir à* + indirect object."
E.g.: *Ce bracelet appartient à Marie.*   *Ce bracelet lui appartient.*
This bracelet belongs to Mary.   This bracelet belongs to her.
(2) Indicating membership = *Faire partie de.*
E.g.: *Ils font partie de la Société des poètes.*
They belong to the Society of Poets.
See **POSSESSION**

BESIDE

(Prepositional construction) = *À côté de.*
E.g.: *Viens t'asseoir à côté de moi.*
Come sit beside me.

BESIDES

(1) (Adverbial expression) = *En outre.*
E.g.: *Je n'ai pas le temps et en outre je n'ai pas d'argent.*
I don't have the time, and besides, I don't have any money.
(2) (Preposition) = *Outre.*
E.g.: *Outre ses parents, il a des cousins en France.*
Besides his parents, he has cousins living in France.
See **EN OUTRE**

BESOIN

See **AVOIR BESOIN DE**

BEST

(Adverb) = *Le mieux.*
E.g.: *C'est le soir qu'elle travaille le mieux.*
She works best at night.

Le mieux c'est d'aller en métro.
It's best to go by subway.
See **ADVERBS, COMPARATIVE AND SUPERLATIVE OF**

BETTER (IT IS BETTER TO)

(Idiomatic construction) = "*Valoir mieux* + infinitive."
E.g.: *Il vaut mieux dormir que d'étudier.*
It is better to sleep than to study.
NOTE:
The second infinitive of the comparison is generally preceded by the construction *Que de*:
E.g.: *Il vaut mieux avoir faim que d'avoir soif.*
It is better to be hungry than to be thirsty.
See **VALOIR**

BIEN

(Adverb) = "Well, very."

E.g.: *Je suis bien content.*   *Tout s'est bien passé.*   *Elle parle bien rapidement.*
      I am very glad.   Everything went well.   She speaks very rapidly.

NOTES:

(1) When it is followed by *des,* it means "Many."

E.g.: *Bien des gens souffrent de la faim.*
      Many people suffer from hunger.

(2) Sometimes *Bien* has a diminishing force on the verb it modifies.

E.g.: *Je t'aime.*
      I love you.

BUT: *Je t'aime bien.*
     I like you.

(3) *Eh bien!* can mark (a) surprise, (b) question, or (c) concession.

E.g.: (a) *Voici Marie! Eh bien, quelle surprise!*
          Here's Mary! Well, what a surprise!

      (b) *Eh bien! Qu'en pensez-vous?*
          Well! What do you think?

      (c) *Vous voulez partir, eh bien, partez.*
          You want to leave? Well, leave.

BIEN QUE

(Conjunction) "*Bien que* + subjunctive" = Though, although, even though."

E.g.: *Bien qu'il soit malade, il ira en France.*
      Though he is sick, he will go to France.

See **SUBJUNCTIVE MOOD**

BILLION

(Masculine noun) = *Un milliard.*

NOTE:

When *Milliard* is followed by a noun, the preposition *de* is needed.

E.g.: *Il y a plus d'un milliard <u>de</u> Chinois.*
      There are more than one billion Chinese.

See **NUMBERS, CARDINAL**

BOIRE

(To drink)

PRÉS.: *bois, bois, boit, buvons, buvez, boivent.*

IMPARF.: *buv-ais, -ais, -ait, -ions, -iez, -aient.*

PASSÉ SIMPLE: *bus, bus, but, bûmes, bûtes, burent.*

FUT.: *boir-ai, -as, -a, -ons, -ez, -ont.*

CONDIT.: *boir-ais, -ais, -ait, -ions, -iez, -aient.*

IMPÉR.: *bois, buvons, buvez.*

SUBJ. PRÉS.: *boive, boives, boive, buvions, buviez, boive.*

SUBJ. IMPARF.: *busse, busses, bût, bussions, bussiez, bussent.*

P. PRÉS.: *buvant.*

P. PASSÉ: *bu(e).*

BON vs. BIEN

(1) *Bon* is an adjective meaning "Good."

E.g.: *C'est un très bon vin.*
      It's a very good wine.

NOTE the idiomatic uses:

(a) *Ça sent bon!*
    That smells good!

(b) *Il fait bon vivre ici.*
    It's good living here.

(2) *Bien* is an adverb meaning "Well."
    E.g.: *Elle chante bien.*
          She sings well.
See **MEILLEUR(E) vs. MIEUX**

BON GRÉ MAL GRÉ

(Idiomatic expression) = "Like it or not, no matter what."
    E.g.: *Tu devras faire ton service militaire bon gré mal gré.*
          You will have to do your military service, like it or not.

BOUILLIR

(To boil)
PRÉS.: *bous, bous, bout, bouillons, bouillez, bouillent.*
IMPARF.: *bouill-ais, -ais, -ait, -ions, -iez, -aient.*
PASSÉ SIMPLE: *bouill-is, -is, -it, -îmes, -îtes, -irent.*
FUT.: *bouillir-ai, -as, -a, -ons, -ez, -ont.*
CONDIT.: *bouillir-ais, -ais, -ait, -ions, -iez, -aient.*
IMPÉR.: *bous, bouillons, bouillez.*
SUBJ. PRÉS.: *bouill-e, -es, -e, -ions, -iez, -ent.*
SUBJ. IMPARF.: *bouill-isse, -isses, -ît, -issions, -issiez, -issent.*
P. PRÉS.: *bouillant.*
P. PASSÉ: *bouilli(e).*

BY

(Preposition) It can (a) indicate the agent or manner: *par;* (b) indicate proximity: *près de;* (c) mean "Across, through, by way of": *par;* (d) introduce the gerund.
    E.g.: (a) *Ce livre a été écrit par Descartes.*
            This book was written by Descartes.
        (b) *Ma maison est près de l'église.*
            My house is by the church.
        (c) *Nous sommes passés par la Suisse.*
            We went by way of Switzerland.
        (d) See **GERUND**
            See also **BY + VERB (-ing)**

BY THE WAY

(Idiomatic expresion) + *À propos.*
    E.g.: *À propos, à quelle heure viendra-t-il?*
          By the way, what time will he come?

BY + VERB (-ING)

"*En* + present participle."
    E.g.: *Il a appris le français en vivant en France.*
          He learned French by living in France.
Do not use *Par* for this construction!
See **GERUND**

C

ÇA

(Demonstrative pronoun, contraction of *Cela*) Used only in spoken language.

E.g.: *Comment ça va?*   *Qu'est-ce que ça veut dire?*
How goes it?   What does that mean?

See **PRONOUNS, DEMONSTRATIVE**

ÇA (CELA) FAIT (FAISAIT) + TIME EXPRESSION + *QUE*

The use of tenses with this expression is very different from the English construction.

(1) If the action is still going on, use the present tense.

E.g.: *Ça fait un an que j'habite ici.*
I have been living here for a year.

(2) If the action was still going on in a past context, use the imperfect (and note that *Fait* becomes *Faisait*).

E.g.: *Ça faisait un an que j'habitais ici quand il est venu me voir.*
I had been living here for a year when he came to see me.

See *IL Y A* + **TIME EXPRESSION** + *QUE*
See also *DEPUIS* + **TIME EXPRESSION**

CAN

(1) Meaning "Able to" = *Pouvoir.*

E.g.: *Il peut venir demain.*
He can come tomorrow.

(2) Meaning "Know how to" = *Pouvoir* or *Savoir.*

E.g.: *Elle peut lire le chinois.*
OR *Elle sait lire le chinois.*
She can read Chinese.

See *POUVOIR*

CAN'T HELP

(Idiomatic expression)
(1) I can't help it = *Je n'y peux rien.*
(2) It can't be helped = *On n'y peut rien.*

CAN'T WAIT

(Idiomatic expression) = *Avoir hâte de* + infinitive.

E.g.: *J'ai hâte de retourner chez moi.*
I can't wait to go home.

CAPITALIZATION

The rules for using capital letters *(les majuscules)* in French are the same as in English EXCEPT in the following cases.

(1) Days of the week and months are not capitalized.

E.g.: *Le mardi douze février.*
Tuesday, February 12.

(2) Such words as *avenue, lac, mer, mont, océan,* and *rue* are not capitalized when they are part of a place name.

E.g.: *l'océan Atlantique*   *la rue de l'Église*   *le mont Everest*
       the Atlantic Ocean   Church Street   Mount Everest

(3) Names of languages are not capitalized.

E.g.: *J'étudie le chinois et le portugais.*
       I study Chinese and Portuguese.

(4) Adjectives of nationality are not capitalized.

E.g.: *Un général américain.*   *L'époque victorienne.*
       An American general.   The Victorian era.

BUT, as in English, names of peoples are capitalized.

E.g.: *Les Français et les Espagnols sont des Européens.*
       Frenchmen and Spaniards are Europeans.

(5) Titles are not capitalized when followed by a person's name.

E.g.: *le professeur Dupont*   *l'oncle Joseph*
       Professor Dupont   Uncle Joseph

CAR

(Conjunction) = "Because, for."

E.g.: *Je n'irai pas avec vous car j'ai du travail à faire.*
       I shall not go with you because I have work to do.

NOTE:

Car is never used at the beginning of a sentence. Use *Comme* instead.

E.g.: Because she was poor, she could not buy any clothes.
       Comme elle était pauvre elle ne pouvait pas acheter de vêtements.

CAUSATIVE CONSTRUCTION WITH *FAIRE*

The "*Faire* + infinitive" construction expresses the idea that someone causes an action to be performed by somebody or something else.

E.g.: *Le professeur fait travailler les élèves.*
       The teacher makes the pupils work.

       Ils ont fait réparer leur voiture.
       They had their car repaired.

NOTE:

If there is only one object, it is a direct object.

(1) If it is a noun, it follows the infinitive.

E.g.: *J'ai fait venir le médecin.*
       I summoned the doctor (I had the doctor come).

(2) If it is a pronoun, it precedes *faire.*

E.g.: *Je l'ai fait venir.*
       I summoned him (her) OR I had him (her) come.

See *FAIRE* **+ INFINITIVE**

CE

As the masculine singular form of the demonstrative adjective, it points (literally or figuratively) to the noun that follows it.

See *CE, CET, CETTE, CES*

As the neuter form of the demonstrative pronoun, it is used:

(1) As the antecedent of a relative pronoun that has no stated antecedent.

E.g.: *Ce qu'il dit est intéressant.*
       What (= that which) he says is interesting.

(2) As the subject of *être* when this verb is followed by (a) a noun, (b) a pronoun, (c) an adjective referring to a general concept or idea.

E.g.: (a) *C'est une fille.*
It's a girl.
(b) *C'est moi.*
It's me.
(c) *C'est étrange.*
It's strange.

See **ADJECTIVES, DEMONSTRATIVE**
See also **PRONOUNS, DEMONSTRATIVE**

CE, CET, CETTE, CES

(Demonstrative adjectives) = "this, these," "that, those."
FORMS:
Masc. sing.: *ce (cet* before a vowel or an unaspirated *h)*
Fem. sing.: *cette*
Masc. and fem. plur.: *ces*

E.g.: *Ce garçon.*   *Cette femme.*
This boy.   This woman.

Cet enfant.   *Ces animaux.*
This child.   These animals.

Cet homme.
This man.

The suffix *-ci* or *-là* can be added to add specificity to the noun.
E.g.: *Cet homme-ci.*   *Cette femme-là.*
This man (here).   That woman (there).

See **ADJECTIVES, DEMONSTRATIVE**

CE QUI vs. CE QUE

(Neuter demonstrative pronoun + relative pronoun) = "What."
(1) *Ce qui* is the <u>subject</u> of a clause that has no expressed antecedent.
E.g.: *Je ne sais pas ce qui se passe.*
I don't know what is happening.
(2) *Ce que* is the <u>object</u> of a clause that has no expressed antecedent.
E.g.: *Je ne comprends pas ce que vous dites.*
I don't understand what you are saying.

See **PRONOUNS, RELATIVE**

CECI, CELA

(Neuter demonstrative pronouns) = "This, that."
These are used to replace an indefinite expression or a general idea. (In informal contexts, they become *ça*.)
E.g.: *Ceci vous intéressera: c'est une lettre qui vient d'arriver.*
This will interest you: It's a letter that has just arrived.

Il pleut. Cela nous obligera à rester ici.
It's raining. That will compel us to stay here.

NOTE:
Before the verb *être*, *ceci* or *cela* is replaced by *c'*.
E.g.: *C'est intéressant à lire.*
It's interesting to read.

CÉDER

(To yield)
The *é* of the stem changes to *è* before a silent syllable that comes at the end of the verb.
Therefore, the following forms are slightly irregular:
PRÉS.: *je cède, tu cèdes, il cède, (nous cédons, vous cédez), ils cèdent.*
SUBJ. PRÉS.: *que je cède, que tu cèdes, qu'il cède, (que nous cédions, que vous cédiez), qu'ils cèdent.*

CEDILLA

The cedilla *(la cédille)* is the symbol (¸) placed under the letter *c* to change its pronunciation from hard to soft (i.e., from a "k" sound to an "s" sound) before the vowels *a, o,* and *u*.
E.g.: *façade, leçon, commençons.*

CELUI, CELLE, CEUX, CELLES (-CI, -LÀ)

(Demonstrative pronoun) = "The one, the ones, those."
(1) Used before:
  (a) A participle:
      E.g.: *Le journal d'aujourd'hui et celui publié hier.*
            Today's newspaper and the one *published* yesterday.
  (b) A preposition and its object:
      E.g.: *Celui d'hier.*
            Yesterday's (= The one *of yesterday*).
  (c) A relative clause:
      E.g.: *Celui que je lis.*
            The one *(that)* I am reading.
(2) Used with the suffix *-ci* or *-là*:
  (a) To point (figuratively):
      E.g.: *Quelle maison vas-tu acheter? Celle-là.*
            Which house are you going to buy? That one.
  (b) To express "The former" and "The latter."
      Note that the order is the opposite of the English equivalent construction.
      E.g.: *Descartes et Bacon étaient de grands penseurs. Celui-ci était anglais, celui-là était français.*
            Descartes and Bacon were two great thinkers. The former was French, and the latter was English.
See **FORMER . . . LATTER**
See also **PRONOUNS, DEMONSTRATIVE**

C'EST vs. *IL EST* or *ELLE EST*

(1) *C'est* is used before (a) a proper name, (b) a noun preceded by an article, (c) a pronoun, (d) a superlative, (e) an adjective or adverb referring to a phrase or an unnamed subject, and (f) a date.
  E.g.: (a) *C'est Jacques.*
            It's James.
        (b) *C'est un livre.*
            It's a book.
        (c) *C'est moi.*   *C'est le mien.*   *C'est celui de Paul.*
            It's me.   It's mine.   It's Paul's.
        (d) *C'est le plus intelligent.*
            He is the most intelligent.
        (e) *C'est vrai (ce qu'il dit).*
            It's true (what he says).
        (f) *C'est le 13 janvier.*
            It's January 13.

(2) *Il (Elle) est* is used before (a) an adjective when the subject is known, (b) an adjective of nationality, (c) a noun (without an article) indicating a profession, (d) an adjective + preposition + infinitive, and (e) the time of day.

E.g.: (a) *Jean? Il est bizarre.*
John? He is odd.

(b) *Elle est américaine.*
She is American.

(c) *Il est médecin.*   *Elle est architecte.*
He is a doctor.   She is an architect.

(d) *Il est difficile de faire cela.*
It's hard to do that.

(e) *Il est trois heures et quart.*
It is a quarter past three.

C'EST vs. IL EST (+ ADJECTIVE + À + INFINITIVE)

(1) "*C'est* + adjective + *à* + infinitive" is used when what the adjective refers to has already been mentioned.

E.g.: *Traduire de la poésie, c'est difficile à faire.*
Translating poetry is hard to do.

(2) "*Il est* + adjective + *de* + infinitive" is used when what the adjective refers to has not yet been mentioned.

E.g.: *Il est difficile de traduire la poésie.*
It is difficult to translate poetry.

C'EST-À-DIRE

(Conjunctional expression) = "That is."

E.g.: *Elle est entomologiste, c'est-à-dire qu'elle étudie les insectes.*
She is an entomologist; that is, she studies insects.

CHACUN(E)

(Indefinite pronoun) = "Each (one)."

E.g.: *Chacun a ses problèmes.*   *Chacune d'elles a sa voiture.*
Each one has his (her) problems.   Each one of them has her car.

Do not confuse with *Chaque,* which is the indefinite adjective.

See **CHAQUE**

CHANGER DE

(Idiomatic construction) = "to change (one thing for another)."

E.g.: *Elle a changé de robe.*   *Nous avons changé de classe.*
She changed her dress.   We changed classes.

NOTE:

The construction "*De* + singular noun" without any possessive adjective, whereas in English the construction requires the possessive ("her") or a plural noun ("classes").

CHAQUE

(Indefinite adjective) = "Each." The masculine and feminine forms are identical.

E.g.: *Chaque garçon fait son travail.*   *Chaque fille a sa propre chambre.*
Each boy does his work.   Each girl has her own room.

Do not confuse with *Chacun,* which is the indefinite pronoun.

See **CHACUN**

CHERCHER

(Transitive verb) = "To look for."
E.g.: *Nous cherchons des champignons.*
   We are looking for mushrooms.
Never say "*Chercher pour.*"

CHEZ

(Preposition) = "At ——'s (house or shop)."
E.g.: *Allons chez moi.*   *Ils sont chez eux.*
   Let's go to my house.   They are at home.

   Chez moi il y a un grand jardin.   *J'ai acheté le rôti chez le boucher.*
   At my house there's a big garden.   I bought the roast at the butcher's.

   Nous allons chez Jeanne.
   We are going to Jeanne's (house).

CHIFFRE vs. NOMBRE vs. NUMÉRO

(1) *Un chiffre* = "A numeral, a digit."
   E.g.: *Écrivez la date en chiffres.*
      Write the date in numerals.
(2) *Un nombre* = "A number, a quantity."
   E.g.: *Il y a un grand nombre de personnes.*
      There is a large number of people.
(3) *Un numéro* = "Number (of house, page, telephone, etc.)."
   E.g.: *Le numéro de téléphone.*   *Il habite au numéro sept.*
      The telephone number.   He lives at number seven.

CI-INCLUS, CI-JOINT

(Adverbial expressions) = "Enclosed, attached."
They are invariable if the noun follows but variable if the noun precedes.
E.g.: *Ci-joint les documents que vous avez demandés.*
   The documents you requested are enclosed.
BUT: *Veuillez lire la lettre ci-incluse.*
   Please read the enclosed letter.

CITIES, PREPOSITIONS WITH
See GEOGRAPHICAL NAMES, PREPOSITIONS WITH

CLAUSE

A clause *(une proposition)* is a group of words that contains a subject and a predicate. It can be independent, subordinate, or relative.
(1) Independent clause *(proposition indépendante)*:
   E.g.: *Tu réussiras à ton examen.*
      You will pass your examination.
(2) Subordinate clause *(proposition subordonnée)*:
   E.g.: *Si tu étudies beaucoup, tu réussiras à ton examen.*
      If you study a lot, you will pass your examination.
      (subordinate clause)   *(main clause)*
(3) Relative clause *(proposition relative)*, which is a subordinate clause beginning with a relative pronoun.
   E.g.: *Voici le professeur qui m'enseigne le français.*
      Here is the professor who teaches me French.
      (main clause)   *(relative clause)*

COLD

(1) (Noun) = *Un rhume.*
   E.g.: *Elle avait un rhume hier.*
      She had a cold yesterday.
(2) "It's cold" (weather) = *Il fait froid.*
   E.g.: *Il fait très froid ici en hiver.*
      It's very cold here in winter.
(3) "To be cold" (person) = *Avoir froid.*
   E.g.: *J'ai toujours froid.*
      I'm always cold.
See **AVOIR FROID**

COLLECTIVE SUBJECT

When the subject of a verb is collective, the predicate is generally singular.
E.g.: *Nous vivons <u>notre vie</u> sur terre.*
   We live our lives on earth.
NOTE:
The corresponding English construction requires the plural: "our live<u>s</u>."

COMMANDS
See **IMPERATIVE MOOD**

COMME

(1) (Conjunction) Indicating comparison or manner = "As, like."
   E.g.: *Sur la terre comme au ciel.*   *Elle chante comme un oiseau.*
      On earth as in heaven.   She sings like a bird.
(2) (Conjunction) Indicating cause = "Since, as, seeing that."
   E.g.: *Comme j'étais malade, je ne suis pas sorti.*
      As I was sick, I did not go out.
(3) (Conjunction) Indicating time = "As."
   E.g.: *Ils sont partis commme j'arrivais.*
      They left as I arrived.
(4) (Adverb of exclamation) = "How."
   E.g.: *Comme il est grand!*
      How tall he is!
   Do not say *"Comment il est grand!"*

COMME IL FAUT

(Invariable idiomatic expression) = "Proper, properly."
E.g.: *Jacqueline est une jeune fille très comme il faut.*
   Jacqueline is a very proper young woman.

   Elle fait toujours son travail comme il faut.
   She always does her homework properly.

COMME SI

(Conjunctional construction) It introduces a contrary-to-fact statement.
See **SI CLAUSES**

COMPARISON OF ADJECTIVES
See **ADJECTIVES, COMPARISON OF**

COMPARISON OF ADVERBS
See **ADVERBS, COMPARATIVE AND SUPERLATIVE OF**

COMPOUND ADJECTIVES
See **ADJECTIVES, COMPOUND**

COMPOUND NOUNS

(Les noms composés) These are nouns made up of two words. Some are written as one word *(un passeport)*, but most are written as two words connected by a hyphen *(un gratte-ciel)*.
PLURAL OF COMPOUND NOUNS:
(1) Nouns written as one word follow the normal rules for the plural of nouns.
E.g.: *Un passeport → des passeports*   A passport
Un portemanteaux → des portemanteaux   A coat hanger
EXCEPTIONS:
Un bonhomme → des bonshommes   A fellow, a guy
Un gentilhomme → des gentilshommes   A gentleman
Madame → mesdames   Madam
Mademoiselle → mesdemoiselles   Miss
Monsieur → messieurs   Mister
(2) Nouns written as two words:
(a) Nouns composed of noun + noun: Both parts are pluralized.
E.g.: *Un chef-lieu → des chefs-lieux*   A county seat (capital)
Un oiseau-lyre → des oiseaux-lyres   A lyre bird
(b) Nouns composed of noun + adjective or adjective + noun: Both parts are pluralized.
E.g.: *Un franc-maçon → des francs-maçons*   A freemason
Un grand-père → des grands-pères   A grandfather
(c) Nouns composed of verb + direct object: In some cases the direct object remains singular, and in other cases it is pluralized.
E.g.: *Un brise-glace → des brise-glace*   An icebreaker
Un gratte-ciel → des gratte-ciel   A skyscraper
BUT: *Un coupe-circuit → des coupe-circuits*   A circuit breaker
Un tire-bouchon → des tire-bouchons   A corkscrew

COMPRENDRE

(To understand)
Conjugated like **PRENDRE**

CONCEVOIR

(To conceive)
PRÉS.: *conçois, conçois, conçoit, concevons, concevez, conçoivent.*
IMPARF.: *concev-ais, -ais, -ait, -ions, -iez, -aient.*
PASSÉ SIMPLE: *conç-us, -us, -ut, -ûmes, -ûtes, -urent.*
FUT.: *concevr-ai, -as, -a, -ons, -ez, -ont.*
CONDIT.: *concevr-ais, -ais, -ait, -ions, -iez, -aient.*
IMPÉR.: *conçois, concevons, concevez.*
SUBJ. PRÉS.: *conçoiv-e, -es, -e, concevions, conceviez, conçoivent.*
SUBJ. IMPARF.: *conç-usse, -usses, -ût, -ussions, -ussiez, -ussent.*
P. PRÉS.: *concevant.*
P. PASSÉ: *conçu(e).*

CONCLURE

(To conclude)
PRÉS.: *conclu-s, -s, -t, -ons, -ez, -ent.*
IMPARF.: *conclu-ais, -ais, -ait, -ions, -iez, -aient.*
PASSÉ SIMPLE: *concl-us, -us, -ut, -ûmes, -ûtes, -urent.*
FUT.: *conclur-ai, -as, -a, -ons, -ez, -ont.*
CONDIT.: *conclur-ais, -ais, -ait, -ions, -iez, -aient.*
IMPÉR.: *conclus, concluons, concluez.*
SUBJ. PRÉS.: *conclu-e, -es, -e, -ions, -iez, -ent.*
SUBJ. IMP.: *concl-usse, -usses, -ût, -ussions, -ussiez, -ussent.*
P. PRÉS.: *concluant.*
P. PASSÉ: *conclu(e).*

CONDITIONAL MOOD

The conditional mood *(le mode conditionnel)* presents the action of the verb as (a) possible or (b) dependent on some condition.

E.g.: (a) *Cet homme travaillerait jour et nuit!*
This man would work day and night!
(b) *Cet homme travaillerait s'il pouvait.*
This man would work if he could.

TENSES: There are two conditional tenses:

(1) PRESENT CONDITIONAL:
FORMATION:
Same stem as that used to form the future + *-ais, -ais, -ait, -ions, -iez, -aient.*
REMEMBER: The future stem = the infinitive (minus the final *e* if there is one).
E.g.: Infinitive: *Manger* → Future: *mangerai* → Conditional: *mangerais*
If the future stem is irregular, the conditional stem has the same irregularity.
E.g.: Infinitive: *Aller* → Future: *irai* → Conditional: *irais*
USAGE:
(a) To state a future action in a past context. That is, if the main verb is in a past tense and the subordinate verb is in the future in relation to the main verb, then the subordinate verb is in the conditional.
E.g.: *Je pensais qu'il viendrait.*
I thought he would come.

Il a dit qu'elle partirait demain.
He said that she would leave tomorrow.
(b) In the result clause of a condition introduced by "*Si* + imperfect."
E.g.: *Si j'avais le temps, je le ferais.*
If I had the time, I would do it.
(c) As a polite way of expressing a desire or asking a question.
This is frequently the case with the verbs *Aimer, pouvoir,* and *vouloir.*
E.g.: *J'aimerais vous poser une question.*
I would like to ask you a question.

Pourriez-vous m'aider?
Could you help me?

Je voudrais du café, s'il vous plaît.
I would like some coffee, please.

(2) PAST CONDITIONAL:
FORMATION:
Conditional of the auxiliary verb + past participle.
E.g.: *J'aurais parlé.*   *Nous serions partis.*
I would have spoken.   We would have left.

USAGE:
(a) In the result clause of an unrealized condition introduced by "*Si* + pluperfect."
  E.g.: *Si j'avais eu le temps, je l'aurais fait.*
    If I had had the time, I would have done it.

    Si tu avais gagné, qu'aurais-tu acheté?
    If you had won, what would you have bought?
(b) To state a past action that is likely but not certain.
  E.g.: *Elle serait morte l'année passée.*
    (= Elle est probablement morte l'année passée.)
    The rumor is that she died last year.

CONDITIONAL SENTENCES
See *SI* **CLAUSES**

CONDUIRE

(To drive, to lead, to take [someone somewhere])
PRÉS.: *condui-s, -s, -t, -sons, -sez, -sent.*
IMPARF.: *conduis-ais, -ais, -ait, -ions, -iez, -aient.*
PASSÉ SIMPLE: *conduis-is, -is, -it, -îmes, -îtes, -irent.*
FUT.: *conduir-ai, -as, -a, -ons, -ez, -ont.*
CONDIT.: *conduir-ais, -ais, -ait, -ions, -iez, -aient.*
IMPÉR.: *conduis, conduisons, conduisez.*
SUBJ. PRÉS.: *conduis-e, -es, -e, -ions, -iez, -ent.*
SUBJ. IMPARF.: *conduis-isse, -isses, -ît, -issions, -issiez, -issent.*
P. PRÉS.: *conduisant.*
P. PASSÉ: *conduit(e).*

CONJUGATION OF "-*CER*" VERBS

Verbs ending in *-cer* take a cedilla (*ç*) before the letters *a* and *o*. (This is to keep the same soft *c* pronunciation as in the infinitive.)
  E.g.: *Avancer → Nous avançons.*
    Commencer → Je commençais.
    Rincer → elle rinça.

CONJUGATION OF "-*ELER*" VERBS

(1) Some verbs ending in *-eler* double the *l* in front of a silent *e*. The resulting *-elle* is pronounced *-èle*.
  E.g.: *Appeler → J'appelle.*
    Amonceler → J'amoncelle.
(2) Some verbs ending in *-eler* change the last *e* of the stem to *è* in front of a silent syllable.
  E.g.: *Geler → Il gèle.*
    Modeler → Je modèle.
    Peler → Je pèle.

CONJUGATION OF "-*ETER*" VERBS

(1) Some verbs ending in *-eter* double the *t* before a silent *e*. The resulting *-ette* is pronounced *-ète.*
  E.g.: *Jeter → Je jette.*
    Étiqueter → J'étiquette.
    Souffleter → Je soufflette.
(2) Some verbs ending in *-eter* change the last *e* of the stem to *è* before a silent syllable.
  E.g.: *Acheter → J'achète.*
    Haleter → Ils halètent.

CONJUGATION OF "-GER" VERBS

Verbs ending in -ger add an e after the g before a or o. (This is to keep the same soft g pronunciation as in the infinitive.)
E.g.: *Manger → Je mangeais.*
      Arranger → Nous arrangeons.

CONJUGATION OF VERBS WITH "É" IN THE LAST SYLLABLE OF THE STEM

These verbs change the é to è before a silent syllable at the end of the verb.
E.g.: *Révéler → Je révèle.*
NOTE:
This change does not take place when the silent syllable is not the final one.
E.g.: *Je révélerai.*

CONJUGATION OF "-YER" VERBS

Verbs ending in -yer change the y to i before a silent e.
E.g.: *Nettoyer → Elle nettoie; je nettoierai.*
NOTE:
This spelling change is optional for verbs ending in -ayer.
E.g.: *Payer → Je paye.*
          OR *Je paie.*

CONJUGATIONS, REGULAR

Verbs are generally divided into four categories, or conjugations, according to the ending of the infinitive.
FIRST CONJUGATION: *"-er"* verbs E.g.: *Aimer*   (To like, to love)
SECOND CONJUGATION: *"-ir"* verbs of which there are two types:
                                            (a) E.g.: *Finir*   (To finish)
                                            (b) E.g.: *Sentir*   (To feel)
THIRD CONJUGATION: *"-oir"* verbs E.g.: *Recevoir* (To receive)
FOURTH CONJUGATION: *"-re"* verbs E.g.: *Rendre* (To give back)
NOTE:
See **PASSIVE VOICE** for an example of a verb conjugated in the passive voice.

FIRST CONJUGATION: "-er" verbs E.g.: *Aimer*

VOIX ACTIVE (Active Voice)
INDICATIF:
PRÉSENT: *aim-e, -es, -e, -ons, -ez, -ent.*
IMPARFAIT.: *aim-ais, -ais, -ait, -ions, -iez, -aient.*
PASSÉ SIMPLE: *aim-ai, -as, -a, -âmes, -âtes, -èrent.*
FUTUR: *aimer-ai, -as, -a, -ons, -ez, -ont.*
PASSÉ COMPOSÉ: *ai aimé, as aimé, a aimé, avons aimé, avez aimé, ont aimé.*
PLUS-QUE-PARFAIT: *avais aimé, avais aimé, avait aimé, avions aimé, aviez aimé, avaient aimé.*
PASSÉ ANTÉRIEUR: *eus aimé, eus aimé, eut aimé, eûmes aimé, eûtes aimé, eurent aimé.*
FUTUR ANTÉRIEUR: *aurai aimé, auras aimé, aura aimé, aurons aimé, aurez aimé, auront aimé.*
CONDITIONNEL:
PRÉSENT: *aimer-ais, -ais, -ait, -ions, -iez, -aient.*
PASSÉ: *aurais aimé, aurais aimé, aurait aimé, aurions aimé, auriez aimé, auraient aimé.*
IMPÉRATIF: *aime, aimons, aimez.*
SUBJONCTIF:
PRÉSENT: *que j'aime, que tu aimes, qu'il aime, que nous aimions, que vous aimiez, qu'ils aiment.*
IMPARFAIT: *que j'aimasse, -asses, -ât, -assions, -assiez, -assent.*
PASSÉ: *que j'aie aimé, que tu aies aimé, qu'il ait aimé, que nous ayons aimé, que vous ayez aimé, qu'ils aient aimé.*
PLUS-QUE-PARFAIT: *que j'eusse aimé, que tu eusses aimé, qu'il eût aimé, que nous eussions aimé, que vous eussiez aimé, qu'ils eussent aimé.*

INFINITIF:
PRÉSENT: aimer.
PASSÉ: avoir aimé.
PARTICIPE:
PRÉSENT: aimant.
PASSÉ: aimé(e); ayant aimé.

SECOND CONJUGATION: (1) *"-ir"* verbs whose present participle ends in *-issant.*
E.g.: *Finir*

VOIX ACTIVE (Active Voice)
INDICATIF:
PRÉSENT: fin-is, -is, -it, -issons, -issez, -issent.
IMPARFAIT: fin-issais, -issais, -issait, -issions, -issiez, -issaient.
PASSÉ SIMPLE: fin-is, -is, -it, -îmes, -îtes, -irent.
FUTUR: finir-ai, -as, -a, -ons, -ez, -ont.
PASSÉ COMPOSÉ: ai fini, as fini, a fini, avons fini, avez fini, ont fini.
PLUS-QUE-PARFAIT: avais fini, avais fini, avait fini, avions fini, aviez fini, avaient fini.
PASSÉ ANTÉRIEUR: eus fini, eus fini, eut fini, eûmes fini, eûtes fini, eurent fini.
FUTUR ANTÉRIEUR: aurai fini, auras fini, aura fini, aurons fini, aurez fini, auront fini.
CONDITIONNEL:
PRÉSENT: finir-ais, -ais, -ait, -ions, -iez, -aient.
PASSÉ: aurais fini, aurais fini, aurait fini, aurions fini, auriez fini, auraient fini.
IMPÉRATIF: finis, finissons, finissez.
SUBJONCTIF:
PRÉSENT: que je finisse, -isses, -isse, -issions, -issiez, -issent.
IMPARFAIT: que je finisse, -isses, -ît, -issions, -issiez, -issent.
PASSÉ: que j'aie fini, aies fini, ait fini, ayons fini, ayez fini, aient fini.
PLUS-QUE-PARFAIT: que j'eusse fini, eusses fini, eût fini, eussions fini, eussiez fini, eussent fini.
INFINITIF:
PRÉSENT: finir.
PASSÉ: avoir fini.
PARTICIPE:
PRÉSENT: finissant.
PASSÉ: fini(e); ayant fini.
NOTE:
For a list of verbs conjugated like *finir,* see *"-IR"* **VERBS**

SECOND CONJUGATION: (2) *"-ir"* verbs whose present participle does not end in *-issant.* E.g.: *Sentir*

VOIX ACTIVE (Active Voice)
INDICATIF:
PRÉSENT: sen-s, -s, -t, -tons, -tez, -tent.
IMPARFAIT: sent-ais, -ais, -ait, -ions, -iez, -aient.
PASSÉ SIMPLE: sent-is, -is, -it, -îmes, -îtes, -irent.
FUTUR: sentir-ai, -as, -a, -ons, -ez, -ont.
PASSÉ COMPOSÉ: ai senti, as senti, a senti, avons senti, avez senti, ont senti.
PLUS-QUE-PARFAIT: avais senti, avais senti, avait senti, avions senti, aviez senti, avaient senti.
PASSÉ ANTÉRIEUR: eus senti, eus senti, eut senti, eûmes senti, eûtes, senti, eurent senti.
FUTUR ANTÉRIEUR: aurai senti, auras senti, aura senti, aurons senti, aurez senti, auront senti.
CONDITIONNEL:
PRÉSENT: sentir-ais, -ais, -ait, -ions, -iez, -aient.
PASSÉ: aurais senti, aurais senti, aurait senti, aurions senti, auriez senti, auraient senti.
IMPÉRATIF: sens, sentons, sentez.

SUBJONCTIF:
PRÉSENT: *que je sent-e, -es, -e, -ions, -iez, -ent.*
IMPARFAIT: *que je senti-isse, -isses, -ît, -issions, -issiez, -issent.*
PASSÉ: *que j'aie senti, aies senti, ait senti, ayons senti, ayez senti, aient senti.*
PLUS-QUE-PARFAIT: *que j'eusse senti, -eusses senti, -eût senti, -eussions senti, -eussiez senti, -eussent senti.*
INFINITIF:
PRÉSENT: *sentir.*
PASSÉ: *avoir senti.*
PARTICIPE:
PRÉSENT: *sentant.*
PASSÉ: *senti(e); ayant senti.*

THIRD CONJUGATION: "-oir" verbs. E.g.: *Recevoir*

VOIX ACTIVE (Active Voice)
INDICATIF:
PRÉSENT: *reçois, reçois, reçoit, recevons, recevez, reçoivent.*
IMPARFAIT: *recev-ais, -ais, -ait, -ions, -iez, -aient.*
PASSÉ SIMPLE: *reç-us, -us, -ut, -ûmes, -ûtes, -urent.*
FUTUR: *recevr-ai, -as, -a, -ons, -ez, -ont.*
PASSÉ COMPOSÉ: *ai reçu, as reçu, a reçu, avons reçu, avez reçu, ont reçu.*
PLUS-QUE-PARFAIT: *avais reçu, avais reçu, avait reçu, avions reçu, aviez reçu, avaient reçu.*
PASSÉ ANTÉRIEUR: *eus reçu, eus reçu, eut reçu, eûmes reçu, eûtes reçu, eurent reçu.*
FUTUR ANTÉRIEUR: *aurai reçu, auras reçu, aura reçu, aurons reçu, aurez reçu, auront reçu.*
CONDITIONNEL:
PRÉSENT: *recevr-ais, -ais, -ait, -ions, -iez, -aient.*
PASSÉ: *aurais reçu, aurais reçu, aurait reçu, aurions reçu, auriez reçu, auraient reçu.*
IMPÉRATIF:
PRÉSENT: *reçois, recevons, recevez.*
SUBJONCTIF:
PRÉSENT: *que je reçoive, reçoives, reçoive, recevions, receviez, reçoivent.*
IMPARFAIT: *que je reç-usse, -usses, -ût, -ussions, -ussiez, -ussent.*
PASSÉ: *que j'aie reçu, aies reçu, ait reçu, ayons reçu, ayez reçu, aient reçu.*
PLUS-QUE-PARFAIT: *que j'eusse reçu, eusses reçu, eût reçu, eussions reçu, eussiez reçu, eussent reçu.*
INFINITIF:
PRÉSENT: *recevoir.*
PASSÉ: *avoir reçu.*
PARTICIPE:
PRÉSENT: *recevant.*
PASSÉ: *reçu(e); ayant reçu.*

FOURTH CONJUGATION: "-re" verbs. E.g.: *Rendre*

VOIX ACTIVE (Active Voice)
INDICATIF:
PRÉSENT: *rends, rends, rend, rendons, rendez, rendent.*
IMPARFAIT: *rend-ais, -ais, -ait, -ions, -iez, -aient.*
PASSÉ SIMPLE: *rend-is, -is, -it, -îmes, -îtes, -irent.*
FUTUR: *rendr-ai, -as, -a, -ons, -ez, -ont.*
PASSÉ COMPOSÉ: *ai rendu, as rendu, a rendu, avons rendu, avez rendu, ont rendu.*
PLUS-QUE-PARFAIT: *avais rendu, avais rendu, avait rendu, avions rendu, aviez rendu, avaient rendu.*
PASSÉ ANTÉRIEUR: *eus rendu, eus rendu, eut rendu, eûmes rendu, eûtes rendu, eurent rendu.*
FUTUR ANTÉRIEUR: *aurai rendu, auras rendu, aura rendu, aurons rendu, aurez rendu, auront rendu.*

CONDITIONNEL:
PRÉSENT: *rendr-ais, -ais, -ait, -ions, -iez, -aient.*
PASSÉ: *aurais rendu, aurais rendu, aurait rendu, aurions rendu, auriez rendu, auraient rendu.*
IMPÉRATIF: *rends, rendons, rendez.*
SUBJONCTIF:
PRÉSENT: *que je rend-e, -es, -e, -ions, -iez, -ent.*
IMPARFAIT: *que je rend-isse, -isses, -ît, -issions, -issiez, -issent.*
PASSÉ: *que j'aie rendu, aies rendu, ait rendu, ayons rendu, ayez rendu, aient rendu.*
PLUS-QUE-PARFAIT: *que j'eusse rendu, eusses rendu, eût rendu, eussions rendu, eussiez rendu, eussent rendu.*
INFINITIF:
PRÉSENT: *rendre.*
PASSÉ: *avoir rendu.*
PRÉSENT: *rendant.*
PASSÉ: *rendu(e); ayant rendu.*

CONJUNCTION

A conjunction *(une conjonction)* is an invariable word that serves to link two clauses or two words in a sentence. There are two kinds of conjunctions: (a) Coordinating conjunctions. E.g.: *Car, donc, et, ni, mais, or, ou.* (b) Subordinating conjunctions. E.g.: *Cependant que, comme, quand, que, quoique, si.*

(1) <u>CONJUNCTIONS THAT TAKE THE SUBJUNCTIVE:</u>
    (a) *À condition que* = "Provided that."
        E.g.: *J'irai à Paris à condition que tu viennes aussi.*
          I shall go to Paris provided that you come too.
    (b) À moins que = "Unless."
        E.g.: *Je sortirai à moins qu'il ne fasse froid.*
          I shall go out unless it is cold.
    (c) *Afin que* = "So that."
        E.g.: *Il ira en France afin que nous le rencontrions.*
          He will go to France so that we might meet him.
    (d) *Avant que* = "Before."
        E.g.: *Je finirai avant que tu (ne) viennes.*
          I shall finish before you come.
    (e) *Bien que* = "Although."
        E.g.: *Elle viendra bien qu'elle soit malade.*
          She will come although she is sick.
    (f) *De crainte que* = "For fear that, lest."
        E.g.: *Nous resterons ici de crainte qu'on ne nous voie.*
          We shall stay here lest we be seen.
    (g) *De peur que* = "For fear that, lest."
         E.g.: *Nous resterons ici de peur qu'on ne nous voie.*
          We shall stay here lest we be seen.
    (h) *De sorte que* = "So that."
        E.g.: *Elle étudiera de sorte que ses parents soient fiers d'elle.*
          She will study so that her parents are proud of her.
NOTE:
De sorte que takes the subjunctive only to indicate an outcome or goal, not a consequence, in which case it takes the indicative.
    (i) *En attendant que* = "While waiting for."
        E.g.: *Reste ici en attendant que je revienne.*
          Stay here while waiting for me to return.
    (j) *Jusqu'à ce que* = "Until."
        E.g.: *Il a dormi jusqu'à ce que nous revenions.*
          He slept until we returned.

    (k) *Malgré que* = "Although."
       E.g.: *Elle est partie malgré que je lui aie dit de rester.*
       She left although I had told her to stay.
    (l) *Pour que* = "So that."
       E.g.: *Nous étudierons pour que le professeur soit content de nous.*
       We shall study so that the teacher is pleased with us.
    (m) *Pourvu que* = "Provided that."
       E.g.: *Ils viendront pourvu qu'ils aient le temps.*
       They will come provided that they have the time.
    (n) *Quoique* = "Although, even though."
       E.g.: *Il réussira quoiqu'il n'ait pas de diplôme.*
       He will succeed even though he has no diploma.
    (o) *Sans que* = "Without."
       E.g.: *Il est parti sans qu'on le voie.*
       He left without anyone seeing him.
(2) <u>CONJUNCTIONS THAT TAKE THE PAST TENSE</u> in relation to the main verb (if the action of the main verb takes place after that of the subordinate verb):
    (a) *Après que* = "After."
       E.g.: *Ils viendront après que la fête sera finie.*
       They will come after the party is finished.
    (b) *Aussitôt que* = "As soon as."
       E.g.: *Je viendrai aussitôt que j'aurai terminé.*
       I shall come as soon as I have finished.
    (c) *Dès que* = "As soon as."
       E.g.: *Je viendrai dès que j'aurai terminé.*
       I shall come as soon as I have finished.
    (d) *Quand* = "When."
       E.g.: *Ils viendront ici quand ils auront achevé leur travail.*
       They will come here when they have completed their work.

CONNAÎTRE

(To know)
PRÉS.: *conn-ais, -ais, -ait, -aissons, -aissez, -aissent.*
IMPARF.: *connaiss-ais, -ais, -ait, -aissions, -aissiez, -aissaient.*
PASSÉ SIMPLE: *conn-us, -us, -ut, -ûmes, -ûtes, -urent.*
FUT.: *connaîtr-ai, -as, -a, -ons, -ez, -ont.*
CONDIT.: *connaîtr-ais, -ais, -ait, -ions, -iez, -aient.*
IMPÉR.: *connais, connaissons, connaissez.*
SUBJ. PRÉS: *connaiss-e, -es, -e, -ions, -iez, -ent.*
SUBJ. IMPARF.: *conn-usse, -usses, -ût, -ussions, -ussiez, -ussent.*
P. PRÉS.: *connaissant.*
P. PASSÉ: *connu(e).*

CONNAÎTRE vs. SAVOIR

Both verbs mean "To know."
(1) *Connaître* means "To be acquainted with" and is used with persons and places.
    E.g.: *Connaissez-vous Jacques Dupont?*   *Je connais bien Paris.*
       Do you know Jacques Dupont?   I know Paris well.
(2) *Savoir* means "To have the knowledge, to know how to" and is used with things that have been learned (facts, reasons, etc.).
    E.g.: *Je ne sais pas nager.*   *Savez-vous pourquoi il est triste?*
       I can't (don't know how to) swim.   Do you know why he is sad?

CONQUÉRIR

(To conquer)
Conjugated like *ACQUÉRIR*

CONSONANT

A consonant *(une consonne)* is a letter other than *a, e, i, o, u,* and *y.* Consonants represent sounds produced by constricting or closing the breath during speech.

CONSTRUIRE

(To build)
Conjugated like *CONDUIRE*

CONTRACTION: *À* + *LES(S)*

The preposition *à* followed by the definite articles *le* and *les* contracts to *au* and *aux*, respectively.
E.g.: *Nous allons au cinéma.*   *Ils sont allés aux courses*
  We go to the movies.   They went to the races.

CONTRACTION: *À* + LEQUEL, LESQUELS, LESQUELLES

The preposition *à* followed by the relative or interrogative pronouns *lequel, lesquels,* and *lesquelles* contracts to *auquel, auxquels,* and *auxquelles,* respectively.
E.g.: *Le bureau auquel je dois aller est loin d'ici.*
  The office to which I have to go is far from here.
  Les gens auxquels il parle sont des étrangers.
  The people to whom he is speaking are foreigners.
  Est-ce que ce sont les personnes auxquelles tu as écrit?
  Are they the people to whom you have written?

CONTRACTION: *DE* + *LE(S)*

The preposition *de* followed by the definite articles *le* and *les* contracts to *du* and *des*, respectively.
E.g.: *Le livre du professeur.*   *Le travail des étudiants.*
  The teacher's book.   The students' work.

CONTRACTION: *DE* + LEQUEL, LESQUELS, LESQUELLES

The preposition *de* followed by the relative or interrogative pronouns *lequel, lesquels,* and *lesquelles* contracts to *duquel, desquels,* and *desquelles*, respectively.
E.g.: *Je vois plusieurs maisons. Desquelles parlez-vous?*
  I see several houses. Which ones are you talking about?
  Tous ces professeurs sont bons. Duquel parlez-vous?
  All these teachers are good. Of which one are you speaking?

CONTRARY-TO-FACT STATEMENTS

Contrary-to-fact statements are conveyed by the "*Si* + imperfect" or "*Si* + pluperfect" construction.
E.g.: *Si j'étais riche j'achèterais une grande maison.*
  If I were rich, I would buy a large house.
  Si elle avait acheté cette voiture-ci elle aurait eu un accident.
  If she had bought this car, she would have had an accident.
See *SI CLAUSES*

CONVAINCRE

(To convince)
PRÉS.: *convaincs, convaincs, convainc, convainqu-ons, -ez, -ent.*
IMPARF.: *convainqu-ais, -ais, -ait, -ions, -iez, -aient.*
PASSÉ SIMPLE: *convainqu-is, -is, -it, -îmes, -îtes, -irent.*
FUT.: *convaincr-ai, -as, -a, -ons, -ez, -ont.*
CONDIT.: *convaincr-ais, -ais, -ait, -ions, -iez, -aient.*
IMPÉR.: *convaincs, convainquons, convainquez.*
SUBJ. PRÉS.: *convainqu-e, -es, -e, -ions, -iez, -ent.*
SUBJ. IMPARF.: *convainque-isse, -isses, -ît, -issions, -issiez, -issent.*
P. PRÉS.: *convainquant*.*
P. PASSÉ: *convaincu(e).*
*The corresponding adjective is spelled *convaincant.*

CORRECT

(Adjective)
(1) Meaning "Right, accurate" = *Exact(e), juste.*
  E.g.: *Ses prévisions ont été tout à fait justes.*
     His forecast was completely correct.

     Je ne sais pas l'heure exacte.
     I don't know the correct time.
(2) Meaning "Proper, seemly" = *Correct, convenable.*
  E.g.: *Il porte une tenue convenable pour cette occasion.*
     He is wearing proper clothing for this occasion.

     Son comportement n'est pas correct.
     His behavior is not proper.

COUDRE

(To sew)
PRÉS.: *couds, couds, coud, cousons, cousez, cousent.*
IMPARF.: *cous-ais, -ais, -ait, -ions, -iez, -aient.*
PASSÉ SIMPLE: *cous-is, -is, -it, -îmes, -îtes, -irent.*
FUT.: *coudr-ai, -as, -a, -ons, -ez, -ont.*
CONDIT.: *coudr-ais, -ais, -ait, -ions, -iez, -aient.*
IMPÉR.: *couds, cousons, cousez.*
SUBJ. PRÉS.: *cous-e, -es, -e, -ions, -iez, -ent.*
SUBJ. IMPARF.: *cous-isse, -isses, -ît, -issions, -issiez, -issent.*
P. PRÉS.: *cousant.*
P. PASSÉ: *cousu(e).*

COULD

(1) As the past tense of "Can" = *Pouvoir* in the *imparfait* or the *passé composé*, depending on the context:
  E.g.: *Elle pouvait jouer du piano pendant des heures.*
     She could play the piano for hours on end.

     Je n'ai pas pu résoudre le problème.
     I couldn't solve the problem.
(2) As the conditional tense of "Can" = *Pouvoir* in the conditional.
  E.g.: *Tu pourrais aller en France si tu voulais.*
     You could go to France if you wanted to.

COUNTRIES, GENDER OF NAMES OF
See GEOGRAPHICAL NAMES

COUNTRIES, PREPOSITIONS WITH
See **GEOGRAPHICAL NAMES, PREPOSITIONS WITH**

COUP, IDIOMS WITH

Un coup means "A blow, a shock, a knock." It is used in many idiomatic expressions, such as these.

Un coup de coude = A nudge
Un coup détat = A coup
Un coup de feu = A gunshot
Un coup de fil = A telephone call
Un coup de foudre = A bolt of lightning; love at first sight
Un coup de fusil = A rifle shot
Un coup de main = A helping hand
Sur le coup de minuit = At the stroke of midnight
Un coup d'œil = A glance
Un coup de pied = A kick
Un coup de poing = A punch
Un coup de revolver = A gunshot
Un coup de soleil = A sunburn
Un coup de tête = An impulse

COURIR

(To run)
PRÉS.: *cours, cours, court, courons, courez, courent.*
IMPARF.: *cour-ais, -ais, -ait, -ions, -iez, -aient.*
PASSÉ SIMPLE: *cour-us, -us, -ut, -ûmes, -ûtes, -urent.*
FUT.: *courrai, courras, courra, courrons, courrez, courront.*
CONDIT.: *courrais, courrais, courrait, courrions, courriez, courraient.*
IMPÉR.: *cours, courons, courez.*
SUBJ. PRÉS. *cour-e, -es, -e, -ions, -iez, -ent.*
SUBJ. IMPARF.: *cour-usse, -usses, -ût, -ussions, -ussiez, -ussent.*
P. PRÉS.: *courant.*
P. PASSÉ: *couru(e).*

COUVRIR

(To cover)
Conjugated like **OUVRIR**

CRAINDRE

(To fear)
PRÉS.: *crains, crains, craint, craign-ons, -ez, -ent.*
IMPARF.: *craign-ais, -ais, -ait, -ions, -iez, -aient.*
PASSÉ SIMPLE: *craign-is, -is, -it, -îmes, -îtes, -irent.*
FUT.: *craindr-ai, -as, -a, -ons, -ez, -ont.*
CONDIT.: *craindr-ais, -ais, -ait, -ions, -iez, -aient.*
IMPÉR.: *crains, craignons, craignez.*
SUBJ. PRÉS.: *craign-e, -es, -e, -ions, -iez, -ent.*
SUBJ. IMPARF.: *craign-isse, -isses, -ît, -issions, -issiez, -issent.*
P. PRÉS.: *craignant.*
P. PASSÉ: *craint(e).*

CRIER

(To shout, to yell)

A regular verb, but note the *ii* in the imperfect and the subjunctive present.

IMPARF.: *je criais, tu criais, il criait, nous cri_i_ons, vous cri_i_ez, ils criaient.*

SUBJ. PRÉS.: *que je crie, que tu cries, qu'il crie, que nous cri_i_ons, que vous cri_i_ez, qu'ils crient.*

CROIRE

(To believe, to think)

PRÉS.: *crois, crois, croit, croyons, croyez, croient.*

IMPARF.: *croy-ais, -ais, -ait, -ions, -iez, -aient.*

PASSÉ SIMPLE: *crus, crus, crut, crûmes, crûtes, crurent.*

FUT.: *croir-ai, -as, -a, -ons, -ez, -ont.*

CONDIT.: *croir-ais, -ais, -ait, -ions, -iez, -aient.*

IMPÉR.: *crois, croyons, croyez.*

SUBJ. PRÉS.: *croie, croies, croie, croyions, croyiez, croient.*

SUBJ. IMP.: *crusse, crusses, crût, crussions, crussiez, crussent.*

P. PRÉS.: *croyant.*

P. PASSÉ: *cru.*

NOTE:

Croire que (affirmative) takes the indicative in the subordinate clause.

E.g.: *Je crois qu'il a raison.*

    I believe he is right.

BUT *Ne pas croire que* (negative) takes the subjunctive in the subordinate clause.

E.g.: *Je ne crois pas qu'il ait raison.*

    I don't believe he is right.

See **SUBJUNCTIVE MOOD**

CROÎTRE

(To grow)

PRÉS.: *croîs, croîs, croît, croiss-ons, -ez, -ent.*

IMPARF.: *croiss-ais, -ais, -ait, -ions, -iez, -aient.*

PASSÉ SIMPLE: *crûs, crûs, crût, crûmes, crûtes, crûrent.*

FUT.: *croîtr-ai, -as, -a, -ons, -ez, -ont.*

CONDIT.: *croîtr-ais, -ais, -ait, -ions, -iez, -aient.*

IMPÉR.: *croîs, croissons, croissez.*

SUBJ. PRÉS.: *croiss-e, -es, -e, -ions, -iez, -ent.*

SUBJ. IMPARF.: *crusse, crusses, crût, cruss-ions, -iez, -ent.*

P. PRÉS.: *croissant.*

P. PASSÉ: *crû, crue.*

CUEILLIR

(To pick)

PRÉS.: *cueill-e, -es, -ons, -ez, -ent.*

IMPARF.: *cueill-ais, -ais, -ait, -ions, -iez, -aient.*

PASSÉ SIMPLE: *cueill-is, -is, -it, -îmes, -îtes, -irent.*

FUT.: *cueiller-ai, -as, -a, -ons, -ez, -ont.*

CONDIT.: *cueiller-ais, -ais, -ait, -ions, -iez, -aient.*

IMPÉR.: *cueille, cueillons, cueillez.*

SUBJ. PRÉS.: *cueill-e, -es, -e, -ions, -iez, -ent.*

SUBJ. IMPARF.: *cueill-isse, -isses, -ît, -issions, -issiez, -issent.*

P. PRÉS.: *cueillant.*

P. PASSÉ: *cueilli(e).*

CUIRE

(To cook)
PRÉS.: *cuis, cuis, cuit, cuisons, cuisez, cuisent.*
IMPARF.: *cuis-ais, -ais, -ait, -ions, -iez, -aient.*
PASSÉ SIMPLE: *cuis-is, -is, -it, -îmes, -îtes, -irent.*
FUT.: *cuir-ai, -as, -a, -ons, -ez, -ont.*
CONDIT.: *cuir-ais, -ais, -ait, -ions, -iez, -aient.*
IMPÉR.: *cuis, cuisons, cuisez.*
SUBJ. PRÉS.: *cuis-e, -es, -e, -ions, -iez, -ent.*
SUBJ. IMPARF.: *cuis-isse, -isses, -ît, -issions, -issiez, -issent.*
P. PRÉS.: *cuisant.*
P. PASSÉ: *cuit(e).*

D

D'ACCORD

(Idiomatic expression) = "In agreement, agreed."
E.g.: *Je suis d'accord avec vous.*
  I am in agreement with you.
See **ÊTRE D'ACCORD (AVEC)**

D'AILLEURS

(Adverbial expression) = "Besides, moreover."
E.g.: *Je n'ai pas vu ce film. D'ailleurs je ne vais jamais au cinéma.*
  I haven't seen that film. Besides, I never go to the movies.

D'APRÈS

(Prepositional expression) = "According to."
E.g.: *D'après le président, la situation économique s'améliore.*
  According to the president, the economic situation is improving.

D'AUTANT

(Adverbial expression) = "In proportion, accordingly."
E.g.: *Les prix ont monté, mais mon salaire a monté d'autant.*
  Prices have risen, but my wages have risen accordingly.

D'AUTANT PLUS

(Adverbial expression) = "All the more" (expressing an additional reason).
E.g.: *Comme j'ai beaucoup de travail je ne peux pas sortir, d'autant plus que je n'ai pas d'argent.*
  As I have a lot of work, I cannot go out, all the more since I have no money.

DANS vs. DEDANS

(1) (Preposition) *Dans* = "in."
  E.g.: *Elle a mis son argent dans son sac.*
    She put her money in her pocketbook.
(2) (Adverb) *Dedans* = "In(side), indoors."
  E.g.: *Où est mon sac? Mon argent est dedans!*
    Where is my pocketbook? My money is in it!

DANS vs. *EN* (with a place)

(Prepositions) = "In."

(1) *Dans* means "Inside." It is more specific, more concrete than *en* and is always followed by an article or an adjective (possessive, demonstrative, etc.).

E.g.: *Pierre travaille dans la prison.*
Peter works in(side) the prison.

(2) *En* is less specific, less concrete than *Dans* and is not followed by an article.

E.g.: *Pierre est en prison.*
Peter is in jail.

It is also used with feminine geographical names.

E.g.: *Ils sont en Italie.*
They are in Italy.

DANS vs. *EN* (with time expressions)

(Prepositions) = "In."

(1) *Dans* indicates the moment.

E.g.: *J'écrirai ma thèse dans un mois.*
I shall write my thesis in a month (= a month from now).

(2) *En* indicates the duration of time.

E.g.: *Il a écrit sa thèse en un mois.*
He wrote his thesis in a month (= over a period of a month).

DATES

For the first day of the month, use the ordinal number.

E.g.: *Le premier janvier.*
January first.

All the other days of the month take cardinal numbers.

E.g.: *Le quatorze juillet.*   *Le vingt-cinq avril.*
July fourteenth.   April twenty-fifth.

The year may be expressed in two ways:

(1) By using *Mille* (or the alternate form *mil*).

E.g.: *Mille (Mil) neuf cent quarante-deux.*
Nineteen (hundred) forty-two.

(2) By counting the hundreds.

E.g.: *Dix-neuf cent soixante-dix-neuf.*
Nineteen (hundred) seventy-nine.

REMEMBER that *cent* (hundred) must be expressed when saying the date in French.

NOTES:

(1) Always use the definite article *le* before the date.

(2) Do not capitalize the name of the month.

(3) When using numbers only to write a date, in English the order is "Month/Day/Year" (e.g.: Christmas Day 1992 = 12/25/92), but in French the order is "Day/Month/Year."

E.g.: *Le jour de Noël 1992 = 25/12/92.*

DAYS OF THE WEEK

The days of the week are all masculine.

Monday = *lundi*   Friday = *vendredi*
Tuesday = *mardi*   Saturday = *samedi*
Wednesday = *mercredi*   Sunday = *dimanche*
Thursday = *jeudi*

NOTES:

(1) Days of the week are not capitalized in French.

(2) If the definite article is used in front of a day of the week, the meaning is "Every" or "On."

E.g.: *Nous n'avons pas de classe le samedi.*
We have no classes on Saturdays.

(3) Without the definite article, the day of the week refers to a specific day.

E.g.: *Mercredi j'irai au théâtre et samedi je verrai le film.*

On Wednesday I'll go to the theater, and Saturday I'll see the film.

DE

(1) The preposition *de* (which contracts to *du* and *des* with *le* and *les*) can have various meanings, depending on context. It can express (a) origin or source: "from," "out of"; (b) belonging: generally translated by the genitive in English; (c) the material of which something is made; (d) the contents; (e) a measurement; (f) the means of doing: "with"; (g) manner; (h) cause or agent; and (i) a link between two nouns.

E.g.: (a) *Il arrive de Paris.*   *Il sortent de la chambre.*

He is arriving from Paris. They come out of the room.

(b) *Le livre de Jeanne.*

Jean's book.

(c) *Une table de bois.*

A wooden table.

(d) *Un verre de vin.*

A glass of wine.

(e) *Une pièce de 10 m².*

A room measuring 10 square meters.

(f) *Elle le montre du doigt.*

She is pointing to it with her finger.

(g) *Elle marche d'un pas rapide.*

She walks along briskly.

(h) *Elle est morte d'une pneumonie.*

She died of pneumonia.

(i) *Le jour de Noël.*

Christmas Day.

(2) The partitive article *de* is used after a negative expression (without any article).

E.g.: *Je n'ai pas de monnaie.*

I have no change.

See **ARTICLES, PARTITIVE**

DE vs. À

See **ADJECTIVE + PREPOSITION + INFINITIVE**

DE BON CŒUR

(Adverbial idiomatic expression) = "Gladly, willingly."

E.g.: *Nous vous recevrons chez nous de bon cœur.*

We'll gladly have you at our house.

See **À CONTRECŒUR**

DE BONNE HEURE

(Idiomatic expression) = "Early."

E.g.: *Nous partirons de bonne heure demain.*

We shall leave early tomorrow.

DE CRAINTE DE vs. DE CRAINTE QUE

(1) The prepositional construction is "*De crainte de* + infinitive or noun" ("For fear of"). It is used when the main clause and the subordinate clause have the same subject.

E.g.: *Il s'est arrêté de crainte d'avoir un accident.*

He stopped for fear of having an accident.

(2) The conjunctional construction is "*De crainte que* + subjunctive" ("For fear that"). It is used when the two clauses have different subjects.
  E.g.: *On l'a arrêté de crainte qu'il n'ait un accident.*
    They stopped him for fear that he might have an accident.

See **DE PEUR DE vs. DE PEUR QUE**

DE LA PART DE

(Prepositional construction) = "On behalf of."
E.g.: *Je vous téléphone de la part de l'association des aveugles.*
    I'm calling on behalf of the association for the blind.

DE MÊME

(Idiomatic expression) = "Likewise."
E.g.: *Mon père ne travaille que trois jours par semaine et ma mère de même.*
    My father only works three days a week, and my mother likewise.

DE NOS JOURS

(Adverbial expression) = "Nowadays."
E.g.: *De nos jours on ne meurt plus de la petite vérole.*
    Nowadays people don't die of smallpox anymore.

DE PEUR DE vs. DE PEUR QUE

(1) The prepositional construction is "*De peur de* + infinitive or noun" ("For fear of"). It is used when both the main clause and the subordinate clause have the same subject.
  E.g.: *Il s'est arrêté de peur d'avoir un accident.*
    He stopped for fear of having an accident.
(2) The conjunctional construction is "*De peur que* + subjunctive" ("For fear that"). It is used when the two clauses have different subjects.
  E.g.: *On l'a arrêté de peur qu'il n'ait un accident.*
    They stopped him for fear that he might have an accident.

See **DE CRAINTE DE vs. DE CRAINTE QUE**

DE MOINS EN MOINS (DE)

(1) (Adverbial construction) *De moins en moins* = "Less and less."
  E.g.: *Elle maigrit parce qu'elle mange de moins en moins.*
    She is losing weight because she is eating less and less.
(2) (Prepositional construction) *De moins en moins de* = "Less and less."
  E.g.: *J'ai de moins en moins de temps libre.*
    I have less and less free time.

See **LESS AND LESS, FEWER AND FEWER**

DE PLUS EN PLUS (DE)

(1) (Adverbial construction) *De plus en plus* = "More and more."
  E.g.: *Ce pays devient de plus en plus industrialisé.*
    That country is getting more and more industrialized.
(2) (Prepositional construction) *De plus en plus de* = "More and more."
  E.g.: *Elle gagne de plus en plus d'argent.*
    She is earning more and more money.

See **MORE AND MORE**

DE QUOI (+ INFINITIVE)

(Idiomatic expression) = "The means to, the reason to, enough to."
E.g.: *Nous n'avons pas de quoi acheter une nouvelle voiture.*
We don't have the means to buy a new car.

DE RIGUEUR

(Idiomatic expression) = "Compulsory, obligatory."
E.g.: *Le port de la cravate est de rigueur.*
Wearing a necktie is compulsory.

DE SORTE QUE

(Conjunction)
(1) "Expressing intention = "*De sorte que* + subjunctive" = "So that."
E.g.: *On l'invitera de sorte qu'il ne soit pas seul.*
We shall invite him so that he will not be alone.
(2) Expressing consequence = "*De sorte que* + indicatif" = "So that"
E.g.: *Il lui a menti de sorti qu'elle est partie*
He lied, so that she left.
See **SO THAT**
See also **SUBJUNCTIVE MOOD**

DE TOUTE FAÇON

(Idiomatic expression) = "In any case."
E.g.: *De toute façon nous nous verrons la semaine prochaine.*
In any case we'll meet next week.

DÉBROUILLER (SE)

See **SE DÉBROUILLER**

DÉCEVOIR

(To disappoint, to let down)
PRÉS.: *déç-ois, -ois, -oit, décevons, décevez, déçoivent.*
IMPARF.: *décev-ais, -ais, -ait, -ions, -iez, -aient.*
PASSÉ SIMPLE: *déç-us, -us, -ut, -ûmes, -ûtes, -urent.*
FUT.: *décevr-ai, -as, -a, -ons, -ez, -ont.*
CONDIT.: *décevr-ais, -ais, -ait, -ions, -iez, -aient.*
IMPÉR.: *déçois, décevons, décevez.*
SUBJ. PRÉS.: *déçoiv-e, -es, -e, décevions, déceviez, déçoivent.*
SUBJ. IMPARF.: *déç-usse, -usses, -ût, -ussions, -ussiez, -ussent.*
P. PRÉS.: *décevant.*
P. PASSÉ: *déçu(e).*

DÉCHOIR

(To lower, to decline)
PRÉS.: *déchois, déchois, déchoit, déchoyons, déchoyez, déchoient.*
PASSÉ SIMPLE: *déch-us, -us, -ut, -ûmes, -ûtes, -urent.*
FUT.: *déchoir-ai, -as, -a, -ons, -ez, -ont.*
CONDIT.: *déchoir-ais, -ais, -ait, -ions, -iez, -aient.*
IMPÉR.: *(not used)*
SUBJ. PRÉS.: *déchoi-e, -es, -e, déchoyions, déchoyiez, déchoient.*
SUBJ. IMPARF.: *déch-usse, -usses, -ût, -ussions, -ussiez, -ussent.*
P. PRÉS.: *(not used)*
P. PASSÉ: *déchu(e).*

DECIMALS

The decimal point is a decimal comma *(la virgule de fraction décimale)* in French.

E.g.: In English: $\pi = 3.141592\ldots$

In French: $\pi = 3,14592\ldots$

Conversely, the use of commas to separate numerals in English is replaced by the use of periods or spaces in French.

E.g.: In English: 1,234,567

In French: 1.234.567 OR 1 234 567

DECLARATIVE SENTENCES

A declarative sentence is one that makes a statement. The normal word order in a declarative sentence is subject-verb-object (or complement).

E.g.: *Robert a étudié la leçon.*

Robert has studied the lesson.

DÉCOUVRIR

(To discover)
Conjugated like *OUVRIR*

DÉCRIRE

(To describe)
Conjugated like *ÉCRIRE*

DEFINITE ARTICLES

See **ARTICLES, DEFINITE**

DEHORS vs. *HORS DE*

(1) (Adverb) *Dehors* = "Outside, outdoors."

E.g.: *Sortons! Il fait beau dehors.*

Let's go out. It's nice weather outside.

(2) (Preposition) *Hors de* = "Outside, out of."

E.g.: *Nous habitons hors de la ville.*

We live outside the city.

DEMANDER

(Transitive verb) = "To ask, to ask for."

NOTE:

"To ask somebody something" = *"Demander quelque chose à quelqu'un."*

(The thing is the direct object, and the person is the indirect object.)

E.g.: *J'ai demandé des renseignements à l'agent de police.*

I asked the policeman for information.

NOTES:

(1) "To ask a question" = *Poser une question.*

E.g.: *Le professeur pose des questions aux élèves.*

The teacher asks the students questions.

(2) "To ask somebody to do something" = *"Demander à quelqu'un de* + infinitive."

E.g.: *Il a demandé à son frère de l'accompagner.*

He asked his brother to accompany him.

(3) The reflexive verb *Se demander* means "To wonder."

E.g.: *Je me demande pourquoi ils ne sont pas venus.*

I wonder why they did not come.

DEMEURER vs. HABITER vs. VIVRE

All three verbs means "To live," but *Demeurer* and *Habiter* mean "To inhabit, to dwell," whereas *Vivre* means "To be alive, to live."

E.g.: *Elle habite* (or *demeure*) *en Angleterre.*   *Elle ne vivra pas longtemps.*
  She lives in England.   She will not live long.

DEMI(E)

See **ADJECTIVES, COMPOUND**

DEMONSTRATIVE ADJECTIVES

See **ADJECTIVES, DEMONSTRATIVE**

DEMONSTRATIVE PRONOUNS

See **PRONOUNS, DEMONSTRATIVE**

DÉPENDRE (DE)

(To depend [on])
Conjugated like **RENDRE**
E.g.: *La solution dépend de toi.*
  The solution depends on you.

DEPUIS + TIME EXPRESSION

(Preposition) = "Since."
The use of tenses with *Depuis* is very different from the English construction.
(1) If the action is still going on, use the present.
  E.g.: *Je suis ici depuis une semaine.*
    I have been here for a week.
(2) If the action was still going on in the past (when something else happened), use the imperfect.
  E.g.: *Il était là depuis une semaine.*
    He had been there for a week.
(3) If the action is completed, use the *passé composé.*
  E.g.: *J'ai fini le livre depuis deux jours.*
    I finished the book two days ago.
(4) If the action was previously completed in a past context (when something else happened), use the past perfect.
  E.g.: *J'avais fini le livre depuis longtemps quand tu m'as téléphoné.*
    I had finished the book a long time before you called me.
See also **IL Y A + TIME EXPRESSION**

DES

(1) Contraction of the preposition *de* and the definite article *les.*
See **ARTICLES, CONTRACTION OF**
(2) Partitive article, plural.
See **ARTICLES, PARTITIVE**

DÈS

(Preposition) = "As early as, as soon as, from . . . on."
E.g.: *Nous serons de retour dès le 15 septembre.*
  We shall be back as early as September 15.

  Dès le XIXᵉ siècle on pouvait voyager en chemin de fer.
  From the nineteenth century on, you could travel by train.
See **DÈS QUE, TENSES WITH**

DÈS QUE, TENSES WITH

(Conjunction) "*Dès que* + indicative."
REMEMBER the rules for the agreement of tenses:
(1) If the two actions are simultaneous, both verbs are in the same tense.
> E.g.: *Dès que tu arriveras, nous partirons.*
> As soon as you arrive, we shall leave. [In French: "you will arrive."]
> *Ils sont partis dès qu'ils ont vu le signal.*
> They departed as soon as they saw the signal.

(2) If the action of the subordinate clause takes place before that of the main verb, the auxiliary of the subordinate clause is in the same tense as the main verb; that is, the tense of the subordinate clause is "once removed" from that of the main clause.
> E.g.: *Dès que j'aurai défait mes bagages, je me coucherai.*
>   *(futur antérieur)*   *(futur)*
> As soon as I have unpacked I shall go to bed. [In French: "will have unpacked."]

> E.g.: *Tout le monde partit dès qu'il eut terminé.*
>   *(passé simple)*   *(passé antérieur)*
> Everybody left as soon as he had finished.

See *AUSSITÔT QUE,* TENSES WITH

DESCENDRE

(To descend, to go down, to take down)
(1) It is transitive (i.e., conjugated with *avoir*) if it has a direct object.
> E.g.: *Il a descendu les valises.*
> He took the suitcases downstairs.
(2) It is intransitive (i.e., conjugated with *être*) if it takes no direct object.
> E.g.: *Ils sont descendus en ville en taxi.*
> They went downtown in a taxi.

Descendre is conjugated like *RENDRE*

DESIRE

There are several ways of expressing desire.
(1) "*Désirer* or *Vouloir* + direct object or infinitive or the subjunctive."
> E.g.: *Je désire une chambre avec salle de bains.*
> I should like a room with bath.

> *Il veut que nous partions tout de suite.*
> He wants us to leave right away.

NOTE:
The conditional of *Vouloir* expresses a softened, polite request.
> E.g.: *Elle voudrait s'en aller.*
> She would like to leave.

See **SUBJUNCTIVE**
(2) "*Avoir envie de* + direct object or infinitive."
See *AVOIR ENVIE DE*

DESPITE

(Preposition) = *Malgré.*
> E.g.: *Nous avons fait une promenade malgré la pluie.*
> We took a walk despite the rain.

See *MALGRÉ*

DESPITE THE FACT THAT

(Conjunction) = "*Bien que* + subjunctive" or "*Malgré que* + subjunctive."
> E.g.: *Il a réussi bien (or malgré) qu'il ne comprenne rien du tout.*
> He succeeded despite the fact that he doesn't understand anything at all.

See *MALGRÉ QUE*

DEVANT vs. *AVANT*

See *AVANT* vs. *DEVANT*

DEVENIR

(To become) (Conjugated with *être*)
PRÉS.: *deviens, deviens, devient, devenons, devenez, deviennent.*
IMPARF.: *deven-ais, -ais, -ait, -ions, -iez, -aient.*
PASSÉ SIMPLE: *dev-ins, -ins, -int, -înmes, -întes, -inrent.*
FUT.: *deviendr-ai, -as, -a, -ons, -ez, -ont.*
CONDIT.: *deviendr-ais, -ais, -ait, -ions, -iez, -aient.*
IMPÉR.: *deviens, devenons, devenez.*
SUBJ. PRÉS.: *devienn-e, -es, -e, devenions, deveniez, deviennent.*
SUBJ. IMPARF.: *dev-insse, -insses, -înt, -inssions, -inssiez, -inssent.*
P. PRÉS.: *devenant.*
P. PASSÉ: *devenu(e).*

DEVOIR

(To owe, ought, should)
PRÉS.: *dois, dois, doit, devons, devez, doivent.*
IMPARF.: *dev-ais, -ais, -ait, -ions, -iez, -aient.*
PASSÉ SIMPLE: *dus, dus, dut, dûmes, dûtes, durent.*
FUT.: *devr-ai, -as, -a, -ons, -ez, -ont.*
CONDIT.: *devr-ais, -ais, -ait, -ions, -iez, -aient.*
IMPÉR.: *dois, devons, devez.*
SUBJ. PRÉS.: *doive, doives, doive, devions, deviez, doivent.*
SUBJ. IMPARF.: *dusse, dusses, dût, dussions, dussiez, dussent.*
P. PRÉS.: *devant.*
P. PASSÉ: *dû, due, dus, dues.*
USAGE: *Devoir* has several meanings and usages.
(1) "to owe."
     E.g.: *Il doit cent francs à ses parents.*
          He owes his parents a hundred francs.
(2) Obligation or necessity (= "To have to, must"): (Any tense) + infinitive.
     E.g.: *Je dois partir.*   *Tu devras étudier*   *Elle a dû se lever tôt.*
          I have to (must) leave.   You will have to study.   She had to get up early.
(3) Suggestion or desirable action: (= "Ought to, should"): Present conditional + infinitive.
     E.g.: *Tu devrais aller voir le médecin.*
          You ought to (should) go see the doctor.
(4) Regret over an action not accomplished (= "Ought to have, should have"): Past conditional + infinitive.
     E.g.: *J'aurais dû étudier hier soir.*
          I ought to (should) have studied last night.
(5) Probability (= "Must, must have"): (Any indicative tense) + infinitive.
     E.g.: *Il doit être malade.*
          He must be sick.
          Il a dû manquer le train.
          He must have missed the train.
          Tu devras (probablement) retourner en France.
          You will (probably) have to return to France.
(6) Intention·(= "To be supposed to, to have to"): Present or imperfect tense + infinitive.
     E.g.: *Ils doivent arriver demain.*
          They are supposed to arrive tomorrow.
          Je devais l'accompagner, mais je suis tombé malade.
          I was supposed to accompany him, but I fell ill.

NOTE:

The <u>imperfect</u> indicates an intention in the past, while the *passé composé* indicates an obligation that was realized in the past.

E.g.: *Je devais aller en ville (mais . . .)*
   I was supposed to go downtown (but . . .)
BUT: *J'ai dû aller en ville (donc . . .)*
   I had to go downtown (so . . .)

DIACRITICAL MARKS

A diacritical mark *(un signe diacritique)* is a mark added to a letter to change its value or its pronunciation. The diacritical marks used in French are:
(1) The accents: *aigu* (´), *grave* (`), *circonflexe* (ˆ).
(2) The diaeresis *(le tréma)* (¨).
(3) The cedilla *(la cédille)* (¸).
See **ACCENTS; CEDILLA;** and **DIAERESIS**

DIAERESIS

The diaeresis *(le tréma)* is an orthographic sign (¨) placed over a vowel to indicate that it must be pronounced separately and not linked to the previous vowel.
E.g.: *Naïf* is pronounced *"na-if"* (not *"nèf"*).

DIMENSIONS
See **SIZES AND MEASUREMENTS**

DIPHTHONG

A diphthong *(une diphtongue)* is a combination into a single syllable of two vowel sounds. For example, in English "toy" is a diphthong. Examples of diphthongs in French are *œil, hier,* and *paille.*

DIRE

(To say)
PRÉS.: *dis, dis, dit, disons, dites,* disent.*
IMPARF.: *dis-ais, -ais, -ait, -ions, -iez, -aient.*
PASSÉ SIMPLE: *dis, dis, dit, dîmes, dîtes, dirent.*
FUT.: *dir-ai, -as, -a, -ons, -ez, -ont.*
CONDIT.: *dir-ais, -ais, -ait, -ions, -iez, -aient.*
IMPÉR.: *dis, disons, dites.*
SUBJ. PRÉS.: *dis-e, -es, -e, -ions, -iez, -ent.*
SUBJ. IMPARF.: *disse, disses, dît, dissions, dissiez, dissent.*
P. PRÉS.: *disant.*
P. PASSÉ: *dit(e).*
*The compounds *contredire* (to contradict) and *interdire* (to forbid) have the forms *contredisez* and *interdisez.*

DIRECT DISCOURSE vs. INDIRECT DISCOURSE
See *DISCOURS INDIRECT* vs. *DISCOURS DIRECT*

DIRECT OBJECT

A direct object *(un complement d'objet direct)* receives the action of the verb.
E.g.: *Je lis <u>le livre</u>.*
   I read <u>the book</u>.

DIRECT OBJECT vs. INDIRECT OBJECT

(1) The direct object follows the verb (with no preposition) to indicate who or what received the action of the verb.

E.g. *J'écris la lettre.*

I write the letter.

(2) The indirect object follows the verb by means of a preposition to indicate to whom or to what (or for whom or for what) the action of the verb is done.

E.g.: *J'écris à Marie.*

I write *to Mary*.

REMEMBER that the indirect object pronoun includes the preposition *(me, te, lui, nous, vous, leur)*.

E.g.: *Je lui écris.*

I write (to him) (her).

NOTE:

Some verbs that take an indirect object in English take a direct object in French, and vice versa.

E.g.: *J'attends Pierre.* = I am waiting for Peter.

Je cherche le livre. = I am looking for the book.

Il demande le journal. = He asks for the newspaper.

Il écoute la radio. = He is listening to the radio.

J'ai payé mes achats. = I paid for my purchases.

Il regarde la jeune fille. = He is looking at the girl.

BUT: *J'obéis à mes parents.* = I obey my parents.

Elle répond à la question. = She answers the letter.

Tu ressembles à ta mère. = You resemble your mother.

DIRECT OBJECT PRONOUNS

See **PRONOUNS, OBJECT OF VERB**

DISCOURS INDIRECT vs. *DISCOURS DIRECT*

In direct discourse (or direct style), the words or thoughts of another person are quoted directly: e.g.: *Il dit: "Je suis fatigué."* He says: "I am tired." In indirect discourse (or indirect style), these words or thoughts are conveyed by subordinating them to a main verb such as *Dire, déclarer,* or *annoncer.*

DIRECT DISCOURSE	INDIRECT DISCOURSE
E.g.: *Il dit: "Je suis fatigué."*	→ *Il dit qu'il est fatigué.*
He says: "I am tired."	→ He says that he is tired.
Elle déclare: "Je vais partir."	→ *Elle déclare qu'elle va partir.*
She declares: "I am going to leave."	→ She declares that she is going to leave.

REMEMBER to make the pronouns in the indirect statement conform to the logic of the sentence. In the foregoing examples, *je* becomes *il* or *elle.*

INDIRECT DISCOURSE IN THE PAST:

If the main verb is in a past tense (e.g.: *imparfait, passé composé, plus-que-parfait*), the verb in the indirect statement will be in:

(1) The imperfect to indicate simultaneity with the main verb.

E.g.: *Il a dit qu'il aimait le champagne.*

He said that he liked champagne.

(2) The present conditional to indicate a future in relation to the main verb.

E.g.: *Il a dit qu'il boirait du champagne.*

He said that he would drink champagne.

(3) The pluperfect to indicate a past in relation to the main verb.

E.g.: *Il a dit qu'il avait bu du champagne.*

He said that he had drunk some champagne.

(4) The infinitive to indicate a command.

E.g.: *Il m'a dit de boire le champagne.*

He told me to drink some champagne.

INDIRECT QUESTIONS:
Same constructions introduced by *si*.
E.g.: *Elle a demandé si je buvais (je boirais, j'avais bu) du champagne.*
  She asked if I was drinking (would drink, had drunk) some champagne.

DISJUNCTIVE PRONOUNS

(*Les pronoms disjonctifs*, also called emphatic pronouns or stressed pronouns)
FORMS:
First person sing.: *moi*
Second person sing.: *toi*
Third person sing., masc.: *lui*
                    fem.: *elle*
First person plur.: *nous*
Second person plur.: *vous*
Third person plur., masc.: *eux*
                    fem.: *elles*
USAGE:
Disjunctive pronouns are used:
(1) When they stand alone, with no verb.
    E.g.: *Qui est là? Moi!*
       Who is there? Me!
(2) After a preposition.
    E.g.: *Nous allons chez lui.*   *Rachel a travaillé avec eux.*
       We are going to his house.   Rachel worked with them.
(3) To add stress or emphasis to a subject pronoun. (They are placed before the subject pronoun and set off from it with a comma.)
    E.g..: *Moi, je n'aime pas le vin blanc.*
       I do not like white wine.

       Vous, vous ne pouvez pas parler.
       You may not speak.
(4) After a comparative.
    E.g.: *Elle est plus grande que moi.*
       She is taller than I.

to DO

Whereas "To do" can be used as an auxiliary verb in English, *Faire* cannot be so used in French (except in the causative construction with *Faire*.)
(1) "to do" is used in English to form a question. But to form a question in French, you must use one of two constructions:
    (a) "*Est-ce que* + normal affirmative word order."
        E.g.: *Est-ce que vous aimez la crème glacée?*
           Do you like ice cream?
    (b) Inversion.
        E.g.: *Aimez-vous la crème glacée?*
           Do you like ice cream?
(2) "To do" can also express emphasis in English. This is not done in French.
    E.g.: I *did* see him, honestly!
       Je l'ai vu, vraiment!
(3) "To do" is also used in English to avoid the repetition of a verb or a full expression. This is not possible in French.
    E.g.: I shall go to France when you do.
       J'irai en France quand tu iras.

See **QUESTIONS, WORD ORDER IN**
See also **CAUSATIVE CONSTRUCTION WITH *FAIRE***

to **DO WITHOUT**

(Idiomatic expression) = *Se passer de.*
E.g.: *Je ne peux pas me passer de ce dictionnaire!*
    I can't do without this dictionary!
See *SE PASSER* vs. *SE PASSER DE*

D'OCCASION

(Idiomatic expression) = ''Secondhand.''
E.g.: *Je cherche une voiture d'occasion.*
    I'm looking for a secondhand car.

DONC

(Conjunction) = ''Therefore, consequently.''
E.g.: *Elle est punie, donc elle devra rester chez elle.*
    She is being punished, so she will have to stay home.

DONT

Relative pronoun that incorporates the preposition *de*. It is used for persons or things. It translates as ''Of whom, of which, whose.''
E.g.: *La fille dont il parle.*
    The girl of whom he is speaking.
    Le livre dont j'ai besoin.
    The book I need (= of which I have need).
    L'homme dont la femme vient de mourir.
    The man whose wife has just died.
    La chaise dont un pied était cassé.
    The chair, one leg of which was broken.
The following commonly used expressions take the relative pronoun *dont*.
Avoir besoin de = To need
Avoir envie de = To want
Avoir honte de = To be ashamed of
Avoir peur de = To be afraid of
Entendre parler de = To hear about
Être certain de = To be sure of
Être content de = To be happy with
Être fier de = To be proud of
Parler de = To talk about
Profiter de = To profit from, to take advantage of
Rire de = To laugh at
Se moquer de = To make fun of
Se passer de = To laugh at
Se servir de = To use
Se souvenir de = To remember
E.g.: *Le chien dont j'ai peur.*
    The dog I am scared of.
    Le résultat dont je suis fier.
    The result I am proud of.
    Le couteau dont je me sers.
    The knife I am using.

NOTES:
(1) In nonprepositional expressions, all constructions using *de* can also use *dont.*
(2) In prepositional expressions (such as *À côté de* and *Près de*), the preposition *de* cannot be changed to *dont.*
   E.g.: *Le musée près duquel j'habite est intéressant.*
      The museum near which I live is interesting
See **PRONOUNS, RELATIVE**

DORMIR

(To sleep)
PRÉS.: *dors, dors, dort, dormons, dormez, dorment.*
IMPARF.: *dorm-ais, -ais, -ait, -ions, -iez, -aient.*
PASSÉ SIMPLE: *dorm-is, -is, -it, -îmes, -îtes, -irent.*
FUT.: *dormir-ai, -as, -a, -ons, -ez, -ont.*
CONDIT.: *dormir-ais, -ais, -ait, -ions, -iez, -aient.*
IMPÉR.: *dors, dormons, dormez.*
SUBJ. PRÉS.: *dorm-e, -es, -e, -ions, -iez, -ent.*
SUBJ. IMPARF.: *dorm-isse, -isses, -ît, -issions, -issiez, -issent.*
P. PRÉS.: *dormant.*
P. PASSÉ: *dormi(e).*

DOUBLE OBJECT PRONOUNS

See **PRONOUNS, DOUBLE OBJECT**

DOUBT

The concept of doubt or uncertainty can be conveyed in two ways:
(1) *Douter que* + subjunctive.
   E.g.: *Je doute qu'elle (ne) vienne avec nous.*
      I doubt that she will come with us.
(2) *Croire* or *Penser* in the negative + subjunctive.
   E.g.: *Je ne pense pas qu'elle sache jouer du violon.*
      I don't think she can play the violin.
See **SUBJUNCTIVE MOOD**

"DR. AND MRS. VANDERTRAMP" VERBS

These are the intransitive verbs conjugated with *être:*

Descendre	**V**enir	**T**omber
Rentrer	**A**ller	**R**etourner
Monter	**N**aître	**A**rriver
Repartir	**D**evenir and **D**emeurer	**M**ourir
Sortir	**E**ntrer	**P**artir
	Rester	

to DRIVE TO

"To drive to" cannot be translated directly into French. Use *aller à* + an expression indicating the mode of transportation.
E.g.: Peter drives to school.
   Pierre va à l'école en voiture.
See **TRANSPORTATION, MEANS OF**
See also **to FLY TO** and **to WALK TO**

DROIT vs. DROITE

(1) (Noun) *Le droit* = "The right."
    E.g.: *Ai-je le droit de parler?*
        Do I have the right to speak?
(2) (Adjective) *droit(e)* = (a) "Straight;" (b) "Right" (as opposed to "Left")
    E.g.: (a) *Dessinez une ligne droite.*
           Draw a straight line.
        (b) *Il écrit de la main droite.*
           He writes with his right hand.
(3) (Adverb) *Droit* = "Straight ahead."
    E.g.: *La poste est droit devant vous.*
        The post office is straight ahead.

DU

(1) Partitive article
See **ARTICLES, PARTITIVE**
(2) Contraction of the preposition *de* + definite article.
See **ARTICLES, CONTRACTION OF**

DU MOINS

(Adverbial construction) = "At least."
E.g.: *Ils ne réussiront pas. Du moins, je le pense.*
    They will not succeed. At least I think not.
When it is at the beginning of a sentence, it is sometimes followed by inversion.
E.g.: *Ils réussiront. Du moins le pensent-ils.*
    They will succeed. At least they think so.

DURATION-OF-TIME CONSTRUCTIONS

(1) To express actions or situations that began in the past and are still going on in the present, use:
    (a) "*Il y a* + time expression + *que* + present tense."
    (b) "Present tense + *depuis* + time expression."
        E.g.: (a) *Il y a deux heures que je vous attends.*
            (b) *Je vous attends depuis deux heures.*
            I have been waiting for you for two hours.
(2) To express actions or situations that began in the past and were continuing at a certain point in time in the past, use:
    (a) "*Il y avait* + time expression + *que* + imperfect tense."
    (b) "Imperfect tense + *depuis* + time expression."
        E.g.: (a) *Il y avait deux heures que je vous attendais (quand vous avez téléphoné).*
            (b) *Je vous attendais depuis deux heures (quand vous avez téléphoné).*
            I had been waiting for you for two hours (when you called).
(3) To express the concept that an action or situation has *not* occurred for a certain period of time, use:
    (a) "*Il y a* + time expression + *que* + *passé composé.*"
    (b) "*Passé composé* + *depuis* + time expression."
        E.g.: (a) *Il y a trois ans que je ne les ai pas vus.*
            (b) *Je ne les ai pas vus depuis trois ans.*
            I have not seen them for three years.
See **IL Y A + TIME EXPRESSION + QUE**

DURING

(Preposition) = *Pendant.*
E.g.: *Elle a habité Paris pendant deux ans.*
    She lived in Paris for (during) two years.
See **PENDANT vs. POUR + TIME EXPRESSION**

E

EACH
See **CHAQUE**

EACH ONE
See **CHACUN**

EACH OTHER
(Reciprocal pronouns)
(1) If the context is clear, simply use the reciprocal pronouns: *nous, vous, se.*
    E.g.: *Pierre et Marie s'aiment.*
        Peter and Mary love each other.
(2) If further clarification is needed, add *l'un(e) l'autre* (for two people), or *les un(e)s les autres* (for more than two people).
    E.g.: *Ces ingénieurs s'aident l'un l'autre.*
        These engineers help each other.

        Jésus a dit: "Aimez-vous les uns les autres."
        Jesus said: ''Love one another.''
NOTE:
If a preposition is used, it must be placed between *l'un* and *l'autre.*
E.g.: Ils se battent l'un contre l'autre.
    They fight against each other.

    Elles vont souvent l'une chez l'autre.
    They often go to each other's house.
See **VERBS, RECIPROCAL**

EARLY
(1) Meaning ''Early in the day'' = *Tôt* or *De bonne heure.*
    E.g.: *Je me suis couché très tôt.*
        I went to bed very early.

        Les moines se lèvent de bonne heure.
        The monks get up early.
(2) Meaning ''Ahead of schedule'' = *En avance.*
    E.g.: *Le train est arrivé en avance.*
        The train arrived early (= ahead of schedule).

ÉCHAPPER BELLE
See **L'ÉCHAPPER BELLE**

ÉCOUTER vs. ENTENDRE
(1) *Écouter* = ''To listen to.''
    E.g.: *Elle écoute la radio.*
        She is listening to the radio.
(2) *Entendre* = ''To hear.''
    E.g.: *Elle entend du bruit dans sa chambre.*
        She hears some noise in her room.

ÉCRIRE

(To write)
PRÉS.: *écris, écris, écrit, écrivons, écrivez, écrivent.*
IMPARF.: *écriv-ais, -ais, -ait, -ions, -iez, -aient.*
PASSÉ SIMPLE: *écriv-is, -is, -it, -îmes, -îtes, irent.*
FUT.: *écrir-ai, -as, -a, -ons, -ez, -ont.*
COND.: *écrir-ais, -ais, -ait, -ions, -iez, -aient.*
IMPÉR.: *écris, écrivons, écrivez.*
SUBJ. PRÉS.: *écriv-e, -es, -e, -ions, -iez, -ent.*
SUBJ. IMPARF.: *écriv-isse, -isses, -ît, -issions, -issiez, -issent.*
P. PRÉS.: *écrivant.*
P. PASSÉ: *écrit(e).*

EH BIEN!

(Exclamation indicating surprise or admiration)
E.g.: *Eh bien, quelle histoire étrange!*
    Well, what a strange story!
See **BIEN**

EITHER . . . OR

(Conjunctions) = *Soit . . . soit . . .*
E.g.: *Prenez soit le train soit l'avion.*
    Take either the train or the plane.
See **SOIT . . . SOIT**
See also **NEITHER . . . NOR**

ELISION

Elison *(l'élision)* is the dropping of the vowel sound, *a, e, i,* or *o* before a word that begins with a vowel or an unaspirated *h.* The dropped vowel is replaced by an apostrophe (*'*).
E.g.: *L'église.*
    L'homme.
    S'il pleut.
    J'aime.
    L'orange.
EXCEPTIONS:
Onze, oui.

EMMENER vs. EMPORTER

(1) *Emmener* (conjugated like **MENER**) = "To take, to lead (away)." It is used for people only.
    E.g.: *Je vais t'emmener à l'aéroport.*
        I'll take you to the airport.
(2) *Emporter* (conjugated like **PORTER**) = "To take (along)." It is used for things.
    E.g.: *Elle a emporté sa valise.*
        She took her suitcase (along).

ÉMOUVOIR

(To affect, disturb [emotionally])
PRÉS.: *émeus, émeus, émeut, émouvons, émouvez, émeuvent.*
IMPARF.: *émouv-ais, -ais, -ait, -ions, -iez, -aient.*
PASSÉ SIMPLE: *émus, émus, émut, émûmes, émûtes, émurent.*
FUT.: *émouvr-ai, -as, -a, -ons, -ez, -ont.*
CONDIT.: *émouvr-ais, -ais, -ait, -ions, -iez, -aient.*
IMPÉR.: *émeus, émouvons, émouvez.*
SUBJ. PRÉS.: *émeuve, -es, -e, émouvions, émouviez, émeuvent.*
SUBJ. IMPARF.: *émusse, émusses, émût, émussions, émussiez, émussent.*
P. PRÉS.: *émouvant.*
P. PASSÉ: *ému(e).*
NOTE:
Unlike *mouvoir,* the past participle has no accent over the *u.*

EMPHATIC PRONOUNS

See **DISJUNCTIVE PRONOUNS**

"E" MUET

See **SILENT "E"**

EN

(1) The preposition *en.*
USAGE:
(a) Before names of feminine countries (i.e., those ending in *e*) and names of American states beginning with a vowel.

    E.g.: *En France.*   *En Algérie.*   *En Alabama.*   *En Iowa.*
          In France.   In Algeria.   In Alabama.   In Iowa.

See **GEOGRAPHICAL NAMES, PREPOSITIONS WITH**
(b) To express duration.
    E.g.: *Il a fait le travail en une heure.*
          He did the work in one hour.
(c) Before the present participle, to form the gerund.
    E.g.: *En arrivant.*   *En mangeant.*
          Upon arriving.   While eating.
See **GERUND**
(d) With means of transportation that one rides in.
    E.g.: *En avion.*   *En autobus.*
          By airplane.   By bus.
See **TRANSPORTATION, MEANS OF**
(e) To indicate composition (i.e., what something is made of).
    E.g.: *Une table en bois.*   *Une boîte en carton.*
          A wooden table.   A cardboard box.
(f) To indicate state or manner.
    E.g.: *Il est en bonne santé.*
          He is in good health.
(g) To express transformation.
    E.g.: *Elle s'est déguisée en danseuse.*
          She dressed up as a dancer.
(h) To introduce subject matter.
    E.g.: *Il est très fort en mathématiques.*
          He is very good in mathematics.

(2) The pronoun *en* is neuter.

As such, it replaces (a) the preposition *de* and the noun (which is a thing or an idea, never a person) or (b) the preposition *de* and the indefinite article *(un, une, des)*.

E.g.: *Elle parle du film.* → *Elle en parle.*

She talks about the film.   She talks about it.

BUT: *Je parle de Monique.* → *Je parle d'elle.*

I'm speaking of Monique.   I'm speaking of her.

J'ai besoin d'argent. → *J'en ai besoin.*

I need money.   I need some.

NOTES:

(1) There is never agreement of the past participle with *en*.

E.g.: *Des livres, j'en ai lu beaucoup.*

Books, I have read a lot (of them).

(2) *En* can never replace "*De* + verb."

E.g.: *J'ai envie d'une pomme* can change to *J'en ai envie.*

BUT: *J'ai envie de manger une pomme* can change to *J'ai envie d'en manger une.*

(3) The adverb *en* replaces the preposition "*De* + a place (location)."

E.g.: *Ils arrivent de New-York.* → *Ils en arrivent.*

They arrive from New York. → They arrive from there.

EN + COUNTRIES

The preposition *en* means "to" or "in" and is used before names of feminine countries, continents, or provinces.

E.g.: *Vous allez en France (en Europe, en Bretagne). Ils sont en Chine (en Asie).*

You are going to France (to Europe, to Brittany). They are in China (in Asia).

See **GEOGRAPHICAL NAMES, PREPOSITIONS WITH**

EN vs. DANS (with a place)

See **DANS vs. EN (with a place)**

EN vs. DANS (with time expressions)

See **DANS vs. EN (with time expression)**

EN ATTENDANT DE vs. EN ATTENDANT QUE

(1) The prepositional construction "*En attendant de* + infinitive" is used if the verb in the subordinate clause has the same subject as the verb of the main clause.

E.g.: *Je resterai ici en attendant de recevoir de tes nouvelles.*

I shall stay here while waiting to hear from you.

(2) The conjunctional construction "*En attendant que* + subjunctive" is used if the two verbs have different subjects.

E.g.: *Il ira en France en attendant que sa femme vienne le rejoindre.*

He will go to France while waiting for his wife to come to join him.

EN AVANCE

(Idiomatic expression) = "Early, ahead of schedule."

E.g.: *Nous sommes arrivés en avance sur l'horaire prévu.*

We arrived ahead of schedule.

EN DÉPIT DE

(Idiomatic expression) = "In spite of."

E.g.: *Ils sont sortis en dépit de la neige.*

They went out in spite of the snow.

EN FACE (DE)

(Adverb and prepositional construction) = "Opposite."
E.g.: *La banque est en face de l'église.*
   The bank is opposite the church.
See **ACROSS**

EN GRÈVE

(Idiomatic expression) = "On strike."
E.g.: *Les pilotes d'avion sont en grève.*
   The airline pilots are on strike.

EN OUTRE

(Idiomatic expression) = "Moreover, furthermore, besides."
E.g.: *Je n'ai pas d'argent et en outre je suis fatigué.*
   I have no money, and furthermore, I am tired.

EN PLEIN AIR

(Idiomatic expression) = "In the open air, outdoors."
E.g.: *Elle a joué en plein air toute la journée.*   *Une piscine en plein air.*
   She played outdoors all day.   An outdoor swimming pool.

EN RETARD

(Idiomatic expression) = "Late, behind schedule."
E.g.: *L'avion est arrivé en retard.*
   The plane arrived late.

EN TANT QUE

(Prepositional construction) = "As, in the capacity of."
E.g.: *Il a parlé en tant que directeur de la compagnie.*
   He spoke as a director of the company.

EN TOUT CAS

(Idiomatic expression) = "In any case."
E.g.: *En tout cas, je ferai ce que je veux.*
   In any case, I will do as I please.

EN TRAIN DE + INFINITIVE

This construction expresses the progressiveness of an action, the fact that it is going on at the moment one is speaking or is in process when something else occurs.
E.g.: *Je suis en train d'écrire une lettre.*
   I am (in the process of) writing a letter.

   Bernard était en train de manger quand nous sommes arrivés.
   Bernard was (in the process of) eating when we arrived.

EN UN MOT

(Idiomatic expression) = "In short."
E.g.: *Il est beau, intelligent et riche. En un mot, il est parfait.*
   He is handsome, intelligent, and rich. In short, he's perfect.

EN VAIN

(Adverbial construction) = "In vain."
E.g.: *J'ai passé tout ce temps à étudier en vain.*
 I spent all that time studying in vain.
When it is at the beginning of a sentence, it is followed by inversion.
E.g.: *En vain a-t-elle cherché à trouver la réponse.*
 In vain did she attempt to find the answer.

EN VOULOIR À

(Idiomatic expression) = "To be angry with, to have a grudge against."
E.g.: *Elle m'en veut parce que je ne suis pas allé avec elle.*
 She is angry with me because I did not go with her.

ENCORE

(Adverb) = "Still, again, more."
E.g.: *Tu es encore ici!*
 You are still here!

 Ma voiture est encore tombée en panne.
 My car broke down again.

 J'en veux encore un.
 I want one more.
When it is at the beginning of a sentence, it means "Even so" and is followed by inversion.
E.g.: *Ce n'est pas difficile. Encore faut-il l'apprendre.*
 It's not difficult. Even so, you have to learn it.

ENDORMIR

(To put to sleep)
Conjugated like **DORMIR**
The reflexive form *S'endormir* = "To fall asleep."
E.g.: *Il s'est endormi pendant la classe.*
 He fell asleep during the class.

ENOUGH + NOUN

(Adverb) = "*Assez de* + noun."
E.g.: *J'ai assez d'argent.*
 I have enough money.
See **ASSEZ DE + NOUN**

ENTENDRE

(To hear)
Conjugated like **RENDRE**
See **ÉCOUTER vs. ENTENDRE**

ENTENDRE DIRE QUE vs. ENTENDRE PARLER DE

(Idiomatic constructions.)
(1) "*Entendre dire que* + indicative" = "It is rumored that, to hear that."
 E.g.: *J'ai entendu dire que ce film est très comique.*
 I have heard that this film is very funny.
(2) "*Entendre parler de*" = "To hear about."
 E.g.: *Avez-vous entendu parler de ce film?*
 Have you heard about this film?

to ENTER

See **ENTRER**

ENTRER

Contrary to the English "to enter," *entrer* is an intransitive verb. It must be followed by the preposition *dans* or *à*.

E.g.: *Ils entrent dans le musée.*   *Elle est entrée à l'université.*
They enter the museum.   She has entered the university.

ENVERS

(Preposition) = "Toward." It is used with expressions of feelings or emotions.
E.g.: *Ils ont été très aimables envers moi.*
They were very kind to me.

ENVIE

See **AVOIR ENVIE DE**

ENVOYER

(To send)
This verb is regular, but note the *yi* in the first and second person plural of the imperfect and the present subjunctive.
IMPARF.: *j'envoyais, tu envoyais, il envoyait, nous envoyions, vous envoyiez, ils envoyaient.*
SUBJ. PRÉS.: *que j'envoie, que tu envoies, qu'il envoie, que nous envoyions, que vous envoyiez, qu'ils envoient.*

ESPÉRER

(To hope)
The *e* of the stem changes to *è* before a silent final syllable. Therefore, the following forms are slightly irregular:
PRÉS.: *j'espère, tu espères, il espère, (nous espérons, vous espérez), ils espèrent.*
SUBJ. PRÉS.: *que j'espère, que tu espères, qu'il espère, (que nous espérions, que vous espériez), qu'ils espèrent.*
NOTE:
Espérer que is an exception in that it takes the indicative (not the subjunctive, as one might have expected).
E.g.: *J'espère que tu viendras avec moi.*
I hope that you will come with me.

EST-CE QUE . . . ?

(Idiomatic interrogative construction) This construction provides the easiest way to form a question. It is followed by normal word order.
   "Interrogative words + *est-ce que* + verb."
E.g.: *Quel livre est-ce que tu lis?*
What book are you reading?

Pourquoi est-ce que vous étudiez le français?
Why do you study French?
See **QUESTIONS, WORD ORDER IN**

ÉTEINDRE

(To extinguish, to put out)
Conjugated like **CRAINDRE**

ÊTRE

(To be)
PRÉS.: *suis, es, est, sommes, êtes, sont.*
IMPARF.: *étais, étais, était, étions, étiez, étaient.*
PASSÉ SIMPLE: *fus, fus, fut, fûmes, fûtes, furent.*
FUT.: *serai, seras, sera, serons, serez, seront.*
CONDIT.: *serais, serais, serait, serions, seriez, seraient.*
IMPÉR.: *sois, soyons, soyez.*
SUBJ. PRÉS.: *sois, sois, soit, soyons, soyez, soient.*
SUBJ. IMPARF.: *fusse, fusses, fût, fussions, fussiez, fussent.*
P. PRÉS.: *étant.*
P. PASSÉ: *été.*
USAGE:
(1) "To be."
   E.g.: *Je suis Pierre Dupont.*   *Nous sommes français.*
         I am Pierre Dupont.   We are French.
(2) Auxiliary verb for certain intransitive verbs.
See **VERBS, INTRANSITIVE**
(3) Auxiliary verb for all reflexive and reciprocal verbs.
See **VERBS, REFLEXIVE**

ÊTRE À + **INFINITIVE**

(Idiomatic construction) It indicates obligation.
E.g.: *Ce travail est à faire tout de suite.*
      This work is to be done at once.

ÊTRE À + **NOUN or PRONOUN**

(Idiomatic construction) It indicates ownership.
E.g.: *Cette robe est à Marie.*
      This dress belongs to Mary.

ÊTRE AMOUREUX (DE)

(Idiomatic construction) = "To be in love with."
E.g.: *Juliette est amoureuse de Roméo.*
      Juliet is in love with Romeo.
See ***TOMBER AMOUREUX (DE)***

ÊTRE ASSIS vs. *S'ASSEOIR*

(1) *Être assis* expresses the state of being, the situation.
   E.g.: *Ils sont assis sur le sofa.*
         They are seated on the sofa.
(2) *S'asseoir* expresses the action.
   E.g.: *Asseyez-vous!*
         Sit down!

ÊTRE CENSÉ + **INFINITIVE**

(Idiomatic construction) = "To be supposed to."
E.g.: *Nous sommes censés aller voir le directeur.*
      We're supposed to go see the director.
See **SUPPOSED TO (meaning OUGHT)**

ÊTRE D'ACCORD (AVEC)

(Idiomatic construction) = "To be in agreement with."
E.g.: *Je ne suis pas du tout d'accord avec votre plan.*
   I do not agree at all with your plan.
See **D'ACCORD** and **TO AGREE (WITH)**

ÊTRE DOUÉ (POUR)

(Idiomatic coonstruction) = "To be gifted for, to be good at."
E.g.: *Caroline est douée pour les langues.*
   Caroline is good at languages.

ÊTRE EN TRAIN DE

See **EN TRAIN DE + INFINITIVE**

ÊTRE RAVI (DE)

(Idiomatic construction) = "To be delighted (to)."
E.g.: *Je suis ravi de faire votre connaissance.*
   I am delighted to make your acquaintance.

ÊTRE REFUSÉ (À)

(Idiomatic construction) = "To be turned down, to fail."
E.g.: *J'ai été refusé à l'examen d'entrée.*
   I failed the entrance examination.

ÊTRE SUR LE POINT DE

(Idiomatic construction) = "To be about to, to be on the verge of."
E.g.: *Elle était sur le point de partir quand je suis arrivé.*
   She was about to leave when I arrived.

ÉTUDIER

(To study)
A regular verb, but note the *ii* in the first and second person plural of the imperfect and the subjunctive present.
IMPARF.: *j'étudiais, tu étudiais, il étudiait, nous étudiions, vous étudiiez, ils étudiaient.*
SUBJ. PRÉS.: *que j'étudie, que tu étudies, qu'il étudie, que nous étudiions, que vous étudiiez, qu'ils étudient.*

EVEN IF

(Conjunctional expression) = "*Même si* + indicative."
E.g.: *Vous sortirez même s'il pleut.*
   You will go out even if it rains.

EVEN THOUGH

(Conjunction) = "*Bien que* + subjunctive" or "*Quoique* + subjunctive."
E.g.: *Elle travaille bien qu' (or quoiqu') elle soit gravement malade.*
   She works even though she is seriously ill.
See **BIEN QUE** and **SUBJUNCTIVE MOOD**

EVERY TIME

(Idiomatic expression) = *Chaque fois.*
E.g.: *Chaque fois qu'il vient il apporte des fleurs.*
   Every time he comes, he brings flowers.
See **FOIS vs. HEURE, TEMPS, MOMENT**

EVERY + TIME EXPRESSION

(Idiomatic construction) = "*Tous (toutes) les* + time expression."

E.g.: *Ils vont nager tous les jeudis.*

They go swimming every Thursday.

Toutes les deux semaines je reçois une lettre de lui.

Every two weeks I receive a letter from him.

EVERYBODY

(Idiomatic expression) = *Tout le monde.*

This expression is masculine singular.

E.g.: *Tout le monde est heureux.*

Everybody is happy.

EVERYTHING

(Noun) = *Tout.*

This expression is masculine singular.

E.g.: *Tout est prêt.*

Everything is ready.

Do not say "Toute chose"!

See **TOUT, TOUTE, TOUS, TOUTES**

EVERYWHERE

(Adverb) = *Partout.*

E.g.: *Il y a des touristes partout.*

There are tourists everywhere.

See **PARTOUT**

EXCLAMATIONS

Exclamations can be introduced using two types of expressions.

(a) The interrogative adjectives *quel, quelle, quels, quelles* (without article) in front of the noun.

E.g.: *Quelle pièce bizarre!*

What an odd play!

(2) The conjunction *Comme* or *Que* before a clause containing an adjective or an adverb.

E.g.: *Comme elle est exigeante!*

How demanding she is!

Commme ils travaillent fort!

How hard they work!

Qu'ils sont fatigants!

How tiresome they are!

See also **EH BIEN!**

to EXPECT

(Idiomatic construction) = "*S'attendre à* + noun or infinitive."

E.g.: *Ils s'attendent à une attaque imminente.*

They are expecting an imminent attack.

Je ne m'attendais pas à vous voir ici.

I did not expect to see you here.

F

FAILLIR

(To fail)
This verb has only the following forms:
PASSÉ SIMPLE: *faill-is, -is, -it, -îmes, -îtes, -irent.*
FUT.: *faillir-ai, -as, -a, -ons, -ez, -ont.*
CONDIT.: *faillir-ais, -ais, -ait, -ions, -iez, -aient.*
P. PRÉS.: *faillissant.*
P. PASSÉ: *failli(e).*
NOTE:
The most frequent use of this verb is in the idiomatic construction: "*Passé composé* of *faillir* + infinitive" = "Almost + verb." It expresses the concept that something very nearly happened but in fact did not.
E.g.: *J'ai failli tomber.*
       I almost fell.
See **ALMOST + VERB (IN PAST TENSE)**

FAIM

See *AVOIR FAIM*

FAIRE

(To do, to make)
PRÉS.: *fais, fais, fait, faisons, faites, font.*
IMPARF.: *fais-ais, -ais, -ait, -ions, -iez, -aient.*
PASSÉ SIMPLE: *fis, fis, fit, fîmes, fîtes, firent.*
FUT.: *fer-ai, -as, -a, -ons, -ez, -ont.*
CONDIT.: *fer-ais, -ais, -ait, -ions, -iez, -aient.*
IMPÉR.: *fais, faisons, faites.*
SUBJ. PRÉS.: *fass-e, -es, -e, -ions, -iez, -ent.*
SUBJ. IMPARF.: *fisse, fisses, fît, fissions, fissiez, fissent.*
P. PRÉS.: *faisant.*
P. PASSÉ: *fait(e).*

FAIRE in CAUSATIVE CONSTRUCTIONS

See *FAIRE* + INFINITIVE

FAIRE + INFINITIVE

"*Faire* + infinitive" is the "causative construction." It corresponds to the English "To have + noun + past participle," "To be having + noun + past participle," or "To make . . . + infinitive."
E.g.: *Je me suis fait couper les cheveux.*
       I had my hair cut.

       Il fait construire une maison.
       He is having a house built.

       Je le fais travailler.
       I make him work.
USE OF OBJECT PRONOUNS with "*Faire* + infinitive":
(1) If there is only one object pronoun, it is a direct object.
       E.g.: *Il la fait parler.*   *Je les ai fait arrêter.*
              He makes her talk.   I had them arrested.

(2) If there are two object pronouns, the person is the indirect object, and the thing is the direct object.

E.g.: *Il lui fait laver la voiture.* *Le professeur leur a fait écrire une rédaction.*
He makes him (her) wash the car. The teacher had them write a composition.

See **CAUSATIVE CONSTRUCTION WITH *FAIRE***

FAIRE DU MAL (À)

(Idiomatic expression) = "To hurt, to harm (morally or mentally)."
E.g.: *Ses actions insensées feront du mal à sa bonne réputation.*
His thoughtless acts will harm his good reputation.

FAIRE MAL (À)

(Idiomatic expression) = "To hurt, to harm (physically)."
E.g.: *Arrête! Tu me fais mal!*
Stop! You're hurting me!

FAIRE PARTIE DE

(Idiomatic expression) = "To belong to, to be a member of."
E.g.: *Je fais partie de l'équipe de football.*
I am a member of the football team.

Nous faisons partie de l'association des écrivains.
We belong to the writers' association.

FAIRE PLAISIR (À)

(Idiomatic expression) = "To please."
E.g.: *Ce cadeau leur fera certainement plaisir.*
This gift will surely please them.

FAIRE SEMBLANT DE

(Idiomatic expression) = "To pretend to + verb"
E.g.: *Il fait semblant de dormir.*
He is pretending to sleep.

FAIRE VENIR

(Idiomatic expression) = "To send for, to summon."
E.g.: *Quand j'étais malade, ma mère a fait venir le médecin.*
When I was ill, my mother sent for the doctor.

to **FALL IN LOVE (WITH)**

(Idiomatic expression) = *Tomber amoureux (de).*
E.g.: *Jean est tombé amoureux de Marie et il va l'épouser.*
John fell in love with Mary and is going to marry her.

See *TOMBER AMOUREUX (DE)*

FALLOIR

(Impersonal verb) = (To be necessary, must)
PRÉS.: *il faut.*
IMPARF.: *il fallait.*
PASSÉ SIMPLE: *il fallut.*
FUT.: *il faudra.*
CONDIT.: *il faudrait.*
SUBJ. PRÉS.: *il faille.*
SUBJ. IMPARF.: *il fallût.*
P. PASSÉ: *fallu.*

NOTE:
This verb takes one of two constructions:
(1) If the statement is generally applicable to anybody: "*Falloir* + infinitive."
      E.g.: *Il faut manger pour vivre.*
          One must eat to live.
(2) If the statement applies to a specific person: "*Falloir que* + subjunctive."
      E.g.: *Il faut que tu manges, sinon tu seras malade.*
          You must eat, or else you will be ill.

FAMILIAR vs. FORMAL FORMS

See *TU vs. VOUS*

FAST

(1) (Adverb) = *Rapidement* or *Vite.*
      E.g.: *Il parle trop rapidement*   OR: *Il parle trop vite.*
          He speaks too rapidly.   He speaks too fast.
      NEVER say *"vitement."* There is no such word!
(2) (Adjective) = *Rapide.*
      E.g.: *Une voiture rapide.* (NOT: *Une voiture vite!*)
          A fast car.

FAUTE DE

(Prepositional construction) = "For lack of."
E.g.: *Faute d'argent, j'ai dû rester à la maison.*
      For lack of money I had to stay home.

to FEEL

(1) Meaning "feeling by touching" = *Toucher.*
      E.g.: *J'ai senti le radiateur pour voir s'il était chaud.*
          I felt the radiator to see if it was hot.
(2) Meaning "to experience" = *Ressentir* or *Éprouver.*
      E.g.: *J'ai ressenti une douleur dans le dos.*
          I felt a pain in my back.
(3) Meaning "to think" = *Avoir l'impression* or *Considérer* or *Estimer.*
      E.g.: *J'estime que tu devrais aller voir un avocat.*
          I feel that you ought to see a lawyer.

          J'ai l'impression qu'elle se trompe.
          I feel that she is wrong.
(4) Meaning "physical condition" = *Se sentir.*
      E.g.: *Je ne me sens pas bien aujourd'hui.*
          I don't feel well today.

to FEEL LIKE

See *AVOIR ENVIE DE*

FEINDRE

(To feign, to pretend)
PRÉS.: *feins, feins, feint, feign-ons, -ez, -ent.*
IMPARF.: *feign-ais, -ais, -ait, -ions, -iez, -aient.*
PASSÉ SIMPLE: *feign-is, -is, -it, -îmes, -îtes, -irent.*
FUT.: *feindr-ai, -as, -a, -ons, -ez, -ont.*
CONDIT.: *feindr-ais, -ais, -ait, -ions, -iez, -aient.*
IMPÉR.: *feins, feignons, feignez.*
SUBJ. PRÉS.: *feign-e, -es, -e, -ions, -iez, -ent.*
SUBJ. IMPARF.: *feign-isse, -isses, -ît, -issions, -issiez, -issent.*
P. PRÉS.: *feignant.*
P. PASSÉ: *feint(e).*

FEMININE OF ADJECTIVES
See **ADJECTIVES, FEMININE OF**

FEMININE NOUNS, IDENTIFIED BY THE ENDING
See **GENDER**

FEW

(Adverb) = "*Peu de* + noun."
E.g.: *Peu de gens parlent basque.*
  Few people speak Basque.
See *PEU*

FEWER AND FEWER
See **LESS AND LESS, FEWER AND FEWER**

FINIR

(To finish)
PRÉS.: *finis, finis, finit, finissons, finissez, finissent.*
IMPARF.: *finiss-ait, -ais, -ait, -issions, -issiez, -issaient.*
PASSÉ SIMPLE: *fin-is, -is, -it, -îmes, -îtes, -irent.*
FUT.: *finir-ai, -as, -a, -ons, -ez, -ont.*
CONDIT.: *finir-ais, -ais, -ait, -ions, -iez, -aient.*
IMPÉR.: *finis, finissons, finissez.*
SUBJ. PRÉS.: *fin-isse, -isses, -isse, -issions, -issiez, -issent.*
SUBJ. IMPARF.: *fin-isse, -isses, -ît, -issions, -issiez, -issent.*
P. PRÉS.: *finissant.*
P. PASSÉ: *fini(e).*
NOTES:
(1) "*Finir de* + infinitive" = "To finish + present participle."
   E.g.: *J'ai fini de lire.*
      I have finished reading.
(2) "*Finir par* + infinitive" = "Finally + present perfect."
   E.g.: *Elle a fini par comprendre mon point de vue.*
      She finally understood my point of view.

FIRST

(1) (Adjective) = *Premier, première.*
   E.g.: *Le premier jour de l'année.*
      The first day of the year.
(2) (Adverb) Meaning "First of all" = *Premièrement, d'abord.*
   E.g.: *Premièrement, je veux vous dire que vous avez tort.*
      First, I want to tell you that you are wrong.
      D'abord, nous écrirons la lettre.
      First of all we'll write the letter.

to FLY TO

(Idiomatic construction) "To fly to" cannot be translated directly into French. Use *aller à* + an expression indicating the mode of transportation.
E.g.: We flew to Algeria.
   Nous sommes allés en Algérie en avion.
See **TRANSPORTATION, MEANS OF**
See also **to DRIVE TO** and **to WALK TO**

FOIS vs. HEURE, TEMPS, MOMENT

All these words are translated as "Time," but note the differences in their usage:

(1) *Fois* indicates repetition and is used with number.

E.g.: *Elle a téléphoné trois fois.*　　*Deux fois cinq font dix.*
She called three times.　　Two times five is ten.

(2) *Heure* means "Hour, o'clock."

E.g.: *J'ai travaillé pendant huit heures.*　　*Il est six heures.*
I worked for eight hours.　　It is six o'clock.

(3) *Temps* means:

(a) Duration of time:

E.g.: *Combien de temps avez-vous passé en Europe?*
How much time did you spend in Europe?

(b) Weather:

E.g.: *Quel temps fait-il?*
What's the weather like?

(4) *Moment* means:

(a) A brief period of time:

E.g.: *Je ne peux rester qu'un moment.*
I can only stay a moment.

(b) An opportunity:

E.g.: *Ce n'est pas le moment de faire cela.*
It is not the time to do that.

FONDRE

(To melt)
Conjugated like **RENDRE**

FOR

(1) (Preposition) Indicating (a) intention: *pour*; (b) destination: *pour* or *à destination de*; (c) purpose: *pour*; (d) period of time in the future: *pour*; (e) period of time that began in the past: *depuis*.

E.g.: (a) *J'ai acheté ce cadeau pour toi.*
I bought this present for you.

(b) *Elle sont parties pour (à destination de) l'Égypte hier.*
They left for Egypt yesterday.

(c) *Je travaille pour gagner ma vie.*
I work (in order) to earn a living.

(d) *Nous partons pour huit jours.*
We are leaving for a week.

(e) See **DEPUIS + TIME EXPRESSION**

(2) (Conjunction) Meaning "Because" = *Car* or *Parce que*.

E.g.: *Il n'a pas voyagé car il n'avait pas d'argent.*
He did not travel because he had no money.

See **POUR**

FOR LACK OF

(Prepositional construction) = *Faute de.*
E.g.: *Faute d'argent, elle n'a pas pu sortir.*
For lack of money she could not go out.
See **FAUTE DE**

FOR + TIME EXPRESSIONS

(1) To express duration use *Pendant* (but it can be omitted altogether).

E.g.: *Je suis resté à Paris pendant trois ans.*
OR: *Je suis resté trois ans à Paris.*
I stayed in Paris (for) three years.

(2) to indicate a period of future time, use *Pour*.
   E.g.: *Il est à Paris pour trois ans (= pour y rester trois ans).*
      He is in Paris for three years (= to stay there three years).

      Elle est revenue pour huit jours (= pour rester huit jours).
      She returned for a week (= to remain a week).

See **PENDANT vs. POUR + TIME EXPRESSION**

FORMAL vs. FAMILIAR FORMS

See **TU vs. VOUS**

FORMER ... LATTER

(Idiomatic construction) = *Celui-ci (celle-ci, etc.) ... celui-là (celle-là, etc.).*
NOTE:
The order is the opposite of the English construction.
   E.g.: *Boston et Bordeaux sont deux belles villes; celle-ci est en France, celle-là est en Amérique.*
      Boston and Bordeaux are two beautiful cities; the former is in America, and the latter is in France.

See **CELUI, CELLE, CEUX, CELLES (-CI, -LÀ)**

FRACTIONS

Use ordinal numbers, as in English.
   E.g.: *1/5 = un cinquième.*
      2/8 = deux huitièmes.
EXCEPTIONS:
      1/4 = un quart.
      1/3 = un tiers.
      1/2 = un demi.
   E.g.: *Les trois quarts du monde.*
      Three quarters of the world.
NOTE:
Demi is invariable before the noun but variable after it.
   E.g.: *Une demi-heure.*
      A half hour.
   BUT: *Une heure et demie.*
      An hour and a half.
La moitié also means "Half."
   E.g.: *La moitié de la classe.*   *La première moitié du livre.*
      Half of the class.   The first half of the book.

FRIRE

(To fry)
This verb has only the following forms:
PRÉS.: *je fris, tu fris, il frit.*
FUT.: *frir-ai, -as, -a, -ons, -ez, -ont.*
CONDIT.: *frir-ais, -ais, -ait, -ions, -iez, -aient.*
IMPÉR.: *fris.*
P. PASSÉ: *frit(e).*
NOTE:
The missing forms are constructed with *faire*.
   E.g.: *J'ai fait frire le poisson.*
      I fried the fish.

FROM + TIME EXPRESSION + ON

(Prepositional construction) = *À partir de.*
   E.g.: *Le magasin sera ouvert à partir de neuf heures.*
      The store will be open from nine o'clock on.

FROM . . . TO . . .

(Prepositions) = *"De . . . à . . . ."*
E.g.: *Il travaille de huit heures à quatre heures.*
He works from eight o'clock to four o'clock.

Elle va de Paris à Lisbonne.
She goes from Paris to Lisbon.

FUIR

(To flee)
PRÉS.: *fuis, fuit, fuit, fuyons, fuyez, fuient.*
IMPARF.: *fuy-ais, -ais, -ait, -ions, -iez, -aient.*
PASSÉ SIMPLE: *fuis, fuis, fuit, fuîmes, fuîtes, fuirent.*
FUT.: *fuir-ai, -as, -a, -ons, -ez, -ont.*
CONDIT.: *fuir-ais, -ais, -ait, -ions, -iez, -aient.*
IMPÉR.: *fuis, fuyons, fuyez.*
SUBJ. PRÉS.: *fui-e, -es, -e, fuyions, fuyiez, fuient.*
SUBJ. IMPARF.: *fuisse, fuisses, fuît, fuissions, fuissiez, fuissent.*
P. PRÉS.: *fuyant.*
P. PASSÉ: *fui(e).*

FURTHERMORE

(Adverbial expression) = *En outre.*
E.g.: *Il prononce mal, et en outre il parle trop vite.*
He pronounces incorrectly, and furthermore, he speaks too fast.
See **EN OUTRE**

FUTUR ANTÉRIEUR

See **FUTURE PERFECT**

FUTURE IN THE PAST

In a past context, that is, if the main clause is in the past, the future is conveyed by using the conditional. This is exactly the same as in English.
E.g.: *Il a dit qu'il <u>irait</u> en France.*
He said that he <u>would go</u> to France.

FUTURE PERFECT

This tense (*le futur antérieur*) describes an action that will take place in the future before a point in time (or another action) that is also in the future.
FORMATION:
Future of the auxiliary verb + past participle.
E.g.: *Elle aura fait son travail.*
She will have done her work.
USAGE:
With *Quand, Lorsque, Aussitôt que,* or *Dès que,* to indicate an action that will occur in the future before another action that is also in the future.
E.g.: *Je vous écrirai dès que j'aurai fini mes examens.*
I shall write you as soon as I have finished my exams.
See **AUSSITÔT QUE**
See also **DÈS QUE; LORSQUE;** and **QUAND, TENSES WITH**
NOTE:
The future perfect can also indicate probability referring to a past action.
E.g.: *Elle est absente? Elle aura eu un accident.*
She is absent? She must (probably) have had an accident.
See **FUTURE TO EXPRESS PROBABILITY**

FUTURE TENSE

The future tense *(le futur)* describes an action that will take place at a future time.

E.g.: *Nous partirons demain.*

We shall leave tomorrow.

FORMATION:

Infinitive [drop the final *e* if there is one] + *-ai, -as, -a, -ons, -ez, -ont.*

NOTE:

The following verbs have an irregular stem for the future:

INFINITIVE	STEM	FUTURE
Aller	→ *Ir-*	*irai, iras, ira, etc.*
Avoir	→ *Aur-*	*aurai, auras, aura, etc.*
Être	→ *Ser-*	*serai, seras, sera, etc.*
Faire	→ *Fer-*	*ferai, feras, fera, etc.*
Pouvoir	→ *Pourr-*	*pourrai, pourras, pourra, etc.*
Savoir	→ *Saur-*	*saurai, sauras, saura, etc.*
Venir	→ *Viendr-*	*viendrai, vendras, viendra, etc.*
Voir	→ *Verr-*	*verrai, verras, verra, etc.*
Vouloir	→ *Voudr-*	*voudrai, voudras, voudra, etc.*

USAGE:

This tense corresponds to the English "Shall" or "Will."

NOTE:

After "When" *(Quand* or *Lorsque)* or "As soon as" *(Aussitôt que* or *Dès que)*, the future is used in French but the present is used in English.

E.g.: *Je la verrai quand elle viendra.*

I shall see her when she comes.

See *AUSSITÔT QUE,* **TENSES WITH** and *QUAND,* **TENSES WITH**

Do not confuse the "*Quand* + future" construction with the "*Si* + present" construction!

E.g.: *Je le ferai quand j'aurai le temps.*

I shall do it when I have the time. (I will have the time.)

BUT: *Je le ferai si j'ai le temps.*

I shall do it if I have time. (I may or may not have the time.)

NOTE:

As in English, the future is sometimes used to express probability.

See **FUTURE TO EXPRESS PROBABILITY**

FUTURE TO EXPRESS PROBABILITY

As in English, the future tense is sometimes used in French to express probability.

E.g.: *Le téléphone sonne. Ce sera Jeanne.*

The telephone is ringing. That will be Jean.

The future perfect can be used to express probability in the past.

E.g.: *Ils auront probablement manqué l'autobus.*

They must have missed the bus.

FUTURE with *ALLER*

This construction is called the *future proche* (proximate future). It corresponds to the English construction "To be going to + verb." Its use generally implies that the action will take place in the relatively near future.

E.g.: *La semaine prochaine je vais aller au théâtre.*

Next week I am going to go to the theater.

FUTUR PROCHE

See **FUTURE with *ALLER*** and **PROXIMATE FUTURE**

G

GENDER

All nouns are either masculine or feminine. Masculine nouns take the definite article *le* (or *l'*) and the indefinite article *un*. Feminine nouns take the definite article *la* (or *l'*) and the indefinite article *une*. While the gender of each noun must be memorized, it is sometimes possible to tell the gender by looking at the ending of the noun. Generally speaking, the following rules apply.

MASCULINE ENDINGS:

-acle	E.g.: *Un spectacle*	*-er*	E.g.: *Un boulanger*
-age	E.g.: *Un village*	*-eur*	E.g.: *Un vendeur*
-al	E.g.: *Un journal*	*-ien*	E.g.: *Un mécanicien*
-asme	E.g.: *Le sarcasme*	*-in*	E.g.: *Un voisin*
-at	E.g.: *Un internat*	*-isme*	E.g.: *Un mécanisme*
-eau	E.g.: *Un bateau*	*-ment*	E.g.: *Un appartement*
-ent	E.g.: *Un client*	*-oir*	E.g.: *Un couloir*

FEMININE ENDINGS:

-ade	E.g.: *Une façade*	*-ine*	E.g.: *Une machine*
-aine	E.g.: *Une fontaine*	*-ique*	E.g.: *Une mécanique*
-ale	E.g.: *Une cathédrale*	*-ise*	E.g.: *Une surprise*
-ance	E.g.: *Une correspondance*	*-oire*	E.g.: *Une histoire*
-ande	E.g.: *Une commande*	*-ole*	E.g.: *Une parole*
-ée	E.g.: *Une soirée*	*-onne*	E.g.: *Une personne*
-eille	E.g.: *Une bouteille*	*-sion*	E.g.: *Une passion*
-ence	E.g.: *Une science*	*-son*	E.g.: *Une maison*
-ère	E.g.: *Une lumière*	*-té*	E.g.: *Une vanité*
-esse	E.g.: *Une maîtresse*	*-tion*	E.g.: *Une conversation*
-ette	E.g.: *Une assiette*	*-trice*	E.g.: *Une monitrice*
-euse	E.g.: *Une danseuse*	*-tude*	E.g.: *Une habitude*
-ie	E.g.: *Une harmonie*	*-ure*	E.g.: *Une voiture*
-ienne	E.g.: *Une persienne*		

GENS

(Masculine plural noun) = "People, folk." It is used only collectively and to indicate a vague, unspecified number of persons.

E.g.: *Les gens.*   *Peu de gens.*   *Beaucoup de gens.*   *De braves gens.*
    People.   Few people.   A lot of people.   Nice people.

With specified (or implied) numbers, use *Personne(s)*.

E.g.: *Quelques personnes.*   *Cinq personnes.*
    A few people.   Five people.

NOTE:

When a verb has both masculine and feminine subjects the predicate is always in the masculine.

E.g.: *Les garçons et les filles sont gentils.*
    The boys and girls are nice.

GEOGRAPHICAL NAMES

Names of countries, like all other nouns, are either masculine or feminine.

GENERAL RULES:

(1) The definite article is always used with names of countries, continents, provinces, regions, states, etc., but not with cities.

E.g.: *la France*   *le Québec*
    les États-Unis   *la Bretagne*
    l'Europe   *la Floride*
BUT: *Paris, New-York, Bordeaux,* etc.

(2) Geographical names ending in *e* are feminine; all others are masculine.

E.g.: *la France*   *le Brésil*
        la Chine   *le Montana*
        la Virginie   *le Japon*
        la Californie   *le Texas*

EXCEPTIONS:

(a) Countries: *le Cambodge*
                 le Mexique
                 le Zaïre

(b) Cities: a few include the definite article in the name:

E.g.: *Le Caire*
        La Havane
        La Nouvelle-Orléans

(3) The names of American states are the same as in English, except the following:

la Californie   *la Louisiane*
la Caroline du Nord   *le Nouveau-Mexique*
la Caroline du Sud   *la Pennsylvanie*
la Floride   *la Virginie*
la Géorgie

GEOGRAPHICAL NAMES, PREPOSITIONS WITH

(1) COUNTRIES, CONTINENTS, REGIONS:

(a) Feminine names (i.e., those ending in *e* EXCEPT *le Cambodge, le Mexique, le Zaïre*) use *en* (= "to, at") and *de* (= "from, of").

E.g.: *Il va en Argentine.*   *Il est parti d'Argentine.*
        He goes to Argentina.   He left Argentina.

        Elle est en Asie.   *Il revient d'Asie.*
        She is in Asia.   He is returning from Asia.

(b) Masculine names (not ending in *e*), use *au* (= "to, at") and *du* (= "from, of").

E.g.: *Il va au Brésil.*   *Il part du Brésil.*
        He is going to Brazil.   He is leaving Brazil.

        Elle est au Maroc.   *Nous revenons du Chili.*
        She is in Morocco.   We are returning from Chile.

EXCEPTIONS:

En Alaska
À Cuba
En Iran
En Israël

If the name is qualified, use "*Dans* + article."

E.g.: *Dans le sud des États-Unis.*   *Dans le nord de l'Europe.*
        In the southern United States.   In northern Europe.

(2) CITIES: Use *à* (= "to, in") and *de* (= "from, of").

E.g.: *Il est à Paris.*   *Elle habite à Lyon.*
        He is in Paris.   She lives in Lyons.

        Ce musée est à New-York.   *Il vient de Paris.*
        This museum is in New York. He comes from Paris.

NOTE:

With names of cities that include the article, make the necessary contraction.

E.g.: *Il va au Havre.*
        He goes to Le Havre.

        Il vient du Havre.
        He comes from Le Havre.

SUMMARY OF PREPOSITIONS WITH PLACE NAMES

To express "to" or "in":		**Examples**
en	+ feminine countries, continents, provinces	*en Allemagne* *en Asie* *en Normandie*
au(x)	+ masculine countries, provinces	*au Portugal* *au Languedoc* *aux États-Unis*
à	+ cities	*à Lyon*
To express "from" or "of":		
de	+ feminine countries, continents, provinces	*de Chine* *d'Afrique* *de Normandie*
du, des	+ masculine countries	*du Canada* *des Pays-Bas*
de	+ cities	*de Paris*

GERUND

(Le gérondif) A verbal phrase used to express: (a) the means, (b) the manner, or (c) the simultaneity of an action with the main verb. It corresponds to the English "By + -ing," "Upon + ing," or "While + -ing."

CONSTRUCTION:
The preposition *en* + present participle.

USAGE:
(a) To indicate the means of doing something.
　　E.g.: *Elle gagne sa vie en écrivant.*
　　　　She earns her living by writing.

(b) To indicate the manner of doing something.
　　E.g.: *Elles sont sorties en courant.*
　　　　They ran out.

(c) To show the simultaneity of two actions.
　　E.g.: *Il s'est endormi en faisant ses devoirs.*
　　　　He fell asleep while doing his homework.
　　　　En arrivant elle a téléphoné à son père.
　　　　Upon arriving, she called her father.

NOTE:
A present participle after *en* always refers to the subject of the main verb.
E.g.: *En entrant dans le restaurant, j'ai vu Jacqueline.*
　　　As I was entering the restaurant, I saw Jacqueline.

BUT: *J'ai vu Jacqueline promenant son chien.*
　　　I saw Jacqueline walking her dog.
Never translate "By + —ing" with "*Par* + present participle"! Always use "*En* + present participle."

to GET

This verb may be translated in many ways, depending on the meaning. It is wise to think of an English synonym and then to translate that synonym into French.

E.g.: I got this in Paris = I bought this in Paris = *J'ai acheté ceci à Paris.*
We got a letter = We received a letter = *Nous avons reçu une lettre.*
Go get your books! = Go fetch your books! = *Va chercher tes livres!*
You must get ready = You must prepare yourself = *Tu dois te préparer.*
They got here at noon = They arrived at noon = *Ils sont arrivés à midi.*

GOING TO + VERB

This is the proximate future construction: "*Aller* + infinitive."

E.g.: *Nous allons partir.*
We are going to leave.

See **PROXIMATE FUTURE** and **FUTURE with *ALLER***

GRÂCE À

(Idiomatic expression) = "Thanks to."

E.g.: *C'est grâce à elle que j'ai trouvé cet emploi.*
It is thanks to her that I found this job.

See **THANKS TO**

GREETINGS

The greeting used depends on the relationship between the persons involved.

(1) When greeting someone you do not know well or who is older than you, use the appropriate title but not the person's name.

E.g.: *Bonjour, Madame.*   *Bonsoir, Monsieur le Professeur.*
Hello, Mrs. (Smith).   Good evening, Professor (Jones).

(2) When greeting a friend or a member of the family, use the first name.

E.g.: *Bonjour, Caroline!*   *Salut, Philippe!*
Hello, Caroline!   Hi, Philip!

See **INTRODUCING SOMEONE**

to GROW

(1) (Intransitive verb) = *Grandir.*
E.g.: *Les enfants grandissent si vite!*
Children grow so fast!

(2) (Transitive verb) = *Cultiver.*
E.g.: *Elle cultive des tomates.*
She grows tomatoes.

NOTE:

When no effort is involved, use *Laisser pousser.*

E.g.: *Il se laisse pousser la barbe.*
He is growing a beard.

H

"H", ASPIRATE and UNASPIRATED (or SILENT)

Like English, French has two kinds of *h* at the beginning of a word: the "aspirate *h*" and the "unaspirated *h*". In French, however, the *h* is never pronounced. Even the so-called aspirate *h* is never heard.

(1) Aspirate *h*: Although it is never pronounced, the aspirate *h* is equivalent to a consonant. This means that there is no elision and no liaison before it.

E.g.: *Le héros.*   NOT: *L'héros.*
La Hollande.   NOT: *L'Hollande.*
Les Hollandais. (pronounced *"Lé Ollandais,"*   NOT *"Lézollandais"*)

(2) Unaspirated *h*: The unaspirated *h* can be ignored, and the word should be considered as beginning with a vowel.

E.g.: *Un homme* (pronounced *"Unnomme"*).
Les hommes (pronounced *"Lézommes"*).

HABITER vs. DEMEURER vs. VIVRE

See **DEMEURER vs. HABITER vs. VIVRE**

HABITUAL ACTIONS

See **IMPERFECT TENSE**

HAÏR

(To hate)
NOTE:
The diaeresis (¨) disappears in the singular forms of the present and the imperative:
PRÉS.: *hais, hais, hait, haïssons, haïssez, haïssent.*
IMPARF.: *haïss-ais, -ais, -ait, -ions, -iez, -aient.*
PASSÉ SIMPLE: *haïs, -ïs, -ït, -ïmes, -ïtes, -ïrent.*
FUT.: *haïr-ai, -as, -a, -ons, -ez, -ont.*
CONDIT.: *haïr-ais, -ais, -ait, -ions, -iez, -aient.*
IMPÉR.: *hais, haïssons, haïssez.*
SUBJ. PRÉS.: *haïss-e, -es, -e, -ions, -iez, -ent.*
SUBJ. IMPARF.: *haïss-e, -es, haït, haïss-ions, -iez, -ent.*
P. PRÉS.: *haïssant.*
P. PASSÉ: *haï(e).*

to HAPPEN

(Verb) = *Se passer* or *Arriver* (used as an impersonal verb).
E.g.: *Qu'est-ce qui s'est passé à la réunion?*
What happened at the meeting?
NOTE:
Arriver conveys an idea of something unpleasant.
E.g.: *Il lui est arrivé un accident terrible.*
A terrible accident happened to him.

HARDLY ANY or SCARCELY ANY + NOUN

"*Ne* + verb + *guère de* + noun."

E.g.: *Je n'ai guère de travail.*

    I have hardly any work.

When the verb is in a compound tense: "*Ne* + auxiliary verb + *guère* + past participle + *de* + noun."

E.g.: *Nous n'avons guère eu de problèmes.*

    We had hardly any problems.

See **NE . . . GUÈRE**

to HAVE A GOOD TIME

(Idiomatic expression) = *S'amuser.*

E.g.: *Nous nous sommes bien amusés hier soir à la surprise-partie.*

    We had a good time at the surprise party last night.

Do not say *"avoir un bon temps."*

to HAVE A MEAL

(Idiomatic construction) = *Prendre un repas* or *Faire un repas.*

E.g.: *Nous prendrons nos repas au réfectoire.*

    We shall have our meals in the dining hall.

    J'ai fait un bon repas.

    I had a good meal.

to HAVE JUST + PAST PARTICIPLE

(Idiomatic construction) = "*Venir de* + infinitive."

E.g.: *Elle vient d'arriver.*

    She has just arrived.

See **RECENT PAST; JUST;** and **VENIR DE + INFINITIVE**

to HAVE TO + VERB

See **DEVOIR**

to HEAR ABOUT vs. HEAR THAT

"To hear" = *Entendre.*

Note the idiomatic usages:

(1) "to hear about" = "*Entendre parler de* + noun or pronoun."

    E.g.: *J'ai entendu parler de ce nouveau roman.*

        I have heard about this new novel.

(2) "To hear that" = "*Entendre dire que* + indicative."

    E.g.: *J'ai entendu dire qu'elle a écrit un nouveau roman.*

        I have heard that she has written a new novel.

See **ENTENDRE DIRE QUE vs. ENTENDRE PARLER DE**

HEIN!

An exclamation that indicates surprise or a question.

E.g.: *Il a dû avoir peur, hein!*
    He must have been afraid, huh!

    —*Tu viens avec moi?* —*Hein? Que dis-tu?*
    "Are you coming with me?" "What? What are you saying?"

HELP (with CAN'T)

See **CAN'T HELP**

HELPING VERBS

See **AUXILIARY VERBS**

HEURE

See **O'CLOCK**

HEURE vs. *FOIS, TEMPS, MOMENT*

See *FOIS* vs. *HEURE, TEMPS, MOMENT*

HOME

(1) (Noun) = *La maison, le foyer.*
    E.g.: *Nous sommes contents de revoir notre maison.*
        We are glad to see our home again.
(2) (Adverb) "At home" = *Chez soi (moi, lui, elle, etc.)* or *À la maison.*
    E.g.: *Nous rentrerons chez nous (à la maison) demain.*
        We shall go home tomorrow.

to HOPE TO + VERB

(1) If both verbs have the same subject: "*Espérer* + infinitive."
    E.g.: *J'espère aller en France.*
        I hope to go to France.
(2) If the two verbs have different subjects: "*Espérer que* + indicative."
    E.g.: *J'espère que tu iras en France.*
        I hope you will go to France.

See **ESPÉRER**

HORS DE vs. *DEHORS*

See *DEHORS* vs. *HORS DE*

HOT

(1) (Adjective) = *Chaud(e).*
    E.g.: *La soupe est chaude.*
        The soup is hot.
(2) "To be hot" (weather) = *Il fait chaud.*
    E.g.: *Il fait très chaud au Zaïre.*
        It's very hot in Zaire.
(3) "To be hot" (person) = *Avoir chaud.*
    E.g.: *J'ai trop chaud.*
        I'm too hot.

See *AVOIR CHAUD*

HOW

(Adverb) = *Comment.*
E.g.: *Comment allez-vous?*
      How are you?

NOTE:

In exclamations, do not use *Comment* but *Comme.*
E.g.: *Commme elle est travailleuse!*
      How hardworking she is!

See **EXCLAMATIONS**

HOW MUCH, HOW MANY

"*Combien de* + noun."
E.g.: *Combien de frères a-t-il?*
      How many brothers does he have?

      Je ne sais pas combien de temps il faut.
      I don't know how much time is needed.

HUNGRY (to be)

(Idiomatic expression) = *Avoir faim.*
E.g.: *J'ai faim. Allons manger!*
      I'm hungry. Let's go eat!

See ***AVOIR FAIM***

to HURT

(Idiomatic expression)
(1) "To hurt (physically)" = *Faire mal.*
    E.g.: *Tu me fais mal!*
          You're hurting me!

NOTE:

"It hurts; my leg hurts," etc. = *Cela me fait mal; ma jambe me fait mal.*
(2) "To hurt (morally)" = *Faire de la peine (à quelqu'un).*
    E.g.: *Je ne veux pas te faire de la peine, mais je dois te quitter.*
          I don't want to hurt you, but I have to leave you.

HYPHEN

The hyphen *(le trait d'union)* is used:
(1) In many compound nouns:
    E.g.: *Les États-Unis; la Grande-Bretagne; grand-père; sourd-muet; moi-même;*
          quelques-uns.
(2) In numerals, between the tens and the units when the conjunction *et* is not used.
    E.g.: *Trente-six; soixante-dix-neuf.*
(3) Between the verb and the inverted subject or object pronoun:
    E.g.: *Dit-elle; donnez-la-moi.*
(4) To join *ci* and *là* to the words they qualify.
    E.g.: *Ces livres-ci; cette femme-là.*

HYPOTHESIZING

See **CONDITIONAL MOOD** and **IMAGINARY STATEMENTS**

I

IDIOMS

Idioms *(les idiotismes)* are expressions whose meaning cannot be derived from the actual meaning of the words they consist of. They are peculiar to a language and cannot be translated literally into another language. Examples of English idioms are "I am fed up" and "You are pulling my leg," whose French equivalents are *J'en ai marre* and *Vous vous payez ma tête* ("You are treating yourself to my head") or *"Vous vous moquez de moi"* ("You are making fun of me").

An example of a French idiom is *J'ai le cafard*, which means "I feel blue." Every language has a large number of idioms, which can only be learned through practice in context.

(1) Some common idioms with *avoir* are *avoir beau, avoir besoin (de), avoir envie (de), avoir faim, avoir lieu, avoir peur, avoir raison, avoir soif, avoir tort.*

(2) Some common idioms with *être* are *être à, être amoureux (de), être 'd accord (avec), être doué (pour), être ravi (de), être refusé, être sur le point de.*

(3) Some common idioms with faire are *faire du mal, faire mal, faire partie de, faire semblant de, faire venir.*

See the alphabetical listing for each of these words and for *par*.

See also **COUP, IDIOMS WITH**

IGNORER

(Transitive verb) = "To be unaware (or ignorant) of, not to know."

E.g.: *J'ignore complètement la littérature russe.*

   I am completely ignorant of Russian literature.

"To ignore someone" = *Faire semblant de ne pas reconnaître.*

E.g.: *J'ai fait semblant de ne pas reconnaître Marie.*

   I completely ignored Mary. (I pretended not to recognize Mary.)

IL EST vs. C'EST

See **C'EST vs. IL EST or ELLE EST**

IL EST vs. C'EST (+ ADJECTIVE + DE + INFINITIVE

See **C'EST vs. IL EST (+ ADJECTIVE + À + INFINITIVE)**

IL SEMBLE QUE vs. IL ME SEMBLE QUE

(1) "*Il semble que* + subjunctive or indicative" depending on the degree of uncertainty.

   (a) If the statement is fairly certain, use the indicative.

      E.g.: *Il semble qu'il a raison.*

         It appears that he is right.

   (b) If the statement is doubtful, use the subjunctive.

      E.g.: *Il semble qu'il ait raison.*

         It appears that he may be right.

(2) "*Il me (te, lui . . .) semble que* + indicative" = "It seems to me (you, him, her, etc.)." This construction always takes the indicative.

   E.g.: *Il me semble que tu as raison.*

      It seems to me that you are right.

IL SEMBLE QUE vs. *IL PARAÎT QUE*

(Idiomatic constructions)
(1) "*Il semble que* + subjunctive" = "It seems (either from appearance or hearsay)."
    E.g.: *Il semble qu'il soit malade.*
        He seems to be sick.
(2) "*Il paraît que* + indicative" = "I've heard that" or "I am told."
    E.g.: *Il paraît qu'il est malade.*
        I am told that he is sick.

IL Y A

(Impersonal construction) = "There is, there are."
It is always used in the singular.
E.g.: *Il y a une voiture dans la rue.*   *Il y a des voitures dans la rue.*
     There is a car in the street.   There are cars in the street.
NOTE:
The *a* of *Il y a* is the third person singular of the present tense of the verb *avoir*. It is conjugated normally:
IMPARF.: *il y avait.*
PASSÉ SIMPLE: *il y eut.*
PASSÉ COMPOSÉ: *il y a eu.*
FUT.: *il y aura.*
CONDIT.: *il y aurait.*
SUBJ. PRÉS.: *qu'il y ait.*
SUBJ. IMPARF.: *qu'il y eût.*
E.g.: *Il y avait des voitures dans la rue.*
     There were some cars in the street.

     Il y aura une surprise-partie samedi prochain.
     There will be a surprise party next Saturday.
NOTE:
Followed by an expression of time, *Il y a* means "Ago."
See **AGO**
See also *IL Y A* + **TIME EXPRESSION** + *QUE*

IL Y A + **TIME EXPRESSION** + *QUE*

The use of tenses in this expression is very different from the English construction.
(1) If the action is still going on, use the present
    E.g.: *Il y a deux heures que je suis ici.*
        I have been here for two hours.
(2) If the action was still going on in a past context, use the imperfect and *Il y avait.*
    E.g.: *Il y avait deux heures que j'étais ici quand tu es arrivé.*
        I had been here for two hours when you arrived.
See also *DEPUIS* + **TIME EXPRESSION**

IMAGINARY STATEMENTS

Imaginary (or hypothetical) statements are conveyed by the conditional mood.
E.g.: *J'irais au cinéma si j'avais le temps.*
     I <u>would</u> *go* to the movies if I had time.
See **CONDITIONAL MOOD**

IMPERATIVE MOOD

The imperative *(l'impératif)* presents the action of the verb as a command or an exhortation.
E.g.: *Faites votre travail!*   *Faisons notre travail!*
     Do your work!   Let's do our work!

FORMS:

There are three persons in the imperative mood:

Second person sing. E.g.: *Finis!*

First person plur. E.g.: *Finissons!*

Second person plur. E.g.: *Finissez!*

FORMATION:

In general, the imperative forms are the same as those of the present tense (minus the subject pronoun).

NOTES:

(1) First conjugation verbs drop the final *s* in the second person singular.

E.g.: *Mange!*

Eat!

(2) *Aller* also drops the final *s*.

E.g.: *Va!*

Go!

EXCEPTIONS:

AVOIR	ÊTRE	SAVOIR	VOULOIR
aie	sois	sache	—
ayons	soyons	sachons	—
ayez	soyez	sachez	veuillez

NOTE:

Before *y* and *en*, the second person singular imperative keeps the final *s*. (This permits the liaison and makes the meaning clearer and the pronunciation easier.)

E.g.: *Donne-le-moi!*   BUT: *Donnes-en à Pierre!*

Give it to me!   Give some to Peter!

Va!   BUT: *Vas-y!*

Go!   Go on!

NEGATIVE IMPERATIVE:

(1) To make a negative command, place *ne* (or *n'*) before the imperative form of the verb and *pas* after it.

E.g.: *Ne sors pas!*   *Ne parlons pas!*   *N'envoyez pas la lettre!*

Don't go out!   Let's not speak!   Don't send the letter!

If the verb is reflexive, the reflexive pronoun goes before the verb.

E.g.: *Ne te trompe pas!*   *Ne nous fâchons pas!*   *Ne vous troublez pas!*

Don't make a mistake!   Let's not get angry!   Don't become flustered!

IMPERATIVE, POSITION OF OBJECT PRONOUNS WITH
See **PRONOUNS, OBJECT OF VERB**

IMPERFECT TENSE

In general, the imperfect *(l'imparfait)* describes an action taking place (or a situation existing) in the past, but without giving any indication as to the beginning or end of this action (or situation). It describes an action under way but not finished.

FORMATION:

Stem of first person plural of the present tense + *-ais, -ais, -ait, -ions, -iez, -aient.*

E.g.: *Je parlais*   *Je peignais*

Tu vendais   *Tu peignais*

Elle finissait   *Il peignait*

Nous écrivions   *Nous peignions*

Vous preniez   *Vous peigniez*

Ils couraient   *Ils peignaient*

EXCEPTIONS:

Être   = *j'étais, tu étais, il était, nous éitons, vous étiez, ils étaient.*

Falloir   = *il fallait.*

Pleuvoir = *il pleuvait.*

USAGE:

The imperfect is used mainly in four instances:

(1) To describe an action in the past that was going on but not yet finished when something else happened.

E.g.: *Je lisais quand il est entré.*   *Elle voulait aller au cinéma.*

I was reading when he came in.   She wanted to go to the movies.

(In English this is frequently conveyed by "was (were) + —ing." E.g.:"I was reading.")

(2) To give a description or express a state of affairs in the past.

E.g.: *Elle avait les yeux bleus.*   *Il était malade quand je l'ai trouvé.*

She had blue eyes.   He was sick when I found him.

(3) After *si*, to express a wish, desire, or suggestion.

E.g.: *Si j'étais riche!*   *Si nous allions au cinéma!*

If only I were rich!   Let's go to the movies!

(4) To describe actions that were performed habitually or repeatedly in the past.

E.g.: *Je me levais toujours tôt.*   *Elle était souvent malade.*

I always used to get up early.   She was often sick.

(In English this is frequently conveyed by "Used to + infinitive" or by the conditional "Would." E.g.: "She would often get up early.")

NOTES:

(1) The interrupted action is expressed in the imperfect, while the interrupting action goes in the *passé composé* (or *passé simple*).

E.g.: *Je dormais quand le téléphone a sonné* (or *sonna*).

I was sleeping when the telephone rang.

(2) The ongoing situation is expressed in the imperfect, while the action that took place goes in the *passé composé* (or *passé simple*).

E.g.: *Il pleuvait quand je suis sorti* (or *je sortis*).

It was raining when I went out.

REMEMBER:

Do not use the conditional in French for repeated actions. The English construction "I would often go swimming when I was little" must be conveyed by using the imperfect.

E.g.: *J'allais souvent nager quand j'étais petit.*

I would often go swimming when I was little.

See **IMPERFECT vs. *PASSÉ COMPOSÉ***

IMPERFECT vs. *PASSÉ COMPOSÉ*

Generally speaking, the imperfect is used for:

(1) Past actions or situations that were going on but were not yet finished.

E.g.: *Je dormais quand le téléphone a sonné.*

I was sleeping when the telephone rang.

(2) Descriptions or state of affairs in the past.

E.g.: *Elle était grande et blonde.*

She was tall and blonde.

(3) Repeated actions in the past.

E.g.: *J'allais souvent au théâtre quand j'étais à Paris.*

I would go to the theater often when I was in Paris.

Generally speaking the *passé composé* is used for:

(1) Actions that ended in the past.

E.g.: *Il est arrivé hier soir.*

He arrived last night.

(2) Actions that occurred at a specific moment in the past.

E.g.: *Le train est parti à trois heures.*

The train left at three o'clock.

(3) Actions whose (a) beginning, (b) duration, or (c) end is known and specified (even if the action lasted a long time).

E.g.: (a) *La classe a commencé à neuf heures.*
The class began at nine o'clock.
(b) *La guerre a duré quatre ans.*
The war lasted four years.
(c) *Il a fait chaud jusqu'en octobre.*
It was hot until October.

See **IMPERFECT TENSE**
See also ***PASSÉ COMPOSÉ***

IMPERSONAL EXPRESSIONS
See **VERBS, IMPERSONAL**

IMPERSONAL VERBS
See **VERBS, IMPERSONAL**

IN (a place)
(Preposition) = *Dans* or *En.*
NOTE:
These two prepositions are not interchangeable.
See ***DANS* vs. *EN* (with a place)**

IN (with time expressions)
(Preposition) = *Dans* or *En.*
NOTE:
These two prepositions are not interchangeable.
See ***DANS* vs. *EN* (with time expressions)**

IN ORDER TO
(Preposition) = *Pour* + infinitive.
E.g.: *Je partirai tôt pour ne pas manquer le train.*
I shall leave early in order not to miss the train.
See ***POUR***
See also ***AFIN DE* vs. *AFIN QUE***

IN SPITE OF
See **DESPITE**
See also ***MALGRÉ***

INCLUDING
(Idiomatic construction) = *Y compris* (invariable expression placed before the noun).
E.g.: *Envoyez-moi la note, y compris les frais de transport.*
Send me the bill including the transportation costs.
See ***Y COMPRIS***

INCLURE

(To include)
PRÉS.: *inclu-s, -s, -t, -ons, -ez, -ent.*
IMPARF.: *inclu-ais, -ais, -ait, -ions, -iez, -aient.*
PASSÉ SIMPLE: *incl-us, -us, -ut, -ûmes, -ûtes, urent.*
FUT.: *inclur-ai, -as, -a, -ons, -ez, -ont.*
CONDIT.: *inclur-ais, -ais, -ait, -ions, -iez, -aient.*
IMPÉR.: *inclus, incluons, incluez.*
SUBJ. PRÉS.: *inclu-e, -es, -e, -ions, -iez, -ent.*
SUBJ. IMPARF.: *incl-usse, -usses, -ût, -ussions, -ussiez, -ussent.*
P. PRÉS.: *incluant.*
P. PASSÉ: *inclus(e).*

INDEFINITE ADJECTIVES

See **ADJECTIVES, INDEFINITE**

INDEFINITE ARTICLES

See **ARTICLES, INDEFINITE**

INDEFINITE PRONOUNS

See **PRONOUNS, INDEFINITE**

INDEFINITE SUBJECT

In English an indefinite subject is generally conveyed by using "They, people, you." This is expressed in French by *on*, which is a third person singular pronoun.
E.g.: They're building a bridge over there.
   On construit un pont là-bas.

You have to work hard at this school.
   On doit travailler dur à cette école.
See **ON**

INDEPENDENT PRONOUNS

See **PRONOUNS, EMPHATIC**

INDICATIVE MOOD

The indicative mood *(l'indicatif)* states the action of the verb as factual.
E.g.: *Cet homme fait tout le travail.*
   This man does all the work.
There are nine tenses in the indicative:

(1) *PRÉSENT:*   E.g.: *Il mange.*
                 He eats, is eating, does eat.
(2) *FUTUR:*   E.g.: *Il mangera.*
                 He will eat.
(3) *IMPARFAIT:*   E.g.: *Il mangeait.*
                 He ate, used to eat, was eating.
(4) *PASSÉ SIMPLE:*   E.g.: *Il mangea.* (Used in literary style only.)
                 He ate.
(5) *PASSÉ COMPOSÉ:*   E.g.: *Il a mangé.*
                 He ate, has eaten.
(6) *FUTUR ANTÉRIEUR:*   E.g.: *Il aura mangé.*
                 He will have eaten.
(7) *PLUS-QUE-PARFAIT:*   E.g.: *Il avait mangé.*
                 He had eaten.

(8) *PASSÉ ANTÉRIEUR:*   E.g.: *Il eut mangé.* (Used in literary style only.)
                                        He had eaten.

(9) *PASSÉ SURCOMPOSÉ:*   E.g.: *Il a eu mangé.* (Used in conversation only.)
                                        He had eaten.

See **PRESENT TENSE; FUTURE TENSE; IMPERFECT TENSE;** *PASSÉ SIMPLE; PASSÉ COMPOSÉ;* **FUTURE PERFECT;** *PLUS-QUE-PARFAIT* **(PLUPERFECT);** *PASSÉ ANTÉRIEUR;* and *PASSÉ SURCOMPOSÉ*

INDICATIVE vs. SUBJUNCTIVE

(1) If the main clause is a simple statement, devoid of emotion, doubt, uncertainty, desire, or will, use the indicative in the subordinate clause.

    E.g.: *Il dit qu'il est préoccupé.*   *Vous connaissez l'homme qui arrive.*
            He says he is worried.   You know the man who is arriving.

            Je pense qu'il est malade.   *Nous resterons ici parce qu'il pleut.*
            I think he is sick.   We shall stay here because it is raining.

            Nous savons que tu as raisons.   *Tu te couches tôt quand tu es fatigué.*
            We know (that) you are right.   You go to bed early when you are tired.

(2) If the main clause contains an idea of emotion, doubt, uncertainty, desire, or will, use the subjunctive in the subordinate clause (provided that the subject is not the same as that of the main clause).

    E.g.: *Je crains qu'il (ne) soit blessé.*
            I am afraid that he is hurt.

            Je doute qu'il soit malade.
            I doubt that he is sick.

            Nous ne sommes pas certains que tu aies raison.
            We are not sure (that) you are right

            Je doute que vous connaissiez l'homme qui arrive.
            I doubt that you know the man who is arriving.

            Il veut que nous restions ici.
            He wants us to stay here.

            Il faut que tu partes tôt.
            You have to leave early.

In the negative, *croire* may be followed by the indicative or the subjunctive.

See *CROIRE*

See also *PENSER*

For complete details, see **SUBJUNCTIVE MOOD**

INDIRECT DISCOURSE

See *DISCOURS INDIRECT* vs. *DISCOURS DIRECT*

INDIRECT OBJECT

An indirect object *(un complément d'object indirect)* tells for whom or to whom the action of the verb is performed.

    E.g.: *Je donne le livre <u>à mon frère</u>.*
         I give the book <u>to my brother</u>.

See **DIRECT OBJECT vs. INDIRECT OBJECT**

INDIRECT OBJECT PRONOUNS

See **PRONOUNS, OBJECT OF VERB**

INDIRECT QUESTIONS

See *DISCOURS INDIRECT* vs. *DISCOURS DIRECT*

INFINITIVE

The infinitive *(l'infinitif)* expresses the action of the verb. It is the noun form of the verb.

E.g.:   *J'aime travailler.*   *Il est humain de se tromper.*

I like to work.   To err is human.

FORMS:

There are two tenses of the infinitive:

(1) PRESENT INFINITIVE:

E.g.:   *Travailler*   *Finir*   *Venir*   *Se lever*

To work   To finish   To come   To get up

(2) PAST INFINITIVE:

(The infinitive of the auxiliary verb + the past participle.)

E.g.:   *Avoir travaillé*   *Avoir fini*   *Être venu*   *S'être levé*

To have worked   To have finished   To have come   To have gotten up

NOTES:

(1) The rules for the agreement of the past participle apply here also.

E.g.: *Après s'être levée, elle est partie.*

After getting up, she left.

(2) Don't forget to conjugate the reflexive pronoun according to the context.

E.g.: *Aprés <u>nous</u> être levés, nous sommes partis.*

After getting up, we left.

REMEMBER:

In English the noun form of the verb can be expressed by the present participle. The French equivalent must be the infinitive.

E.g.: I like <u>watching</u> TV. = *J'aime <u>regarder</u> la télé.*

INFINITIVE AFTER PREPOSITIONS

Whereas in English the present participle is frequently used after prepositions, in French the infinitive is used after most prepositions.

E.g.: *Avant de partir.*   *Pour réussir.*

Before leaving.   In order to succeed.

EXCEPTION:

The preposition *en* is followed by the present participle.

E.g.: *En arrivant.*

Upon arriving. (OR: While arriving.)

En courant.

While running. (OR: By running.)

See **GERUND**

SPECIAL CASE:

The preposition *Après* is always followed by the past infinitive.

E.g.:   *Après être arrivé(e)(s).*   *Après avoir mangé.*

After arriving.   After eating.

See ***APRÈS* vs. *APRÈS QUE***

INFINITIVE IN THE NEGATIVE

To make an infinitive negative, place *Ne pas* before the infinitive.

E.g.: *Ne pas fumer.*

Do not smoke.

INFINITIVE INTRODUCED BY A VERB

See **PREPOSITIONS + INFINITIVES**

INFINITIVE OF REFLEXIVE VERBS

The reflexive pronoun is always placed before the reflexive verb in the infinitive. REMEMBER that the reflexive pronoun must agree with the subject.

E.g.: *Je vais me coucher.*   *Voulez-vous vous dépêcher?*
       I am going to go to bed.   Will you hurry up?

See **VERBS, REFLEXIVE**

INFINITIVE WITH *FAIRE*

See *FAIRE* + **INFINITIVE**

INFINITIVES PRECEDED BY *À*

See **PREPOSITIONS + INFINITIVES**

INFINITIVES PRECEDED BY *DE*

See **PREPOSITIONS + INFINITIVES**

INQUIÉTER

(To worry, to cause worry)
The *e* of the stem changes to *è* before a silent syllable at the end of the verb. Therefore, the following forms are slightly irregular.

PRÉS.: *j'inquiète, tu inquiètes, il inquiète, (nous inquiétons, vous inquiétez), ils inquiètent.*
SUBJ. PRÉS.: *que j'inquiète, que tu inquiètes, qu'il inquiète, (que nous inquiétions, que vous inquiétiez), qu'ils inquiètent.*
The reflexive verb *S'inquiéter* means "To worry, to be worried."

E.g.: *Il s'inquiète de sa santé.* (reflexive)
       He worries about his health.

       Ta santé inquiète le docteur. (not reflexive)
       Your health worries the doctor.

INSIDE

(1) (Adverb) = *Dedans* or *À l'intérieur.*
    E.g.: *Il fait plus chaud dedans (à l'intérieur) que dehors.*
          It is warmer inside than outside (or outdoors).
(2) Preposition) = *Dans* or *À l'intérieur de.*
    E.g.: *Elle est dans (à l'intérieur de) la maison.*
          She is inside the house.

INSIDE OUT

(Idiomatic construction) = *À l'envers.*
E.g.: *Tu as mis ta chemise à l'envers.*
      You put your shirt on inside out.

See *À L'ENVERS*

INSTRUIRE

(To instruct, to teach, to educate)
Conjugated like *CONDUIRE*

to be INTERESTED IN

(Idiomatic construction) = "*S'intéresser à* + object of preposition."
E.g.: *Elle commence à s'intéresser à lui.*
      She is beginning to be interested in him.

See *S'INTÉRESSER À*

INTERJECTIONS

Interjections *(les interjections)* are expressions of surprise, fear, or another emotion that do not have any true grammatical meaning but are rather more like cries or shouts. These are some common French interjections:

Aïe! = Ouch!	*Merde!* (vulgar) = Damn!
Bon alors! = Well, then!	*Mince alors!* = Gee whiz!
Ça alors! = Gosh!	*Ouf!* = Whew!
Eh bien! = Gee!	*Tiens!* = What do you know!
Formidable! = Terrific!	*Zut!* = Darn!

INTERROGATIVE PRONOUNS
See PRONOUNS, INTERROGATIVE

INTERROGATIVE SENTENCES

An interrogative sentence is one that asks a question. The normal word order in an interrogative sentence is as follows.

(1) In conversational style:

(Interrogative word) + *est-ce que* + subject + verb + object.

E.g.: *Est-ce que Pierre lit le livre?*
   Is Peter reading the book?

   Pourquoi est-ce que Pierre lit le livre?
   Why is Peter reading the book?

(2) In formal or literary style:

(a) If the subject is a pronoun:

(Interrogative word) + verb + subject + object.

E.g.: *Pourquoi lit-il le livre?*
   Why is he reading the book?

(Except with *je*: E.g.: *Pourquoi est-ce que je lis le livre?* NOT: *Pourquoi lis-je le livre?*)

(b) If the subject is a noun, it remains before the verb and the corresponding subject pronoun is added (and hyphenated to) the verb:

(Interrogative word) + noun subject + verb + pronoun subject + object.

E.g.: *Pourquoi Pierre lit-il le livre?*
   Why is Peter reading the book?

(Except with the interrogative pronoun *que*: E.g.: *Que fait Pierre?* NOT: *Que Pierre fait-il?*)

See *EST-CE QUE . . . ?*
See also **QUESTIONS, WORD ORDER IN**

INTERROGATIVE SENTENCES IN THE NEGATIVE

(1) With inversion, use *ne* before the verb and *pas* after the pronoun.

E.g.: *N'aimez-vous pas la musique?*
   Don't you like music?

(2) If the verb is in a compound tense, place *ne* before the auxiliary verb and *pas* after the subject pronoun.

E.g.: *N'avez-vous pas aimé le film?*
   Didn't you like the film?

(3) In the case of reflexive verbs, place *ne* before the auxiliary verb and *pas* after the subject pronoun.

E.g.: *Ne vous couchez-vous pas?*
   Aren't you going to bed?

INTRANSITIVE VERBS
See VERBS, INTRANSITIVE

INTRODUCING SOMEONE

Formulas used when introducing someone:

E.g.: *Je voudrais vous présenter mes parents.*
  I'd like to introduce my parents.

  Je vous présente ma fiancée.
  I'd like to introduce my fiancée.

An appropriate response is:

  (Je suis très) heureux de faire votre connaissance.
  (I'm very) glad to meet you.

See **GREETINGS**

INVERSION

The normal word order in an affirmative or negative sentence is:
  Subject—verb—object (or predicate).
There is inversion *(l'inversion)* when the order is changed as follows:
  Verb—subject—object (or predicate).
Inversion is used in the following instances.

(1) Interrogative sentences, if the question bears on the verb itself.
  E.g.: *Viens-tu?*   *Comprenez-vous?*
      Are you coming?   Do you understand?

(2) Interrogative sentences beginning with an interrogative word.
  E.g.: *Que faites-vous?*
      What are you doing? (OR: What do you do?)

      Quand partiras-tu?
      When will you leave?

NOTE:

If the question does not begin with an interrogative word and if the subject is a noun or a pronoun, this noun or pronoun remains before the verb and the corresponding subject pronoun is added after the verb.

  E.g.: *Jacques vient-il?*   *Cela est-il difficile?*
      Is James coming?   Is that difficult?

      Pierre est-il ici?   *Jacqueline est-elle arrivée?*
      Is Peter here?   Has Jacqueline arrived?

REMEMBER:

There is no inversion when the question begins with *Est-ce que.*

  E.g.: *Est-ce que Jacques vient?*   *Est-ce que c'est difficile?*
      Is James coming?   Is it difficult?

      Est-ce que Pierre est ici?   *Est-ce que Jacqueline est arrivée?*
      Is Peter here?   Did Jacqueline arrive?

(3) In sentences beginning with *À peine, À plus forte raison, Ainsi, Aussi, Aussi bien, Du moins, Encore, En vain, Peut-être, Sans doute,* and *Tout au plus,* inversion is frequently used.
  E.g.: *À peine fut-il rentré qu'il sortit de nouveau.*
      He had hardly returned when he went out again.

      Peut-être avez-vous raison.
      Maybe you are right.

(4) Incised clauses such as *dit-il, cria-t-elle, demanda-t-il, annonça-t-on,* and *cria madame Lebrun.*
  E.g.: *"Allez-vous-en!" s'écria le professeur.*
      "Go away!" the teacher exclaimed.

"IR" VERBS CONJUGATED LIKE *FINIR* (*-ISS-* VERBS)

The following verbs have the *-iss-* infix in the first person plural of the present indicative and in the tenses derived from that form (imperfect, subjunctive present):

Accomplir = To accomplish	*Mugir* = To bellow, to roar
Adoucir = To sweeten	*Mûrir* = To ripen, to mature
Affaiblir = To weaken	*Noircir* = To blacken
Affermir = To strengthen	*Haïr* = To hate
Agir = To act	*Jaillir* = To gush forth
Agrandir = To enlarge	*Nourrir* = To nourish
Applaudir = To applaud	*Obéir* = To obey
Assagir = To subdue	*Obscurcir* = To darken
Assombrir = To darken	*Pâlir* = To turn pale
Assouplir = To soften	*Périr* = To perish
Atterrir = To land	*Polir* = To polish
Avertir = To warn	*Pourrir* = To rot
Bâtir = To build	*Punir* = To punish
Blanchir = To whiten	*Raccourcir* = To shorten
Blêmir = To turn pale	*Rafraîchir* = To refresh
Bleuir = To turn blue	*Rajeunir* = To rejuvenate
Bondir = To jump	*Ralentir* = To slow down
Bruire = To rustle, to hum	*Ravir* = To delight
Chérir = To cherish	*Réfléchir* = To think
Choisir = To choose	*Refroidir* = To cool
Convertir = To convert	*Réjouir* = To rejoice
Démolir = To demolish	*Remplir* = To fill
Désobéir = To disobey	*Répartir* = To divide up
Durcir = To harden	*Resplendir* = To shine
Éblouir = To dazzle	*Retentir* = To ring out, to reverberate
Éclaircir = To lighten, to clear up	*Rétrécir* = To shrink
Élargir = To widen	*Réunir* = To gather
Embellir = To embellish	*Réussir* = To succeed
Emplir = To fill	*Rôtir* = To roast
Endurcir = To harden	*Rougir* = To blush
Enrichir = To enrich	*Rugir* = To roar
Envahir = To invade	*Saisir* = To seize, to grab
Établir = To establish	*Salir* = To soil
Farcir = To stuff	*S'évanouir* = To faint
Fleurir = To flourish, to bloom	*Surgir* = To come into view
Frémir = To shudder	*Ternir* = To tarnish
Garantir = To guarantee	*Trahir* = To betray
Gémir = To groan	*Unir* = To unite
Grandir = To grow	*Verdir* = To turn green
Grossir = To get fat	*Vieillir* = To age
Guérir = To cure, to heal	*Vomir* = To vomit

IT

"It" is sometimes translated by *c'est*, sometimes by *Il est* or *Elle est*.
See **C'EST vs. IL EST or ELLE EST**
"It" can also be the subject of an impersonal verb.
See **VERBS, IMPERSONAL**

J

JETER

(To throw)

PRÉS.: *jette, jettes, jette, jetons, jetez, jettent.*
IMPARF.: *jet-ais, -ais, -ait, -ions, -iez, -aient.*
PASSÉ SIMPLE: *jet-ai, -as, -a, -âmes, -âtes, -èrent.*
FUT.: *jetter-ai, -as, -a, -ons, -ez, -ont.*
CONDIT.: *jetter-ais, -ais, -ait, -ions, -iez, -aient.*
IMPÉR.: *jette, jetons, jetez.*
SUBJ. PRÉS.: *jett-e, -es, -e, jetions, jetiez, jettent.*
SUBJ. IMPARF.: *jet-asse, -asses, -ât, -assions, -assiez, -assent.*
P. PRÉS.: *jetant*
P. PASSÉ: *jeté(e).*

to JOIN

(1) Meaning "To link" = *Joindre* or *Unir.*
    E.g.: *Les deux candidats ont uni leurs forces.*
        The two candidates joined forces.
(2) Meaning "to become member of" + *Devenir membre de.*
    E.g.: *Je suis devenu membre du club de tennis.*
        I joined the tennis club.

JOINDRE

(To join)

PRÉS.: *joins, joins, joint, joign-ons, -ez, -ent.*
IMPARF.: *joign-ais, -ais, -ait, -ions, -iez, -aient.*
PASSÉ SIMPLE: *joign-is, -is, -it, -îmes, -îtes, -irent.*
FUT.: *joindr-ai, -as, -a, -ons, -ez, -ont.*
CONDIT.: *joindr-ais, -ais, -ait, -ions, -iez, -aient.*
IMPÉR.: *joins, joignons, joignez.*
SUBJ. PRÉS.: *joign-e, -es, -e, -ions, -iez, -ent.*
SUBJ. IMPARF.: *joign-isse, -isses, -ît, -issions, -issiez, -issent.*
P. PRÉS.: *joignant.*
P. PASSÉ: *joint(e).*

JOUER À vs. JOUER DE

(1) *Jouer à* with sports, games, etc.
    E.g.: *Nous jouons au tennis.*   *Il joue aux cartes.*
        We play tennis.   He plays cards.
(2) *Jouer de* with musical instruments.
    E.g.: *Elle joue du piano.*   *Vous jouez de la guitare.*
        She plays the piano.   You play the guitar.
NOTE:
When *jouer* takes a direct object (e.g., the name of the tune played), use the preposition *à* with the instrument.
E.g.: *Elle a joué "La Marseillaise" au piano.*
        She played the Marseillaise on the piano.

JOUR vs. *JOURNÉE*

The two words are not always interchangeable.
(1) *Le jour* generally refers to the unit of time.
    E.g.: *Je passerai trois jours à Paris.*
        I shall spend three days in Paris.

        Elle est arrivée deux jours plus tard.
        She arrived three days later.
(2) *La journée* generally refers to the duration.
    E.g.: *Il dort pendant la journée et il travaille la nuit.*
        He sleeps during the day(time) and works at night.

        Une journée de travail.
        A day's work.

JUSQU'À CE QUE

(Conjunction) "*Jusqu'à ce que* + subjunctive" = "Until."
E.g.: *Il restera en France jusqu'à ce qu'il obtienne son diplôme.*
    He will stay in France until he obtains his diploma.
See **UNTIL vs. NOT . . . UNTIL**

JUSQUE, JUSQU'À

The preposition *Jusque* = "To, as far as, right up to, all the way to" is used for both time and distance.
E.g.: *Il a dormi jusqu'à onze heures.*
    He slept until eleven o'clock.

    Jusqu'où ira-t-il? Jusqu'ici.
    How far will he go? Up to here.
NOTE:
When followed by a noun, it takes the preposition *à*.
E.g.: *Jusqu'à demain.*   *Jusqu'à Paris.*
    Until tomorrow.   As far as (All the way to) Paris.

JUST

"To have just + past participle" = "*Venir de* + infinitive." (This is the recent past construction.)
E.g.: *Nous venons d'apprendre la nouvelle.*
    We have just learned the news.
NOTE:
Since this construction describes a state of affairs or a state of being, not an action, when it is in the past, it must always be in the *imparfait*.
E.g.: *Je venais d'entrer quand tu m'as vu.*
    I had just come in when you saw me.

    Nous venions d'apprendre la nouvelle.
    We had just learned the news.

JUST AS + CLAUSE

(Idiomatic construction) = *Au moment où.*
E.g.: *On fermait le magasin au moment où nous sommes arrivés.*
    They were closing the store just as we arrived.

L

for LACK OF

(Prepositional construction) = *Faute de.*

E.g.: *Je n'ai pas pu finir le livre, faute de temps.*
        I was not able to finish the book for lack of time.

See ***FAUTE DE***

to LACK

(Idiomatic construction) = *Manquer de.*

E.g.: *Il manque de courage.*
        He lacks courage.

See ***MANQUER vs. MANQUER À vs. MANQUER DE***

LAISSER + INFINITIVE

"*Laisser* + infinitive" = "To let (someone) + verb."

E.g.: *Nous laissons les enfants dormir.*
        We let the children sleep.

NOTES:

(1) The past participle agrees with the preceding direct object only if the object performs the action stated by the infinitive.

E.g.: *Les enfants que j'ai laissés dormir.*
        The children whom I let sleep.

(2) For the "Let's + verb" construction, use the imperative mood in French.

See **IMPERATIVE MOOD**

LAISSER vs. PARTIR, QUITTER, S'EN ALLER, SORTIR

All these verbs mean "To leave."

(1) *Laisser* means:

(a) "To leave behind."

E.g.: *J'ai laissé mon livre dans ma chambre.*
        I left my book in my room.

(b) "To let (someone) + verb."

E.g.: *Laissez-moi partir!*
        Let me leave!

See ***LAISSER* + INFINITIVE**

(2) *Partir* means "To leave, to go away, to depart."

E.g.: *Ils partent demain matin.*
        They leave tomorrow morning.

(3) *Quitter* means "To leave (a place or a person)."

E.g.: *Il a quitté sa femme.*   *Nous quittons la France demain.*
        He has left his wife.   We leave France tomorrow.

(4) *S'en aller* means "To go away."

E.g.: *Allez-vous en!*   *Je m'en vais.*
        Go away!   I am leaving.

(5) *Sortir* means "To go out of a place, to go out (with someone), to take out."

E.g.: *Elle est sortie de la pièce sans bruit.*
        She left the room without a sound.

Je vais vous demander de sortir un instant.
        I'll have to ask you to leave for a moment.

LANGUAGES, NAMES OF

The names of languages *(les langues)* are masculine and are preceded by the definite article *le* (except after the verb *parler*). Most names of languages are the same as the masculine singular form of the adjective of nationality. Names of languages are not capitalized.

E.g.: *L'allemand est une langue difficile.*

German is a difficult language.

Il étudie l'italien.

He studies Italian.

BUT: *Il parle italien.*

He speaks Italian.

LAST

(1) (Adjective) = *Dernier, dernière.*

E.g.: *Le dernier jour de l'année est le 31 décembre.*

The last day of the year is December 31.

NOTE:

Le mois dernier.	*La semaine dernière.*	*L'année dernière.*
Last month.	Last week.	Last year.
BUT: *Le dernier mois.*	*La dernière semaine.*	*La dernière année.*
The last month.	The last week.	The last year.

REMEMBER: "Last night" = *Hier soir.*

(2) (Adverb) Meaning "Last of all, finally" = *Finalement.*

E.g.: *J'irai d'abord en France, puis en Belgique et finalement en Allemagne.*

I shall go first to France, then to Belgium, and finally to Germany.

to LAST

(Verb) = *Durer.*

E.g.: *L'examen dure deux heures.*

The examination lasts two hours.

to LEAVE

(Verb)

(1) Meaning "To go away" = *Quitter* (transitive) or *Partir (de).*

E.g.: *Ils quitteront Paris demain.*   *Ils partiront de Paris demain.*

They will leave Paris tomorrow.   They will depart from Paris tomorrow.

(2) Meaning "To leave behind" = *Laisser.*

E.g.: *J'ai laissé ma voiture au garage.*

I left my car in the garage.

See **LAISSER + INFINITIVE**

LEAVE-TAKING

Various formulas used for leave-taking:

À bientôt! = See you soon!

À demain! = See you tomorrow!

À la semaine prochaine! = See you next week!

Adieu! = Farewell!

Au plaisir de vous revoir! = I'll look forward to seeing you again!

Au revoir! = Goodbye!

Bon voyage! = Have a good trip!

L'ÉCHAPPER BELLE

(Idiomatic expression) = "To have a narrow escape."

E.g.: *Je l'ai échappé belle: une minute plus tôt j'aurais été tué.*

I had a narrow escape: one minute earlier I would have been killed.

LEFT

  (1) (Adjective) = *Gauche.*
      E.g.: *Elle écrit de la main gauche.*
            She writes with her left hand.
  (2) "To be left (over)" = *Rester.*
      E.g.: *Il me reste cinquante francs.*
            I have fifty francs left.

LEQUEL, LAQUELLE, LESQUELS, LESQUELLES

  (1) Relative pronouns used as the object of prepositions and referring generally to things.
      E.g.: *La table sur laquelle j'écris.*
            The table on which I write.
  (2) Interrogative pronouns used to choose among various options. They may be used for things or persons.
      E.g.: *Laquelle de ces deux maisons préfères-tu?*
            Which of these two houses do you prefer?

            Laquelle de ces jeunes filles aimerais-tu connaître?
            Which one of these girls would you like to know?

See **PRONOUNS, RELATIVE**

LESS AND LESS, FEWER AND FEWER

(Adverbial expressions)
  (1) "Less and less" = *De moins en moins (de).*
      E.g.: *J'ai de moins en moins de temps.*
            I have less and less time.
  (2) "Fewer and fewer" = *De moins en moins (de).*
      E.g.: *Il y a de moins en moins de gens.*
            There are fewer and fewer people.

See ***DE MOINS EN MOINS (DE)***

LEST

(Conjunction)
  (1) If the subject of the two clauses is the same: "*De peur de* + infinitive" or "*De crainte de* + infinitive."
      E.g.: *Je te confie ce livre de peur de (de crainte de) le perdre.*
            I entrust this book to you lest I lose it.
  (2) If the subject of the two clauses is different: "*De peur que* + subjunctive" or "*De crainte que* + subjunctive."
      E.g.: *Je t'accompagnerai de crainte que (de peur que) tu ne te perdes.*
            I shall accompany you lest you get lost.

See ***DE PEUR DE* vs. *DE PEUR QUE***

to LET

See ***LAISSER* + INFINITIVE**

LET'S

(English idiomatic construction) "Let's + verb" is the first person plural form of the imperative mood. The French equivalent is therefore the imperative in the first person plural.
See **IMPERATIVE MOOD**

LETTER WRITING

Conventions for writing letters differ somewhat from those used in English.
(1) PAGE LAYOUT AND FORMAT:
 • The sender's name and address are written in the top left corner of the page.
 • The city and date are written a little lower, on the right side of the page.
 • The addressee's name and address are written on the right, a little under the date.
 • A comma is placed between the house number and the name of the street.
 • The words *avenue, boulevard, rue,* and the like are not capitalized.
 • The postal code is written before the name of the city.
 • The city is written in all capitals.
 • Last names are written in all capitals.
E.g.:

Arthur VERDOUX
25, avenue de la Victoire
75261 PARIS

Paris, le 30 janvier 1990

Monsieur P. DURAND
120, rue Broca
75006 PARIS

Monsieur,

---

(2) MODE OF ADDRESS and CONCLUDING PHRASES:
 This tends to be much more formal in French than in English.

MODE OF ADDRESS	*CONCLUDING PHRASES*
	(examples)

(a) *When writing to someone you do not know well or who is older than you:*

Madame,	*Veuillez agréer, Madame, l'expression de mes sentiments dévoués.*
Mademoiselle,	*Je vous prie de croire à mes sentiments les meilleurs.*
Monsieur,	*Je vous prie d'accepter mes sentiments très dévoués.*
	Veuillez agréer, Monsieur, l'expression de mes sentiments distingués.

(b) *When writing to someone you know quite well:*

Chère Madame,	*Soyez assurée, chère Madame, de mes fidèles sentiments.*
Cher Monsieur,	*Je vous adresse l'expression de mes sentiments les plus cordiaux.*
Cher ami,	*Veuillez croire, cher ami, à mes sentiments les plus fidèles.*
Chère amie,	*Je vous envoie mes sentiments très amicaux. Dans l'attente de recevoir de vos nouvelles, je vous envoie mes cordiales salutations.*

(c) *When writing to a friend:*

Cher ami,	*Cordialement,*
Chère amie,	*À bientôt,*
Cher Georges,	*Meilleures amitiés,*
Ma chère Anne-Marie,	*Je t'embrasse,*
Mon cher Bernard,	*Je vous embrasse tous bien fort,*
Amicalement,	*Bons baisers,*

(3) STYLE:

The style used in formal correspondence, business letters, and letters addressed to offices is more formal than in English. A few examples follow.

Madame la Directrice,
J'ai l'honneur de vous envoyer ci-inclus une photocopie du document que vous m'avez demandé . . . .

Monsieur,
Vous êtes prié de vous présenter en nos bureaux dans les plus brefs délais afin de . . .

Monsieur le Professeur,
Je vous serais très obligé de bien vouloir excuser ma fille, dont l'absence a été motivée par un séjour à l'hôpital . . . .

Monsieur l'Abbé,
J'ai l'honneur de solliciter votre participation à la conférence qui aura lieu le 24 courc

(4) THE ENVELOPE:

The same conventions are used as for the heading of the letter itself.

E.g.:

Monsieur Jacques DUPONT
16, rue du Lac
38000 GRENOBLE
FRANCE

NOTE:

The return address is on the back, not on the front as in the United States.

LEVER

(To raise)

The *e* of the stem changes to *è* before a silent syllable. Therefore, the following forms are slightly irregular.

PRÉS.: *je lève, tu lèves, il lève, (nous levons, vous levez), ils lèvent.*
FUTUR.: *je lèverai, tu lèveras, il lèvera, nous lèverons, vous lèverez, ils lèveront.*
CONDIT.: *je lèverais, tu lèverais, il lèverait, nous lèverions, vous lèveriez, ils lèveraient.*
SUBJ. PRÉS.: *que je lève, que tu lèves, qu'il lève, (que nous levions, que vous leviez), qu'ils lèvent.*

NOTE:

The reflexive verb *Se lever* = "To get up."

E.g.: *Nous nous levons à sept heures du matin.*
   We get up at seven o'clock in the morning.

LIAISON

The liaison *(la liaison)* is the adding, in the spoken language, of a consonant sound between two words.

(1) COMPULSORY LIAISONS:
    (a) With the plural pronouns *nous, vous, ils, elles.*
        E.g.: *Vous allez.*   *Elles iront.*
               z   z

    (b) With adjectives preceding the noun:
        E.g.: *Les bons amis.*
                   z

    (c) After *est* and *sont*:
        E.g.: *Il est ingénieur.*   *Elles sont ici.*
                t   t

    (d) After the articles *les, un,* and *une*:
        E.g.: *Les enfants.*   *Un enfant.*   *Une affaire.*
             z   n   n

    (e) After *pas*:
        E.g.: *Elle n'est pas ici.*
                    z

    (f) After prepositions:
        E.g.: *En arrivant.*
              n

    (g) When there is inversion:
        E.g.: *Dit-elle.*   *Plaît-il.*
             t   t

    (h) With the adverb *très*:
        E.g.: *Très élégante.*
             z

(2) FORBIDDEN LIAISONS: No liaison is permitted:
    (a) With the conjunction *et*:
        E.g.: *Français | et | Américains.*
    (b) Between a noun subject and the verb:
        E.g.: *Les enfants | arrivent.*
    (c) With proper names:
        E.g.: *Charles | est fatigué.*
    (d) After a word ending with *an* or *on*:
        E.g.: *Un an | et demi.*   *Le garçon | est malade.*
    (e) Before the words *oui, huit,* and *onze*:
        E.g.: *C'est un | oui définitif.*   *Ils sont | huit.*   *Nous sommes | onze.*

(3) OPTIONAL LIAISONS: There are many cases where the liaison may be used or omitted. Generally speaking, it is omitted in casual conversation but is used in more formal speech.
    E.g.: *Nous allons en France.*   or   *Nous allons | en France.*
                          z

NOTE:

When the liaison is used, some changes in sound occur:

(1) *d* is pronounced *t*:   E.g.: *Quand il est arrivé.*
                                   t

(2) *f* is pronounced *v*:   E.g.: *Neuf heures.*
                                  v

(3) *s* and *x* are pronounced *z*:   E.g.: *Les heureux accidents.*
                                     z   z

LIEU

See *AVOIR LIEU*

to LIKE

(Verb) = *Aimer*. But this verb also means "To love." Thus *J'aime ma voisine.* = "I love my neighbor" (rather than "I like my neighbor").
NOTE:
There are two ways of avoiding ambiguity and confusion:
(1) Add the adverb *Bien*, which in this case decreases the force of the verb.
    E.g.: *J'aime bien ma voisine.*
        I like my neighbor.
(2) Use "*Plaire à* + indirect object." But remember that it means "To be pleasing to." It is constructed differently from the English equivalent.
    E.g.: *Ma voisine me plaît.*
        I like my neighbor.

LIRE

(To read)
PRÉS.: *lis, lis, lit, lisons, lisez, lisent.*
IMPARF.: *lis-ais, -ais, -ait, -ions, -iez, -aient.*
PASSÉ SIMPLE: *lus, lus, lut, lûmes, lûtes, lurent.*
FUT.: *lir-ai, -as, -a, -ons, -ez, -ont.*
CONDIT.: *lir-ais, -ais, -ait, -ions, -iez, -aient.*
IMPÉR.: *lis, lisons, lisez.*
SUBJ. PRÉS.: *lis-e, -es, -e, -ions, -iez, -ent.*
SUBJ. IMPARF.: *lusse, lusses, lût, lussions, lussiez, lussent.*
P. PRÉS.: *lisant.*
P. PASSÉ: *lu(e).*

to LISTEN TO

(Transitive verb) = *Écouter*. (The preposition "To" is included in the verb *Écouter*.)
E.g.: *Nous écoutons la musique.*
    We are listening to the music.

LITERARY STYLE

Written, literary, or formal style *(le style littéraire)* is loftier and more elegant than conversational style. This means, for example, using:
(1) The *passé simple* rather than the *passé composé*.
    E.g.: LITERARY STYLE: *Ils allèrent en vacances.*
        CONVERSATIONAL STYLE: *Ils sont allés en vacances.*
                                 They went on vacation.
(2) Inversion rather than the *est-ce que* construction in questions.
    E.g.: LITERARY STYLE: *Comprend-elle sa situation?*
        CONVERSATIONAL STYLE: *Est-ce qu'elle comprend sa situation?*
                                 Does she understand her situation?
(3) The imperfect and past perfect subjunctive in *si* clauses.
    E.g.: LITERARY STYLE: *Si j'eusse le temps, je vous accompagnerais.*
        CONVERSATIONAL STYLE: *Si j'avais le temps, je vous accompagnerais.*
                                 If I had the time, I would accompany you.
        LITERARY STYLE: *S'ils eussent pu, ils seraient partis.*
        CONVERSATIONAL STYLE: *S'ils avaient pu, ils seraient partis.*
                                 If they had been able, they would have left.

LITTLE

(1) (Adjective) = *Petit(e)*.
  E.g.: *Une petite fille.*   *Les petits chiens.*
     A little girl.   The little dogs.
(2) (Adverb) = *Peu*.
  E.g.: *Elle mange peu.*
     She eats little.
See **PEU**

L'ON

See **ON**

to LOOK AT

(Transitive verb) = *Regarder*. (The preposition "At" is included in the verb *Regarder*.)
E.g.: *Elle regarde le paysage.*
   She is looking at the scenery.

to LOOK FOR

(Transitive verb) = *Chercher*. (The preposition "For" is included in the verb *Chercher*.)
E.g.: *Il cherche sa cravate.*
   He is looking for his necktie.

LORSQUE

(Conjunction) Interchangeable with *Quand* (= "When"). It is followed by the indicative.
E.g.: *Lorsque je suis fatigué, je me couche.*
   When I am tired, I go to bed.
NOTE:
When the context is the future, use the future tense in both the main clause and the subordinate clause. This contrasts with the English construction, which uses the present tense in the subordinate clause.
E.g.: *J'irai à Paris lorsque je serai en France.*
   I shall go to Paris when I am in France.

a LOT (OF)

(1) (Adverb) = *Beaucoup*.
  E.g.: *Vous mangez beaucoup!*
     You eat a lot!
(2) (Expression of quantity) = *Beaucoup de* (NOT *des*).
  E.g.: *Nous avons beaucoup de temps.*
     We have a lot of time.

LUIRE

(To shine)
PRÉS.: *luis, luis, luit, luisons, luisez, luisent.*
IMPARF.: *luis-ais, -ais, -ait, -ions, -iez, -aient.*
PASSÉ SIMPLE: *luis-is, -is, -it, -îmes, -îtes, -irent.*
FUT.: *luir-ai, -as, -a, -ons, -ez, -ont.*
CONDIT.: *luir-ais, -ais, -ait, -ions, -iez, -aient.*
IMPÉR.: *luis, luisons, luisez.*
SUBJ. PRÉS.: *luis-e, -es, -e, -ions, -iez, -ent.*
SUBJ. IMPARF.: *luis-isse, -isses, -ît, -issions, -issiez, -issent.*
P. PRÉS.: *luisant.*
P. PASSÉ: *lui.*

M

MAINT(E)(S)

(Adjective) = "A great many + plural noun."

E.g.: *Il est allé maintes fois en Afrique.*

He has gone to Africa a great many times.

MAKE + ADJECTIVE

See **RENDRE + ADJECTIVE**

to MAKE + INFINITIVE

See **FAIRE + INFINITIVE**

MAL vs. MAUVAIS

See **MAUVAIS vs. MAL**

MALGRÉ

(Preposition) = "In spite of, despite."

E.g.: *Ils sont partis malgré la tempête.*

They left despite the storm.

MALGRÉ QUE

(Conjunction) "*Malgré que* + subjunctive" = "Even though, despite the fact that."

E.g.: *Il ira en France malgré que sa femme soit malade.*

He will go to France even though his wife is ill.

NOTE:

Malgré que is colloquial. It is better to use *Bien que* or *Quoique*.

See **BIEN QUE** and **QUOIQUE**

MANQUER vs. MANQUER À vs. MANQUER DE

(1) *Manquer* means "To miss."

   E.g.: *J'ai manqué mon avion.*

   I missed my plane (my flight).

(2) *Manquer à* means "To be missed by."

   E.g.: *Jeanne me manque.*

   I miss Jean. ("Jean is missed by me.")

(3) *Manquer de* means "To lack, to be lacking."

   E.g.: *Nous manquons de temps.*

   We lack time.

(4) *Manquer (de)* + infinitive = "Nearly (do something)." The *de* may be omitted.

   E.g.: *Il a manqué (de) se casser la jambe.*

   He nearly broke his leg.

MANY + NOUN

(Adverbial expression of quantity) = "*Beaucoup de* + noun."

E.g.: *Elle a beaucoup d'enfants.*

She has many children.

Beaucoup de also means "Much, a lot of."

E.g.: *J'ai beaucoup de travail.*

I have a lot of work.

See **BEAUCOUP (DE + NOUN)**

MARIER vs. SE MARIER

(1) *Marier* (Transitive verb) = "To marry off" or "To join in matrimony."
  E.g.: *M. Legrand a marié sa fille à un politicien.*
    Mr. Legrand married off his daughter to a politician.
    Le curé nous a mariés dans l'église du village.
    The parish priest married us in the village church.
(2) *Se marier* (Reflexive verb) = "To get married."
  E.g.: *Elle va se marier le mois prochain.*
    She is going to get married next month.

to MARRY

See **MARIER vs. SE MARIER**

MASCULINE NOUNS IDENTIFIED BY ENDING

See **GENDER**

MATIN vs. MATINÉE

(1) *Le matin* = "The morning."
  E.g.: *Je me lève à six heures du matin.*
    I get up at six o'clock in the morning.
    Nous avons des classes le matin, mais pas l'après-midi.
    We have classes in the morning but not in the afternoon.
(2) *La matinée* =
 (a) "The whole morning."
   E.g.: *Nous avons des classes toute la matinée.*
     We have classes all morning long.
 (b) "A matinee (i.e., afternoon) performance."
   E.g.: *On joue la pièce en matinée à 3 heures et en soirée à 8 heures.*
     There is a matinee performance of the play at 3 o'clock and an evening performance at 8 o'clock.

MATTER

(Idiomatic expressions)
(1) It doesn't matter = *Cela n'a pas d'importance* or *Cela ne fait rien.*
(2) What does it matter if . . . = *Qu'est-ce que cela fait si . . .*
(3) What's the matter? = *Qu'est-ce qu'il y a?*
(4) What's the matter with you? = *Qu'est-ce que tu as?*
(5) It's a matter of politics. = *C'est une question (une affaire) de politique.*

MAUVAIS vs. MAL

(1) *Mauvais(e)* is an adjective.
  E.g.: *Cette route est mauvaise.*
    This road is bad.
(2) *Mal* is an adverb.
  E.g.: *Il conduit mal.*
    He drives badly.
    Ce travail a été mal fait.
    This job was badly done.
  BUT: *Ça sent mauvais.*
    That smells bad.

MAY

(1) Indicating possibility: Use the adverb *Peut-être* (= "Maybe, perhaps") or "*Il se peut que* + subjunctive."
   E.g.: *Elle viendra peut-être demain.*   *Il se peut qu'elle vienne demain.*
   She may come tomorrow.   She may come tomorrow.

(2) Indicating permission: Use "*Pouvoir* + infinitive."
   E.g.: *Puis-je vous poser une question?*
   May I ask you a question?

to MEAN

(Verbal idiom) = *Vouloir dire* or *Signifier.*
The more frequently used expression is *Vouloir dire.*
E.g.: *Qu'est-ce que ça veut dire?*
   What does that mean?

MEASUREMENTS

See **SIZES AND MEASUREMENTS**
See also **METRIC SYSTEM**

MEILLEUR(E) vs. MIEUX

(1) *Meilleur(e)* is the comparative form of the adjective *Bon.*
   E.g.: *La tarte est bonne, mais le gâteau est meilleur.*
   The pie is good, but the cake is better.

(2) *Mieux* is the comparative form of the adverb *bien.*
   E.g.: *Je chante bien, mais vous chantez mieux.*
   I sing well, but you sing better.

See **BON vs. BIEN**

MÊME

(Adjective)

(1) Before the noun, *Même* means "Same."
   E.g.: *Le même jour.*
   The same day.

(2) After the noun, *Même* means "Very, actual."
   E.g.: *Le jour même.*
   The very day.

(3) Added to the stressed pronoun, *Même* adds emphasis.
   E.g.: *Je l'ai fait moi-même.*   *Faites-le vous-mêmes!*
   I did it myself.   Do it yourselves!

MENER

(To lead)
The *e* of the stem changes to *è* before a silent syllable. Therefore, the following forms are slightly irregular.

PRÉS.: *je mène, tu mènes, il mène, (nous menons, vous menez), ils mènent.*

FUT.: *je mènerai, tu mèneras, il mènera, nous mènerons, vous mènerez, ils mèneront.*

CONDIT.: *je mènerais, tu mènerais, il mènerait, nous mènerions, vous mèneriez, ils mèneraient.*

IMPÈR.: *mène, menons, menez.*

SUBJ. PRÉS.: *que je mène, que tu mènes, qu'il mène, (que nous menions, que vous meniez), qu'ils mènent.*

MENTIR

(To lie, to tell a lie)
PRÉS.: *mens, mens, ment, mentons, mentez, mentent.*
IMPARF.: *ment-ais, -ais, -ait, -ions, -iez, -aient.*
PASSÉ SIMPLE: *ment-is, -is, -it, -îmes, -ites, -irent.*
FUT.: *mentir-ai, -as, -a, -ons, -ez, -ont.*
CONDIT.: *mentir-ais, -ais, -ait, -ions, -iez, -aient.*
IMPÉR.: *mens, mentons, mentez.*
SUBJ. PRÉS.: *ment-e, -es, -e, -ions, -iez, -ent.*
SUBJ. IMPARF.: *ment-isse, -isses, -ît, -issions, -issiez, -issent.*
P. PRÉS. *mentant.*
P. PASSÉ: *menti(e).*

METRIC SYSTEM

The metric system *(le système métrique)*, used in most countries, is based on the number 10.

EQUIVALENTS

MEASURES OF LENGTH:
1 mètre	*= 10 décimètres*	1 m = 1.0936 yd.
1 décimètre	*= 10 centimètres*	
1 centimètre	*= 10 millimètres*	
10 mètres	*= 1 décamètre*	
1000 mètres	*= 1 kilomètre*	1 km = 0.6214 mi.

MEASURES OF AREA:
1 are	*= 100 mètres carrés*	1 a = 119.6 sq. yd.
1 hectare	*= 100 ares*	1 ha = 2.4711 acres
100 hectares	*= 1 kilomètre carré*	1 km^2 = 0.3861 sq. mi.

WEIGHT MEASURES:
1 kilo (gramme)	*= 1000 grammes*	1 kg = 2.2046 lb.
1 tonne	*= 1000 kilos*	1 t = 1.1023 short tons

LIQUID MEASURES:
1 litre	*= 10 décilitres*	1 l = 0.2642 U.S. gal.
		0.2200 imp. gal.
1 décilitre	*= 10 centilitres*	
1 centilitre	*= 10 millilitres*	

METTRE

(To put, to put on [clothing])
PRÉS.: *mets, mets, met, mettons, mettez, mettent.*
IMPARF.: *mett-ais, -ais, -ait, -ions, -iez, -aient.*
PASSÉ SIMPLE: *mis, mis, mit, mîmes, mîtes, mirent.*
FUT.: *mettr-ai, -as, -a, -ons, -ez, -ont.*
CONDIT.: *mettr-ais, -ais, -ait, -ions, -iez, -aient.*
IMPÉR.: *mets, mettons, mettez.*
SUBJ. PRÉS.: *mett-e, -es, -e, -ions, -iez, -ent.*
SUBJ. IMPARF.: *misse, misses, mît, missions, missiez, missent.*
P. PRÉS.: *mettant.*
P. PASSÉ: *mis(e).*

MIEUX vs. *MEILLEUR(E)*

See *MEILLEUR(E)* vs. *MIEUX*

MIGHT

(1) Indicating suggestion: Use the conditional of *Pouvoir.*
E.g.: *Tu pourrais essayer de lui téléphoner.*
You might try to call him.
(2) Expressing a wish: Use the subjunctive present.
E.g.: *Qu'elle réussisse enfin à son examen!*
Might she at last pass her examination!
(3) Indicating possibility: Use "*Il se peut que* + subjunctive."
E.g.: *Il se peut que nous soyons en retard.*
We might be late.

MILLE

(Invariable numeric adjective) Without any numeral before it, it means "One thousand." It does not take the numeral *Un.*
E.g.: *Mille hommes.*
One thousand men.
It does not take an *s* in the plural.
E.g.: *Cinq mille personnes.*
Five thousand people.
The alternate form *Mil* is used only in dates.
E.g.: *Mil* (or *mille*) *huit cent douze.*
Eighteen (hundred) twelve.
See **NUMBERS, CARDINAL**

MILLION

(Masculine noun) It takes the preposition *De* before a noun.
E.g.: *Elle a gagné trois millions de dollars.*
She won three million dollars.
See **NUMBERS, CARDINAL**

MISS

(Noun) = *Mademoiselle* (plural: *Mesdemoiselles*).
Abbreviated *Mlle* and *Mlles* (without a period).
E.g.: *Mlle Delattre.*   *Mlles Delattre et Gobineau.*
Miss Delattre.   The Misses Delattre and Gobineau.

to MISS

(Transitive verb)
(1) "To miss (a goal, a target)" = "*Manquer* + direct object."
E.g.: *Il a manqué le train.*
He missed the train.
(2) "To miss" = "To long for (someone or something)" = *Manquer,* but remember the construction!
"*Quelqu'un* or *quelque chose manque à* + indirect object."
In this sense, *Manquer* has the meaning "To be missed by."
E.g.:I miss my little dog.   Her family misses her.
Mon petit chien me manque.   *Elle manque à sa famille.*
See **MANQUER vs. MANQUER À vs. MANQUER DE**

MOINS + NUMBERS

See **PLUS, MOINS + NUMBERS**

MOINS . . . MOINS

(Idiomatic construction) = "The less . . . , the less . . ."
E.g.: *Moins j'ai d'argent, moins je dépense.*
    The less money I have, the less I spend.

MOIS

See **MONTHS**

MOMENT vs. FOIS, HEURE, TEMPS

See *FOIS vs. HEURE, TEMPS, MOMENT*

MONDE

Le monde = "The world." It is used in a number of idiomatic expressions to mean "People."
Beaucoup de monde. = A lot of people.
Il y a du monde. = There is a crowd.
Peu de monde. = Not a large crowd.
Tout le monde. = Everybody.

MONTER

"To go up(stairs), to take up(stairs)."
(1) If *Monter* has no direct object, it is intransitive (i.e., conjugated with *Être*).
    E.g.: *Elle est montée dans sa chambre.*
        She went up to her room.
(2) If *Monter* takes a direct object, it is transitive (i.e., conjugated with *Avoir*).
    E.g.: *Elle a monté les valises dans sa chambre.*
        She took the suitcases up to her room.

MONTHS

The names of the months are all masculine. They are not capitalized in French: *janvier, février, mars, avril, mai, juin, juillet, août, septembre, octobre, novembre, décembre.*
The preposition *en* is used to say "In (+ name of a month)."
E.g.: *Elle est née en juillet.*
    She was born in July.

MOOD (or MODE)

The mood *(le mode)* is the manner by which the verb expresses a state or an action. In French there are six moods: the indicative, the subjunctive, the conditional, the imperative, the infinitive, and the participle.

MORE AND MORE

(Adverbial expression)
De plus en plus (de).
E.g.: *Il fait de plus en plus de fautes.*
    He makes more and more mistakes.
See *DE PLUS EN PLUS (DE)*
See also **LESS AND LESS, FEWER AND FEWER**

MOREOVER

(Adverbial expression) = *En outre* or *En plus.*
E.g.: *Il prononce mal, et en outre il parle trop vite.*
    He pronounces incorrectly, and moreover, he speaks too fast.

MOST + ADJECTIVE or ADVERB (SUPERLATIVE)

The corresponding French construction is the superlative form of the adjective or adverb.

E.g.: *C'est le problème le plus difficile.*   *Elle parle le mieux de toutes les étudiantes.*
     It is the most difficult problem.   She speaks the best of all the female students.

See **ADJECTIVES, SUPERLATIVE OF** and **ADVERBS, COMPARATIVE AND SUPERLATIVE OF**

MOST (meaning LARGEST PART)

See **PLUPART**

MOTS COMPOSÉS

See **COMPOUND NOUNS**

MOUDRE

(To grind)

PRÉS.: *mouds, mouds, moud, moulons, moulez, moulent.*
IMPARF.: *moul-ais, -ais, -ait, -ions, -iez, -aient.*
PASSÉ SIMPLE: *moul-us, -us, -ut, -ûmes, -ûtes, -urent.*
FUT.: *moudr-ai, -as, -a, -ons, -ez, -ont.*
CONDIT.: *moudr-ais, -ais, -ions, -iez, -aient.*
IMPÉR.: *mouds, moulons, moulez.*
SUBJ. PRÉS.: *moul-e, -es, -e, -ions, -iez, -ent.*
SUBJ. IMPARF.: *moul-usse, -usses, -ût, -ussions, -ussiez, -ussent.*
P. PRÉS.: *moulant.*
P. PASSÉ: *moulu(e).*

MOURIR

(To die) (Conjugated with *être*)

PRÉS.: *meurs, meurs, meurt, mourons, mourez, meurent.*
IMPARF.: *mour-ais, -ais, -ait, -ions, -iez, -aient.*
PASSÉ SIMPLE: *mour-us, -us, -ut, -ûmes, -ûtes, urent.*
FUT.: *mourrai, mourras, -mourra, mourrons, mourrez, mourront.*
CONDIT.: *mourrais, mourrais, mourrait, mourrions, mourriez, mourraient.*
IMPÉR.: *meurs, mourons, mourez.*
SUBJ. PRÉS.: *meure, meures, meure, mourions, mouriez, meurent.*
SUBJ. IMPARF.: *mour-usse, -usses, -ût, -ussions, -ussiez, -ussent.*
P. PRÉS.: *mourant.*
P. PASSÉ: *mort(e).*

MOUVOIR

(To drive, to power, to move)

PRÉS.: *meus, meus, meut, mouvons, mouvez, meuvent.*
IMPARF.: *mouv-ais, -ais, -ait, -ions, -iez, -aient.*
PASSÉ SIMPLE: *mus, mus, mut, mûmes, mûtes, murent.*
FUT.: *mouvr-ai, -as, -a, -ons, -ez, -ont.*
CONDIT.: *mouvr-ais, -ais, -ait, -ions, -iez, -aient.*
IMPÉR.: *meus, mouvons, mouvez.*
SUBJ. PRÉS.: *meuv-e, -es, -e, mouvions, mouviez, meuvent.*
SUBJ. IMPARF.: *musse, musses, mût, mussions, mussiez, mussent.*
P. PRÉS.: *mouvant.*
P. PASSÉ: *mû, mue, mus, mues.*

MR.

M. (with a period) (plural: *MM.*).

E.g.: *M. Delacre.*   *MM. Delacre et Lafond.*
      Mr. Delacre.   Messrs. Delacre and Lafond.

MRS.

Mme (without a period) (plural: *Mmes*).

E.g.: *Mme Dumont*   *Mmes Dumont et Lemeland.*
    Mrs. Dumont.   Mesdames Dumont and Lemeland.

MS.

There is no French equivalent for this abbreviation. Use *Mlle* ("Miss") or *Mme* ("Mrs.") as appropriate.

MUCH

(Adverb) = *Beaucoup* or *Fort*.

E.g.: *Elle ne travaille pas beaucoup.*
    She doesn't work much.

NOTE:

Beaucoup never takes a modifier. Do not say "*très beaucoup*"! "Very much" is simply *beaucoup*.

E.g.: *Je t'aime beaucoup.*
    I love you very much.

MUCH + NOUN.

"*Beaucoup de* + noun."

E.g.: *Ils ont beaucoup d'argent.*
    They have much money.

See **BEAUCOUP (DE + NOUN)**
See also **MANY + NOUN**

MULTIPLE OBJECT PRONOUNS

See **PRONOUNS, OBJECT OF VERB**

MUST

See **DEVOIR**

N

NAÎTRE

(To be born)

PRÉS.: *nais, nais, naît, naissons, naissez, naissent.*
IMPARF.: *naiss-ais, -ais, -ait, -ions, -iez, -aient.*
PASSÉ SIMPLE: *naqu-is, -is, -it, -îmes, -îtes, -irent.*
FUT.: *naîtr-ai, -as, -a, -ons, -ez, -ont.*
CONDIT.: *naîtr-ais, -ais, -ait, -ions, -iez, -aient.*
IMPÉR.: *nais, naissons, naissez.*
SUBJ. PRÉS.: *naiss-e, -es, -e, -ions, -iez, -ent.*
SUBJ. IMPARF.: *naqu-isse, -isses, -ît, -issions, -issiez, -issent.*
P. PRÉS.: *naissant.*
P. PASSÉ: *né(e).*

REMEMBER that in the past tense, this verb refers to a completed action. So use the *passé composé*. Do not say "*J'étais né*"!

E.g.: *Je suis né en France.*
    I was born in France.

NAMES, PROPER

Proper names *(les noms propres)* do not change in the plural. This is contrary to the English usage.

E.g.: *Les Dupont et les Lebrun sont arrivés.*
The Duponts and the Lebruns have arrived.

NE . . . AUCUN(E)

(Negative construction) = "None, not any."

E.g.: *Il n'a aucune raison de se plaindre.*
He has no reason to complain.

When it is the subject of the verb: *Aucun(e) . . . ne.*

E.g.: *Aucune nouvelle ne nous est parvenue.*
No news has reached us.

NE, EXPLETIVE

The expletive (meaningless) *Ne* is sometimes used. It "pads" the sentence without changing its meaning. It has nothing to do with the negative particle *Ne.* (This usage is gradually disappearing.)

(1) After expressions of fear (where it is akin to the English "lest").

E.g.: *J'ai peur qu'il (ne) vienne.*   BUT: *J'ai peur qu'il ne vienne pas.*
I fear that he might come.   I fear that he might not come.

(2) After expressions of precaution or prohibition.

E.g.: *Évitons qu'il (ne) nous voie.*
Let's avoid his seeing us.

(3) After comparisons of inequality.

E.g.: *Il est plus tard que vous (ne) croyez.*
It is later than you think.

(4) After *Avant que.*

E.g.: *Partons avant qu'il (ne) pleuve.*
Let's leave before it rains.

(5) After *À moins que.*

E.g.: *Je viendrai à moins qu'il (ne) fasse mauvais.*
I shall come unless the weather is bad.

NE . . . GUÈRE

(Negative construction) = "Scarcely, hardly, almost not."

E.g.: *Nous n'avons guère de temps.*
We have hardly any time.

NE . . . JAMAIS

(Negative construction) = "Never."

E.g.: *Je ne suis jamais allé en Chine.*
I have never been to China.

For emphasis *jamais* can be placed at the beginning of the sentence:

E.g.: *Jamais je n'ai vu cela.*
Never have I seen that.

NE . . . NI . . . NI

(Negative construction) = "Neither . . . nor."

E.g.: *Nous n'avons ni chien ni chat.*
We have neither a dog nor a cat.

Note that contrary to the English construction, no indefinite article is used in French.

NE . . . PAS

This is the basic negative construction. The *ne* goes before the verb (or before the object pronouns, if there are any), and the *pas* goes after the verb (or the conjugated part of the verb, in compound tenses).

E.g.: *Je ne lis pas le livre.*   *Je ne l'ai pas lu.*
    I do not read the book.   I have not read it.

When the verb is in the infinitive, *Ne pas* goes before it.

E.g.: *Je lui ai demandé de ne pas le faire.*
    I asked him not to do it.

NE . . . PAS ENCORE

(Negative construction) = "Not yet."

E.g.: *Il n'a pas encore fini de travailler.*
    He has not finished working yet.

NE . . . PERSONNE

(Negative construction) = "Nobody."

E.g.: *Je ne parlerai à personne.*
    I shall speak to nobody.

When it is the subject of the verb: *Personne . . . ne.*

E.g.: *Personne n'a appelé.*
    Nobody called.

NE . . . PLUS

(Negative construction) = "No longer, no more, not anymore."

E.g.: *Elle n'habite plus ici.*
    She doesn't live here anymore.

NE . . . POINT

(Negative construction) = "Not."
NOTE:
This construction is the literary equivalent of *Ne . . . pas.*

E.g.: *Ils n'eurent point de difficultés.*
    They had no difficulties.

NE . . . QUE

(Negative construction) = "Only."

E.g.: *Je n'ai que cinquante dollars.*
    I have only fifty dollars.

NE . . . RIEN

(Negative construction) = "Nothing."

E.g.: *Il ne mange rien.*
    He doesn't eat anything.

When it is the subject of the verb: *Rien . . . ne.*

E.g.: *Rien n'a changé.*
    Nothing has changed.

N'EST-CE PAS?

(Adverbial expression) = "Isn't it? Don't you? Aren't they? etc."

E.g.: *Tu as fini le livre, n'est-ce pas?*
    You have finished the book, haven't you?

NEARLY + VERB

(Idiomatic construction) = "*Manquer (de)* + infinitive."
E.g.: *J'ai manqué de tomber.*
    I nearly fell.
See **MANQUER vs. MANQUER À vs. MANQUER DE**

NECESSITY

The concept of necessity can be rendered by:
(1) *Devoir* + infinitive.
    E.g.: *Nous devons trouver un emploi.*
        We have to find a job.
(2) "*Il faut que* or *Il est nécessaire que* + subjunctive" (or "*il faut* or *il est nécessaire de* + infinitive").
    E.g.: *Il faut que nous trouvions un emploi.*   *Il faut travailler pour réussir.*
        We have to find a job.   One has to work (in order) to succeed.
See **DEVOIR**
See also **FALLOIR**

NEED

See **AVOIR BESOIN DE**

NEGATIVE COMMANDS

See **IMPERATIVE MOOD**

NEGATIVE EXPRESSIONS

Negative expressions are composed of two parts: *ne*, which goes before the verb, and another word, which goes after the verb. When the verb is in the infinitive, *ne pas* goes before it.
The most common negative expressions are these:
(1) *Ne . . . aucun(e)* (= "Not any at all").
    E.g.: *Je n'ai aucun livre.*
        I do not have any book.
    When it is the subject of the verb: "*Aucun (e) . . . ne.*"
    E.g.: *Aucune femme n'est venue.*
        No woman came.
(2) *Ne . . . guère* (= "Scarcely, hardly").
    E.g.: *Ils ne voyagent guère.*
        They hardly travel.
(3) *Ne . . . jamais* (= "Never").
    E.g.: *Je n'ai jamais visité le Louvre.*
        I have never visited the Louvre.
    For emphasis: *Jamais . . . ne.*
    E.g.: *Jamais je n'ai vu cela.*
        Never have I seen that.
(4) *Ne . . . ni . . . ni* (= "Neither . . . nor").
    E.g.: *Elle n'a ni frère ni sœur.*
        She has neither a brother nor a sister.
(5) *Ne . . . pas* (= "Not").
    E.g.: *Il ne parle pas.*
        He does not speak.

(6) *Ne . . . personne* (= "No one, nobody").
    E.g.: *Il ne parle à personne.*
        He does not speak to anyone.
    When it is the subject of the verb: *"Personne . . . ne."*
    E.g.: *Personne n'a téléphoné.*
        Nobody called.

(7) *Ne . . . plus* (= "No longer, not anymore").
    E.g.: *Ils ne vont plus en France.*
        They no longer go to France.

(8) *Ne . . . que* (= "Only").
    E.g.: *Elle n'a que deux enfants.*
        She has only two children.

(9) *Ne . . . rien* (= "Nothing, not anything").
    E.g.: *Je ne vois rien.*
        I do not see anything.
    When it is the subject of the verb: *"Rien . . . ne."*
    E.g.: *Rien ne lui fait peur.*
        Nothing scares him.

NOTE:
In compound tenses, the second half of the expression goes immediately after the auxiliary verb.
E.g.: *Il n'a pas parlé.*
      He did not speak.

      Vous n'êtes jamais allé en France?
      You have never been to France?

      Ils n'ont rien fait.
      They did not do anything.

EXCEPTIONS:
Aucun, ni . . . ni, personne, and *que* are placed after the past participle.
E.g.: *Je n'en ai vu aucun.*
      I did not see any.

      Elle n'a appris ni l'allemand ni le russe.
      She learned neither German nor Russian.

      Je n'ai rencontré personne.
      I met nobody.

      Ils n'ont eu que dix minutes pour le faire.
      They had only ten minutes to do it.

NEGATIVE IMPERATIVE
See **IMPERATIVE MOOD**

NEGATIVE INTERROGATIVE
See **INTERROGATIVE SENTENCES IN THE NEGATIVE**

NEGATIVE OF COMPOUND TENSES
For the negative of compound tenses, place *ne* before the auxiliary verb and *pas* after it.
E.g.: *Tu n'as pas mangé.*
      You did not eat.

NEGATIVE PARTITIVE
See **ARTICLES, PARTITIVE**

NEGATIVE QUESTIONS
See **INTERROGATIVE SENTENCES IN THE NEGATIVE**

NEITHER . . . NOR

(Negative construction) = *"Ne + verb + ni . . . ni."*
E.g.: *Elle n'a ni frère ni sœur.*
    She has neither a brother nor a sister.
NOTE:
There is no article (definite or indefinite) with this construction unless reference is made to specific objects.
E.g.: *Je n'ai ni stylo ni crayon.*
    I have neither a pen nor a pencil.
BUT: *Je n'ai ni le stylo ni le crayon que tu cherches.*
    I have neither the pen nor the pencil that you are looking for.
See **NE . . . NI . . . NI**

NEITHER, NOT . . . EITHER

(Conjunction) = *"Ne . . . non plus."*
E.g.: *Si vous ne partez pas, je ne partirai pas non plus.*
    If you don't leave, I won't leave either.
See **EITHER . . . OR**
See also **NON PLUS**

NEUTER

The only neuter words in French are *ceci, cela, ça, ce,* and *le* when they stand for a vague concept or a general idea.
E.g.: *C'est intéressant!*
    It's interesting!

    Ça ne m'intéresse pas.
    That doesn't interest me.

    Vous êtes fatigué, je le vois.
    You are tired, I can see it.

NEVER

(Adverb) = *"Ne + verb + jamais."*
E.g.: *Elle ne sort jamais.*
    She never goes out.
If the verb is in a compound tense, *jamais* is placed after the auxiliary verb and before the past participle.
E.g.: *Elle n'est jamais sortie.*
    She has never gone out.
NOTE:
Without *ne, jamais* means "Ever."
E.g.: *Si jamais tu vas en France.*
    If ever you go to France.
See **NE . . . JAMAIS**

NEXT

(1) (Adjective) Meaning "Forthcoming" = *Prochain(e).*
    E.g.: *Nous irons en Italie la semaine prochaine.*
        We shall go to Italy next week.
(2) (Adjective) Meaning "Following" = *Suivant(e).*
    E.g.: *Nous visiterons la Grèce le mois suivant.*
        We shall visit Greece the following month.
(3) (Adverb) Expressing an order of events = *Ensuite.*
    E.g.: *D'abord nous nous sommes levés, ensuite nous avons mangé.*
        First we got up, and next we ate.

NEXT TO

(Prepositional construction) = À *côté de.*
E.g.: *Leur maison est à côté de l'église.*
      Their house is next to the church.

NI . . . NI

See *NE . . . NI . . . NI*

NIGHT

(1) Meaning "Evening" = *Le soir.*
    E.g.: *Ils regardent la télévision tous les soirs.*
          They watch television every night (= evening).
(2) Meaning the opposite of "Day" = *La nuit.*
    E.g.: *Il ne voit jamais ses enfants, parce qu'il travaille la nuit.*
          He never sees his children because he works at night.

N'IMPORTE COMMENT

(Adverbial expression) = "Anyhow, in a haphazard manner."
E.g.: *Cet élève fait son travail n'importe comment.*
      This pupil does his work any old way.
See **ANYHOW, ANYWAY**

N'IMPORTE LEQUEL (LAQUELLE, LESQUELS, LESQUELLES)

(Indefinite pronoun) = "Any one, no matter which one (referring to a thing)."
E.g.: *Quel livre voulez-vous? N'importe lequel.*
      Which book do you want? Any one.

N'IMPORTE QUI

(Indefinite pronoun) = "Anybody, anyone."
E.g.: *N'importe qui peut comprendre cela.*
      Anybody can understand that.
See **ANYONE, ANYBODY**

N'IMPORTE QUAND

(Adverbial expression) = "Anytime."
E.g.: *Vous pouvez venir n'importe quand.*
      You may come anytime.
See **ANYTIME**

N'IMPORTE QUEL (QUELLE, QUELS, QUELLES)

(Indefinite adjective) = "Any, no matter which."
E.g.: *Entrez dans n'importe quel magasin.*
      Go into any store.

N'IMPORTE QUI

(Indefinite pronoun) = "Anybody, anyone."
E.g.: *N'importe qui peut comprendre cela.*
      Anybody can understand that.
See **ANYONE, ANYBODY**

N'IMPORTE QUOI

(Indefinite pronoun) = "Anything."
E.g.: *Dites n'importe quoi, mais dites quelque chose.*
    Say anything, but say something.
See **ANYTHING**

NO (meaning NOT ANY)

See **NOT ANY, NO + NOUN**
See also **ARTICLES, PARTITIVE**

NO LONGER, NO MORE, NOT ANYMORE

(Negative expression) = "*Ne* + verb + *plus.*"
E.g.: *Elle ne danse plus.*
    She no longer dances.
If the verb is in a compound tense, *plus* comes after the auxiliary verb and before the past participle.
E.g.: *Elle n'a plus dansé.*
    She no longer danced.
See *NE . . . PLUS*

NOBODY

(Negative construction)
(1) As subject: "*Personne ne* + verb"
    E.g.: *Personne ne parle.*
        Nobody speaks.
(2) As object: "*Ne* + verb + *personne.*"
    E.g.: *Je ne vois personne.*
        I don't see anybody.
See *NE . . . PERSONNE*
See also *PERSONNE*

NOMBRE vs. CHIFFRE vs. NUMÉRO

See *CHIFFRE vs. NOMBRE vs. NUMÉRO*

NOMS COMPOSÉS

See **COMPOUND NOUNS**

NON PLUS

(Adverbial construction) = "Neither, not either."
E.g.: *Il n'y est pas allé, (ni) moi non plus.*
    He didn't go, neither did I.
See **NEITHER, NOT . . . EITHER**

NOT

See **NEGATIVE EXPRESSIONS**

NOT ANY, NO + NOUN

(Negative partitive construction) = "*Pas de* + noun (with no article)."
E.g.: *Elle n'a pas de frère.*   *Nous n'avions pas d'argent.*
    She has no brother.   We did not have any money.
Never say *"Pas un"* unless you mean "Not a single one."
E.g.: *Je n'ai pas de livre.*
    I do not have a book.
BUT: *Je n'ai pas un sou sur moi.*
    I don't have a (single) penny on me.
See **ARTICLES, PARTITIVE**

NOT YET

(Negative expression) = *Pas encore.*
E.g.: *Elles ne sont pas encore arrivées.*
    They have not arrived yet.
See ***NE . . . PAS ENCORE***

NOTHING

(Indefinite pronoun)
(1) As subject: *"Rien ne + verb."*
    E.g.: *Rien ne l'intéresse.*
        Nothing interests him.
(2) As object: *"Ne + verb + rien."*
    E.g.: *Il ne mange rien.*
        He eats nothing.
If the verb is in a compound tense, *rien* goes after the auxiliary verb and before the past participle.
E.g.: *Il n'a rien mangé.*
    He didn't eat anything.
See ***NE . . . RIEN***

NOTHING + ADJECTIVE

Rien takes the preposition *de* before an adjective (which is always in the masculine singular).
E.g.: *Rien de nouveau.*
    Nothing new.

NOUN

A noun *(un substantif)* is a word that names a person, thing, idea, or place. All French nouns are either masculine or feminine.
E.g.: *Un monument.*   *La famille.*
Nouns are either proper *(un nom propre)* or common *(un nom commun)*. A proper noun is the name of a particular place, person, or thing and is capitalized.
E.g.: *Pierre.*   *Paris.*   *Le Louvre.*
    Peter.   Paris.   The Louvre.
A common noun does not name a particular place, person, or thing and is not capitalized but is almost always preceded by a definite article, an indefinite article, a demonstrative adjective, a possessive adjective, or an interrogative adjective.
E.g.: *Un homme.*   *Une ville.*   *Un musée.*
    A man.   A city.   A museum.

NOUNS, GENDER OF
See **GENDER**

NOUNS, PLURAL OF

GENERAL RULE:

Add *s*:

E.g.: *Un homme → des hommes*

SPECIAL CASES:

(1) Nouns ending in *s, x,* or *z* do not change:

E.g.: *Un pois → des pois*   A pea

Une croix → des croix   A cross

Un nez → des nez   A nose

(2) Nouns ending in *al* change to *aux*:

E.g.: *Un cheval → des chevaux*   A horse

EXCEPTIONS:

Un bal → des bals   A ball (= dance)

Un carnaval → des carnaval   A carnival

Un chacal → des chacals   A jackal

Un festival → des festivals   A festival

Un récital → des récitals   A recital

Un régal → des régals   A delight, a treat

(3) Nouns ending in *eau* or *eu* add *x*:

E.g.: *Un chameau → des chameaux*   A camel

Un cheveu → des cheveux   A hair

(4) Some nouns ending in *ail* change to *aux*:

E.g.: *Un travail → des travaux*   A project

Un vitrail → des vitraux   A stained-glass window

BUT: *Un éventail → des éventails*   A fan

(5) Some nouns ending in *ou* add *x*:

E.g.: *Un bijou → des bijoux*   A jewel

Un caillou → des cailloux   A pebble

Un chou → des choux   A cabbage

Un genou → des genoux   A knee

Un hibou → des hiboux   An owl

Un pou → des poux   A louse

BUT: *Un clou → des clous*   A nail

Un sou → des sous   A penny

SPECIAL CASES:

Le ciel → les cieux   The sky

Un œil → des yeux   An eye

Madame → Mesdames   Mrs.

Mademoiselle → Mesdemoiselles   Miss

Monsieur → Messieurs   Mr.

NOTE:

Proper names are invariable:

E.g.: *Les Dupont.*

Les Tocqueville.

Les Smith.

NOTE:

Some English nouns are collective and imply a plural quantity without being plural. The French equivalent has a singular and a plural.

E.g.: Furniture   *Un meuble, des meubles*

Luggage   *Un bagage, des bagages*

Advice   *Un conseil, des conseils*

For the plural of compound nouns, see **COMPOUND NOUNS**

NOUNS, PROPER

Proper nouns *(les noms propres)* are the names of particular persons, things, or places. In French they are always invariable.

E.g.: *Marianne.*   *La France.*   *Les Durand.*

NOUVEAU, NOUVEL, NOUVELLE

(Adjective)

Before a masculine singular noun beginning with a vowel or an unaspirated *h*, *nouveau* changes to *nouvel*.

E.g.: *Il a un nouvel ami.*   *Le Nouvel An.*
       A new friend.   The New Year.

The feminine form is *nouvelle*.

E.g.: *C'est une nouvelle voiture.*
       It's a new car.

NOWHERE

(Adverb) = *Nulle part.*

E.g.: *Il n'est allé nulle part.*
       He went nowhere.

See **NULLE PART**

NUIRE

(To harm, to damage)

PRÉS.: *nuis, nuis, nuit, nuisons, nuisez, nuisent.*
IMPARF.: *nuis-ais, -ais, -ait, -ions, -iez, -aient.*
PASSÉ SIMPLE: *nuis-is, -is, -it, -îmes, -îtes, -irent.*
FUT.: *nuir-ai, -as, -a, -ons, -ez, -ont.*
CONDIT.: *nuir-ais, -ais, -ait, -ions, -iez, -aient.*
IMPÉR.: *nuis, nuisons, nuisez.*
SUBJ. PRÉS.: *nuis-e, -es, -e, -ions, -iez, -ent.*
SUBJ. IMPARF.: *nuis-isse, -isses, -isse, -ît, -issions, -issiez, -issent.*
P. PRÉS.: *nuisant.*
P. PASSÉ: *nui.*

NUL(LE)

(Indefinite adjective) = ''No, not any (whatsoever).''

E.g.: *Je n'ai nulle envie de sortir.*
       I have no desire (whatsoever) to go out.

NULLE PART

(Adverb) = ''Nowhere.''

E.g.: *Ils ne sont allés nulle part pendant les vacances.*
       They went nowhere during the vacation.

NOTE:

Ne must precede the verb.

See **NOWHERE**

See also **ANYWHERE**

NUMBER

See **CHIFFRE vs. NOMBRE vs. NUMÉRO**

NUMBERS, CARDINAL

(Les nombres cardinaux)
Un, deux, trois, quatre, cinq, six, sept, huit, neuf, dix, onze, douze, treize, quatorze, quinze, seize, dix-sept, dix-huit, dix-neuf, vingt, ving et un, vingt-deux, vingt-trois, vingt-quatre, vingt-cinq, vingt-six, ving-sept, ving-huit, vingt-neuf,
trente, trente et un, trento doux, . . .
quarante, quarante et un, quarante-deux, . . .
cinquante, cinquante et un, cinquante-deux, . . .
soixante, soixante et un, soixante-deux, . . .
soixante-dix, soixante et onze, soixante-douze, . . .
quatre-vingts, quatre-vingt-un, quatre-vingt-deux, . . .
quatre-vingt-dix, quatre-vingt-onze, quatre-vingt-douze, . . .
cent, cent un, cent deux, . . .
deux cents, deux cent un, deux cent deux, . . .
mille, mille un, mille deux, . . .

HYPHEN RULE:
A hyphen is placed between the parts when both are numbers less than one hundred.

E.g.: *Trente-deux.*   *Cent vingt-quatre.*
     Thirty-two.   One hundred twenty-four.

     Soixante-six.   *Quinze mille sept cent quarante-trois.*
     Sixty-six.   Fifteen thousand seven hundred forty-three.

Note that 21, 31, 41, 51, 61, and 71 do not contain hyphens.

NOTES:

(1) *Vingt* takes an *s* when it is multiplied by another number and comes at the end of the numeral.
    E.g.: *Quatre-vingts.*
       Eighty.
    BUT: *Quatre-vingt-trois.*
       Eighty-three.

(2) *Cent* takes an *s* when it is multiplied by another number and comes at the end of the numeral.
    E.g.: *Six cents.*
       Six hundred.
    BUT: *Six cent trente.*
       Six hundred thirty.

(3) *Mille* is invariable.
    E.g.: *Quatre mille personnes.*
       Four thousand people.

       Dix-sept mille trois cent vingt-trois.
       Seventeen thousand three hundred twenty-three.
    BUT: *Un millier* ("A group of around one thousand") can be used in the plural.
    E.g.: *Il y avait des milliers de gens.*
       Thousands of people were there.

(4) "One thousand" is simple *mille.* It never takes *un.*
    E.g.: *Mille francs.*
       One thousand francs.

(5) *Million* and *milliard* (= "billion") take the preposition *de* before a noun.
    E.g.: *Un million de francs.*   *Cinq milliards de personnes.*
       One million francs.   Five billion people.

(6) In Arabic numerals, a space or a period (.) is used to separate groups of three digits.
    E.g.: *3 000* or *3.000* = "3,000"
       28 765 or *28.765* = "28,765"

(7) A comma (,) is the equivalent of the English decimal point.
    E.g.: π = *3,141592* . . .   "π = 3.141592 . . ."

(8) In titles of rulers, use cardinal numbers except for the first one of the series.

E.g.: *Louis quatorze (Louis XIV).*
Louis the Fourteenth.

Pie douze (Pie XII).
Pius the Twelfth.

BUT: *François premier (François Ier)*
Francis the First.

(9) For days of the month, use cardinal numbers except for the first.

E.g.: *Le cinq janvier.*
January 5.

BUT: *Le premier avril.*
April first.

NUMBERS, COLLECTIVE

The cardinal numbers 8, 10, 12, 15, 20, 30, 40, 50, 60, and 100 take the suffix -*aine* to indicate an approximation:

E.g.: *Il y a une dizaine de personnes.*
There are about ten people.

Elle a une vingtaine d'années.
She is about twenty years old.

Une centaine d'habitants.
About a hundred inhabitants.

NOTES:

(1) *Un millier* = "Approximately 1,000."

E.g.: *Il y avait un millier de personnes.*
There were about a thousand people.

(2) Some collective numbers can also indicate an exact number.

E.g.: *Une douzaine d'œufs.*   *Une quinzaine (de jours).*
A dozen eggs.   A fortnight.

NUMBERS, ORDINAL

(Adjectives) *(Les nombres ordinaux)*

Premier, Première	*Septième*	*Treizième*	*Dix-neuvième*
Deuxième	*Huitième*	*Quatorzième*	*Vingtième*
Troisième	*Neuvième*	*Quinzième*	*Vingt et unième*
Quatrième	*Dixième*	*Seizième*	*Vingt-deuxième*
Cinquième	*Onzième*	*Dix-septième*	*Vingt-troisième*
Sixième	*Douzième*	*Dix-huitième*	etc.

NOTES:

(1) In titles of rulers, use ordinal numbers only for the first of the series. Also, use ordinal numbers only for the first day of the month.

E.g.: *Louis premier (Louis Ier).*   BUT: *Louis deux, Louis trois (Louis II, Louis III).*
Louis the First.   Louis the Second, Louis the Third.

Pie douze (Pie XII).   *Henri quatre (Henri IV)*
Pius the Twelfth.   Henry the Fourth

Le premier avril.   *Le cinq mars.*
The first of April.   The fifth of March.

(2) When referring to only two items, *Deuxième* is often replaced by *Second(e)*.

NUMÉRO

See *CHIFFRE* vs. *NOMBRE* vs. *NUMÉRO*

O

to OBEY

Obéir.

This verb is intransitive in French. It takes an indirect object.

E.g.: *Elle obéit à ses parents.*

She obeys her parents.

OBJECT, DIRECT

See **DIRECT OBJECT vs. INDIRECT OBJECT**

OBJECT, INDIRECT

DIRECT OBJECT vs. INDIRECT OBJECT

OBLIGATION

The concept of obligation or necessity can be rendered by:

(1) "*Devoir* + infinitive."

E.g.: *Je dois aller au bureau de police.*

I have to go to the police station.

See **DEVOIR**

(2) "*Il faut que* + subjunctive" or "*Il faut* + infinitive."

E.g.: *Il faut que j'aille au bureau de police.*

I have to go to the police station.

Il faut travailler pour réussir.

One has to work in order to succeed.

See **FALLOIR**

See also **NECESSITY**

OBTENIR

(To obtain)

Conjugated like **TENIR**

O'CLOCK

"It is . . . o'clock" = *Il est . . . heures.*

E.g.: *Il est trois heures vingt-cinq.*

It is three twenty-five (o'clock).

(1) "Noon" = *midi.*

(2) "Midnight" = *minuit.*

(3) "Quarter past" = . . . *et quart.*

E.g.: *Il est dix heures et quart.*

It is a quarter past ten.

(4) "A quarter of (to)" = *moins le quart.*

E.g.: *Il est sept heures moins le quart.*

It is a quarter of (to) ten.

(5) "Half past" = . . . *et demie.*

E.g.: *Il est cinq heures et demie.*

It is half past five.

(6) A.M. = *du matin.*

P.M. = *de l'après-midi, du soir.*

NOTES:

(1) *Demi* is in the masculine after *midi* and *minuit.*

    E.g.: *Il est midi et demi.*   *Il est minuit et demi.*

         It is half past noon.   It is half past midnight.

(2) Use no article for minutes past the hour or before the hour.

    E.g.: *Quatre heures vingt-cinq.*   *Six heures moins dix.*

         Twenty-five past four.   Ten to six.

(3) In official schedules and timetables, the 24-hour clock is used.

    Note also that the abbreviation for "hour" is *h* rather than a colon (:).

    E.g.: 8:50 A.M. = *8h50.*

         3:45 P.M. = *15h45.*

OFFRIR

(To offer)

PRÉS.: *offr-e, -es, -e, -ons, -ez, -ent.*

IMPARF.: *offr-ais, -ais, -ait, -ions, -iez, -aient.*

PASSÉ SIMPLE: *offr-is, -is, -it, -îmes, -îtes, -irent.*

FUT.: *offrir-ai, -as, -a, -ons, -ez, -ont.*

CONDIT.: *offrir-ais, -ais, -ait, -ions, -iez, -aient.*

IMPÉR.: *offre, offrons, offrez.*

SUBJ. PRÉS.: *offr-e, -es, -e, -ions, -iez, -ent.*

SUBJ. IMPARF.: *offr-isse, -isses, -ît, -issions, -issiez, -issent.*

P. PRÉS.: *offrant.*

P. PASSÉ: *offert(e).*

OMISSION OF THE DEFINITE ARTICLE
See **ARTICLES, DEFINITE**

ON

(Preposition)

(1) "On the train, the plane" = *Dans le train, dans l'avion.*

(2) "On the street" = *Dans la rue.*

(3) "On the radio, on TV" = *À la télévision, à la radio.*

ON

(Indefinite pronoun) = "One, you, we, they, people."

It is used only as subject and is in the third person singular.

E.g.: *On doit se reposer quand on est fatigué.*   *Que fait-on là-bas?*

     One has to rest when one is tired.   What are they doing over there?

     On ne peut pas parler ici.   *On va au cinéma?*

     One (you) mustn't talk here.   Shall we go to the movies?

NOTE:

The article *l'* is placed before *on* in the written language for reasons of euphony, that is, to make it sound better.

E.g.: *Si l'on savait la vérité.*

     If we (one) knew the truth.

Also, *on* is often used when a passive construction is used in English.

E.g.: English is spoken in Canada.

     On parle anglais au Canada.

     It is said that . . .

     On dit que . . .

ONE ANOTHER
See **EACH OTHER**

ONLY

This can be translated in one of two ways:
(1) By the adverb *Seulement.*
    E.g.: *J'ai seulement cinquante francs.*
      I have only fifty francs.
(2) By the construction "*Ne* + verb + *que.*"
    E.g.: *Je n'ai que cinquante francs.*
      I have only fifty francs.
See **NE . . . QUE**

OPINION, EXPRESSING AN

Various ways of stating one's opinion:
(1) *À mon avis* = "In my opinion."
    E.g.: *A mon avis on devrait partir tout de suite.*
      In my opinion we ought to leave right away.
(2) "*Penser que* or *Trouver que* + indicative."
    E.g.: *Je pense que ça ne vaut pas la peine.*
      I don't think it's worth it.
      Moi, je trouve que c'est magnifique.
      I think it's wonderful.

ORDER OF OBJECT PRONOUNS
See **PRONOUNS, DOUBLE OBJECT**

ORIGIN

To state where a person was born use *Être originaire de.*
E.g.: *Mes parents sont originaires du Languedoc.*
    My parents are from Languedoc.

OÙ vs. OU

(1) *Où* is an adverb meaning "Where" or "When." It is used in two ways:
    (a) As a relative pronoun indicating place or time.
      E.g.: *La ville où j'habite.*
        The city where I live.
        Le jour où il est arrivé.
        The day (when) he arrived.
    (b) As an interrogative adverb:
      E.g.: *Où allez-vous?*
        Where are you going?
(2) *Ou* (without accent) is a conjunction that means "Or."
    E.g.: *Apportez-moi du café ou du thé.*
      Bring me some coffee or some tea.

OUGHT TO + VERB
See **DEVOIR**

OUTSIDE, OUTDOORS

(1) (Adverb) = *Dehors* or *À l'extérieur.*
    E.g.: *Les enfants jouent dehors.*
      The children are playing outside.
(2) (Preposition) = *Hors de* or *À l'extérieur de.*
    E.g.: *Elle est restée hors du pays pendant dix ans.*
      She stayed outside the country for ten years.
See **DEHORS vs. HORS DE**
See also **EN PLEIN AIR**

OUVRIR

(To open)
PRÉS.: *ouvr-e, -es, -e, -ons, -ez, -ent.*
IMPARF.: *ouvr-ais, -ais, -ait, -ions, -iez, -aient.*
PASSÉ SIMPLE: *ouvr-is, -is, -it, -îmes, -îtes, -irent.*
FUT.: *ouvrir-ai, -as, -a, -ons, -ez, -ont.*
CONDIT.: *ouvrir-ais, -ais, -ait, -ions, -iez, -aient.*
IMPÉR.: *ouvre, ouvrons, ouvrez.*
SUBJ. PRÉS.: *ouvr-e, -es, -e, -ions, -iez, -ent.*
SUBJ. IMPARF.: *ouvr-isse, -isses, -ît, -issions, -issiez, -issent.*
P. PRÉS.: *ouvrant.*
P. PASSÉ: *ouvert(e).*

OVER

(Preposition) Meaning "Above" = *par-dessus.*
E.g.: *Il a lancé la balle par-dessus le mur.*
    He threw the ball over the wall.
"Over" is used as both a preposition and an adverb in many idiomatic constructions, which must be conveyed by the appropriate construction in French.
E.g.: It's all over. = *C'est fini.*
    All over the world. = *Dans le monde entier.*
    You must do this over. = *Vous devez refaire ceci.*
    They started over again. = *Ils ont recommencé.*
    Over here, over there. = *Ici, là-bas.*
    I went over to John's house. = *Je suis allé chez Jean.*
    The teacher looked over my work. = *Le professeur a jeté un coup d'œil sur mon travail.*

OVER (meaning "TURN THE PAGE")

(Idiomatic expression) = *T. S. V. P.,* which stands for *Tournez la page, s'il vous plaît.*

P

PAR

(Preposition) Used to indicate (a) the agent or cause: "by"; (b) the place or direction: "Across," "along," "by way of," "through"; (c) the manner or means: "by," "with," "through"; (d) the distribution or measure: "a," "by," "per"; (e) the atmosphere: "in," "on;" and (f) the subordination of an infinitive to verbs such as *commencer* and *finir.*
E.g.: (a) *Ce livre a été écrit par Descartes.*
      This book was written by Descartes.
   (b) *Il est entré par la fenêtre.*
      He entered through the window.
   (c) *Payez par chèque ou carte de crédit.*   *Ils sont passés par le Sahara.*
      Pay by check or with a credit card.   They went across the Sahara.
   (d) *Une fois par semaine.*
      Once a week.
   (e) *Par une belle journée de printemps.*
      On a beautiful spring day.
   (f) *Elle a fini par s'endormir.*
      She finally fell asleep.

PAR AILLEURS

(Idiomatic expression) = "Moreover."
E.g.: *Ça ne coûte pas cher, par ailleurs c'est de la très bonne qualité.*
It's not very expensive; moreover, it's of very good quality.

PAR BONHEUR

(Idiomatic expression) = "Fortunately."
E.g.: *Par bonheur il n'a pas plu hier.*
Fortunately, it didn't rain yesterday.

PAR CHANCE

(Idiomatic expression) = "Fortunately."
E.g.: *Par chance nous avons trouvé une petite auberge.*
Fortunately, we found a little inn.

PAR CONSÉQUENT

(Idiomatic expression) = "Consequently."
E.g.: *Il a échoué, par conséquent il a dû repasser ses examens.*
He failed; consequently, he had to take his exams over again.

PAR CONTRE

(Idiomatic expression) = "On the other hand."
E.g.: *C'est compliqué; par contre ce n'est pas très long.*
It's complicated; on the other hand, it's not very long.

PAR ERREUR

(Idiomatic expression) = "By mistake."
E.g.: *Nous sommes montées dans ce train par erreur.*
We boarded this train by mistake.

PAR EXEMPLE

(Idiomatic expression) = "For example."
The abbreviation is *p. ex.*
E.g.: *Tu pourrais faire ceci, par exemple.*
You could do this, for example.

PAR HASARD

(Idiomatic expression) = "By chance, by accident."
E.g.: *Nous les avons rencontrés par hasard.*
We met them by accident.

PAR MALHEUR

(Idiomatic expression) = "Unfortunately."
E.g.: *Par malheur nous avons raté l'avion.*
Unfortunately, we missed the plane.

PAR MÉGARDE

(Idiomatic expression) = "Inadvertently."
E.g.: *J'ai laissé tomber le bocal par mégarde.*
I dropped the jar inadvertently.

PAR SUITE

(Idiomatic expression) = "Consequently, therefore."
E.g.: *Elle est partie en retard, par suite elle a raté son avion.*
She left late; consequently, she missed her plane.

PAR TERRE

(Idiomatic expression) = "On the ground, on the floor."
E.g.: *Ne jetez pas les papiers par terre!*
Don't throw papers on the floor!

PARAÎTRE

(To appear, to seem)
PRÉS.: *par-ais, -ais, -aît, -aissons, -aissez, -aissent.*
IMPARF.: *paraiss-ais, -ais, -ait, -ions, -iez, -aient.*
PASSÉ SIMPLE: *par-us, -us, -ut, -ûmes, -ûtes, -urent.*
FUT.: *paraîtr-ai, -as, -a, -ons, -ez, -ont.*
CONDIT.: *paraîtr-ais, -ais, -ait, -ions, -iez, -aient.*
IMPÉR.: *parais, paraissons, paraissez.*
SUBJ. PRÉS.: *paraiss-e, -es, -e, -ions, -iez, -ent.*
SUBJ. IMPARF.: *par-usse, -usses, -ût, -ussions, -ussiez, -ussent.*
P. PRÉS.: *paraissant.*
P. PASSÉ: *paru(e).*

PARCE QUE vs. À CAUSE DE

See **À CAUSE DE vs. PARCE QUE**

PARLER

(To speak, to talk)
PRÉS.: *parl-e, -es, -e, -ons, -ez, -ent.*
IMPARF.: *parl-ais, -ais, -ait, -ions, -iez, -aient.*
PASSÉ SIMPLE: *parl-ai, -as, -a, -âmes, -âtes, -èrent.*
FUT.: *parler-ai, -as, -a, -ons, -ez, -ont.*
CONDIT.: *parler-ais, -ais, -ait, -ions, -iez, -aient.*
IMPÉR.: *parle, parlons, parlez.*
SUBJ. PRÉS.: *parl-e, -es, -e, -ions, -iez, -ent.*
SUBJ. IMPARF.: *parl-asse, -asses, -ât, -assions, -assiez, -assent.*
P. PRÉS.: *parlant.*
P. PASSÉ: *parlé(e).*
NOTE:
Parler à quelqu'un = To talk to someone (indirect object).
E.g.: *Je parle à Jeanne.*   *Je lui parle.*
I am talking to Jean.   I am talking to her.
BUT: *Parler de quelqu'un* = To talk about someone (object of the preposition *de*).
E.g.: *Je parle de Jeanne.*   *Je parle d'elle.*
I am talking about Jean.   I am talking about her.

PARMI

(Preposition) = "Among."
E.g.: *Elle a passé dix ans parmi les chimpanzés.*
She spent ten years among the chimpanzees.

PARTICIPE PASSÉ

See **PARTICIPLE, PAST**

PARTICIPE PRÉSENT
See **PARTICIPLE, PRESENT**

PARTICIPLE, PAST

The past participle *(le participe passé)* conveys a sense of a finished action. It is an adjective form of the verb. When used as a simple adjective, it agrees, like any adjective, with the noun it qualifies.

E.g.: *La lettre écrite le dix juin.*
> The letter written on June tenth.
>
> *Les soldats blessés à la guerre.*
> The soldiers injured in the war.

FORMATION:

(1) *"-er"* verbs: Stem + é.
E.g.: *Parlé, étudié, arrivé.*

(2) *"-ir"* verbs: Stem + i.
E.g.: *Fini, choisi, sali.*

Many verbs have irregular past participles. These are some of the most common:

Acquis = Acquired	*Ouvert* = Opened
Conquis = Conquered	*Souffert* = Suffered
Couru = Run	*Tenu* = Held
Couvert = Covered	*Venu* = Come
Mort = Dead	*Vêtu* = Dressed
Offert = Offered	

(3) *"-re"* verbs: Stem + u.
E.g.: *Perdu, vaincu, vendu.*

Some verbs have an irregular stem for the past participle, among them:

Bu = Drunk	*Paru* = Appeared
Connu = Known	*Plu* = Pleased
Cousu = Sewn	*Repu* = Satiated
Cru = Believed	*Résolu* = Resolved
Crû = Grown	*Tu* = Kept silent
Lu = Read	*Vécu* = Lived
Moulu = Ground	

IRREGULAR PAST PARTICIPLES:

Absous, absoute = Absolved	*Fait* = Done, made
Clos = Closed	*Frit* = Fried
Conduit = Driven	*Extrait* = Abstracted, drawn from
Craint = Feared	*Joint* = Joined
Cuit = Cooked	*Mis* = Put
Dit = Said	*Né* = Born
Éclos = Blossomed	*Nui* = Harmed
Écrit = Written	*Pris* = Taken
Éclos = Closed in	*Ri* = Laughed
Été = Been	*Suffi* = Sufficed
Éteint = Extinguished	*Suivi* = Followed

(4) *"-oir"* verbs: Stem + u.
E.g.: *Fallu, vu, voulu.*

Some verbs have an irregular stem for the past participle, among them:

Aperçu = Noticed	*Plu* = Rained
Assis = Seated	*Pu* = Able
Déçu = Disappointed	*Reçu* = Received
Dû = Owed	*Su* – Known
Eu = Had	*Sursis* = Postponed
Mû = Moved	

USAGE:

The past participle is used to form all the compound tenses of all verbs: *passé composé, plus-que-parfait, futur antérieur, conditionnel passé, subjonctif passé.*

See **PAST PARTICIPLES, AGREEMENT OF**

PARTICIPLE, PRESENT

The present participle *(le participe présent)* conveys a sense of ongoing action. It is an adjective form of the verb.

FORMATION:

Stem of the first person plural of the indicative present + *ant.*

E.g.: *Parler → parlant.*
 Finir → finissant.
 Prendre → prenant.

EXCEPTIONS:

Avoir → ayant.
Être → étant.
Savoir → sachant.

USAGE:

It can be used in two ways:

(1) As a verb form. It is then invariable.
 E.g.: *Je la vois encore arrivant avec son chapeau sur la tête.*
  I can still see her arriving with her hat on her head.

(2) As an adjective. It then agrees with the noun it modifies.
 E.g.: *Une voix chantante.*
  A singing voice.

NOTES:

(1) Some adjectives are slightly different from the corresponding present participle forms:

PRESENT PARTICIPLE	ADJECTIVE
Différant = Differing	*Différent* = Different
Négligeant = Neglecting	*Négligent* = Negligent

(2) The past form of the present participle is simply the present participle of the auxiliary verb + the past participle.
 E.g.: *Ayant mangé.* *Étant parti.*
  Having eaten. Having departed.

(3) Unlike English, in French prepositions are never followed by the present participle but always by an infinitive. The only exception to this is the preposition *en.*
 E.g.: *Elle est entrée en souriant.*
  She came in smiling.

See *EN*
See also **GERUND**

PARTIR

(To leave) (Conjugated with *être*)

PRÉS.: *pars, pars, part, partons, partez, partent*
IMPARF.: *part-ais, -ais, -ait, -ions, -iez, -aient.*
PASSÉ SIMPLE: *part-is, -is, -it, -îmes, -îtes, -irent.*
FUT.: *partir-ai, -as, -a, -ons, -ez, -ont.*
CONDIT.: *partir-ais, -ais, -ait, -ions, -iez, -aient.*
IMPÉR.: *pars, partons, partez.*
SUBJ. PRÉS.: *part-e, -es, -e, -ions, -iez, -ent.*
SUBJ. IMPARF.: *part-isse, -isses, -ît, -issions, -issiez, -issent.*
P. PRÉS.: *partant.*
P. PASSÉ: *parti(e).*

PARTIR vs. LAISSER, QUITTER, S'EN ALLER, SORTIR
See *LAISSER vs. PARTIR, QUITTER, S'EN ALLER, SORTIR*

PARTITIVE ARTICLES
See **ARTICLES, PARTITIVE**

PARTOUT

(Adverb) = "Everywhere."
E.g.: *Il y a des restaurants partout dans cette ville.*
    There are restaurants everywhere in this city.
See **EVERYWHERE**

PARTS OF THE BODY, ARTICLES WITH

The definite article, rather than the possessive adjective, is used with parts of the body in three instances:
(1) When talking about frequent or habitual actions, where no confusion is possible.
    E.g.: *Elle a haussé les épaules.*
        She shrugged (her shoulders).
(2) When talking about physical appearance.
    E.g.: *Il a les cheveux blonds et les yeux bruns.*
        He has blond hair and brown eyes.
(3) When using reflexive verbs.
    E.g.: *Elle s'est coupé la main.*
        She cut her hand.

PARVENIR

(To reach)
Conjugated like *VENIR*

PAS

See *NE . . . PAS*
See also **NEGATIVE EXPRESSIONS** and **ARTICLES, PARTITIVE**

PAS ENCORE

See *NE . . . PAS ENCORE*
See also **NEGATIVE EXPRESSIONS**

PAS MAL (DE)

(Idiomatic expression) = "Quite a bit."
E.g.: *Elles gagnent pas mal d'argent.*
    They earn quite a bit of money.

PASSÉ ANTÉRIEUR

The *passé antérieur* ("past perfect") in French is a literary tense that expresses an action that occurred in the past before another action in the past.
FORMATION:
Passé simple of the auxiliary verb + past participle.
E.g.: *J'eus fini.*   *Elles furent parties.*
    I had finished.   They had left.

USAGE:

The *passé antérieur* is used in the literary style after *quand, lorsque, aussitôt que, dès que,* and *après que* when the main verb is in the *passé simple.*

E.g.: *Tout le monde partit quand il eut fini.*
Everybody left when he had finished.

Il se coucha dès qu'elles furent parties.
He went to bed as soon as they had left.

PASSÉ COMPOSÉ

The *passé composé* ("compound past") corresponds in form to the English present perfect. It is composed of two parts:

FORMATION:

Present tense of *être* or *avoir* + past participle of the verb.

(REMEMBER that *être* is the auxiliary verb for intransitive and reflexive verbs and *avoir* is the auxiliary verb for transitive verbs.)

E.g.: *J'ai mangé.*   *Il est arrivé.*
I have eaten.   He has arrived.

See **VERBS, INTRANSITIVE** and **VERBS, REFLEXIVE**
See also **AUXILIARY VERBS**

USAGE:

The *passé composé* is used in three types of situations:

(1) To express an action that ended in the past.
E.g.: *J'ai lu le livre.*   *Il a plu hier.*
I (have) read the book.   It rained yesterday.

(2) To express an action that occurred at a certain moment (e.g., a specific time or date in the past).
E.g.: *Il est arrivé à deux heures.*
He arrived at two o'clock.

Elle a ri quand j'ai dit cela.
She laughed when I said that.

Elles sont parties le trois janvier.
They left on January third.

(3) To express an action whose (a) beginning, (b) end, or (c) duration is known and specified (even if it lasted a long time).
E.g.: (a) *La vente a commencé à neuf heures.*
The sale began at nine o'clock.
(b) *Elle est restée en France jusqu'à Noël.*
She remained in France until Christmas.
(c) *La famine a duré cinq ans.*
The famine lasted five years.

Nous ne l'avons pas vu depuis cinq ans.
We have not seen him for five years.

PASSÉ COMPOSÉ vs. IMPERFECT

See **IMPERFECT vs. *PASSÉ COMPOSÉ***

PASSÉ RÉCENT

See **RECENT PAST**

PASSÉ SIMPLE

The *passé simple* (''simple past'') is so called because it is composed of only one part (as opposed to the *passé composé*).

FORMATION:

The *passé simple* is one of the principal parts of the verb. That is, it is not derived from any other tense. Therefore, it must be memorized. (Frequently, but not always, the *passé simple* resembles the past participle.)

(1) FIRST CONJUGATION: *''-er''* verbs:

Stem + *-ai, -as, -a, -âmes, -âtes, -èrent.*

E.g.: *je parlai* = I spoke
    tu entras = you entered
    il chanta = he sang
    nous étudiâmes = we studied
    vous dansâtes = you danced
    ils allèrent = they went

(2) SECOND AND THIRD CONJUGATIONS: *''-ir''* and *''-re''* verbs:

Stem + *-is, -is, -it, -îmes, -îtes, -irent.*

E.g.: *je finis* = I finished
    tu écrivis = you wrote
    il sortit = he went out
    nous dîmes = we said
    vous fîtes = you did, made
    ils salirent = they soiled

(3) FOURTH CONJUGATION: *''-oir''* verbs:

Stem + *-us, -us, -ut, -ûmes, -ûtes, -urent.*

E.g.: *je voulus* = I wanted
    tu valus = you were worth
    il fallut = it was necessary
    nous voulûmes = we wanted
    vous voulûtes = you wanted
    ils voulurent = they wanted

IRREGULAR VERBS:

(1) **Être**

je fus
tu fus
il fut
nous fûmes
vous fûtes
ils furent

(2) **Tenir** **Venir**

(and compounds such as contenir, retenir, etc.)	(and compounds such as devenir, parvenir, etc.)
je vins	*je tins*
tu vins	*tu tins*
il vint	*il tint*
nous vînmes	*nous tînmes*
vous vîntes	*vous tîntes*
ils vinrent	*ils tinrent*

(3) **Courir** **Mourir**

je courus	*je mourus*
tu courus	*tu mourus*
il courut	*il mourut*
nous courûmes	*nous mourûmes*
voous courûtes	*vous mourûtes*
ils coururent	*ils moururent*

(4)

Avoir	**Devoir**	**Pleuvoir**	**Pouvoir**	**Recevoir**	**Savoir**	**Vouloir**
j'eus	je dus	il plut	je pus	je reçus	je sus	je voulus
tu eus	tu dus		tu pus	tu reçus	tu sus	tu voulus
il eut	il dut		il put	il reçut	il sut	il voulut
nous eûmes	nous dûmes		nous pûmes	nous reçûmes	nous sûmes	nous voulûmes
vous eûtes	vous dûtes		vous pûtes	vous reçûtes	vous sûtes	vous voulûtes
ils eurent	ils durent		ils purent	ils reçurent	ils surent	ils voulurent

BUT:

S'asseoir	**Voir**
je m'assis	je vis
tu t'assis	tu vis
il s'assit	il vit
nous nous assîmes	nous vîmes
vous vous assîtes	vous vîtes
ils s'assirent	ils virent

(5) The following verbs ending in *-re* also take the *-us, -us, -ut* . . . endings:

Boire	**Conclure**	**Connaître**	**Croire**	**Croître**
je bus	je conclus	je connus	je crus	je crûs
tu bus	tu conclus	tu connus	tu crus	tu crûs
il but	il conclut	il connut	il crut	il crût
nous bûmes	nous conclûmes	nous connûmes	nous crûmes	nous crûmes
vous bûtes	vous conclûtes	vous connûtes	vous crûtes	vous crûtes
ils burent	ils conclurent	ils connurent	ils crurent	ils crûrent

Lire	**Moudre***	**Paraître**	**Plaire**	**Résoudre***
je lus	je moulus	je parus	je plus	je résolus
tu lus	tu moulus	tu parus	tu plus	tu résolus
il lut	il moulut	il parut	il plut	il résolut
nous lûmes	nous moulûmes	nous parûmes	nous plûmes	nous résolûmes
vous lûtes	vous moulûtes	vous parûtes	vous plûtes	vous résolûtes
ils lurent	ils moulurent	ils parurent	ils plurent	ils résolurent

* Note stem change.

Taire	**Vivre***
je tus	je vécus
tu tus	tu vécus
il tut	il vécut
nous tûmes	nous vécûmes
vous tûtes	vous vécûtes
ils turent	ils vécurent

* Note stem change

USAGE:

The *passé simple* is used only in the literary style. It is the literary equivalent of the *passé composé* and is used in the same way:

(1) To describe a completed action.
  E.g.: *Il écrivit une lettre.*
    He wrote a letter.
    Il neigea beaucoup cette année-là.
    It snowed a lot that year.

(2) To describe an action that occurred at a certain moment in the past.
  E.g.: *Elle quitta la ville le lendemain.*
    She left the town the next day.
    Ils rirent quand ils apprirent cela.
    They laughed when they learned that.

(3) To describe an action whose (a) beginning, (b) end, or (c) duration is known and specified (even if it lasted a long time).

E.g.: (a) *La vente commença dès sept heures.*
The sale began at seven o'clock.

(b) *Elle resta à Paris jusqu'à Noël.*
She stayed in Paris until Christmas.

(c) *La guerre dura trois ans.*
The war lasted three years.

PASSÉ SURCOMPOSÉ

There is no English equivalent of this tense. It is a past tense used to describe an action that took place before another action in the past.

FORMATION:

Passé composé of the auxiliary verb + past participle.

E.g.: *J'ai eu terminé.*
I had finished.

USAGE:

This tense is used only in conversation. (Its literary counterpart is the *passé antérieur.*) It describes a past action that occurred before another action in the past and is used only in subordinate clauses after *après que, aussitôt que, dès que, lorsque,* and *quand.*

E.g.: *Quand il a eu fini son travail, il s'est couché.*
When he had finished his work, he went to bed.

On est parti après que Mariette a été revenue.
We left after Mariette had returned.

PASSER

(To pass, to go past, to go through, to spend [time])

(1) It is transitive (i.e., conjugated with *avoir*) if it takes a direct object.

E.g.: *Il a passé ses examens la semaine dernière.*
He took his examinations last week.

Elle passe son temps à bavarder.
She spends her time chatting.

(2) It is intransitive (i.e., conjugated with *être*) if it takes no direct object.

E.g.: *Elle est passée devant le musée.*
She went past the museum.

NOTES:

(1) *Se passer* = "To happen, to take place."

E.g.: *La cérémonie s'est passée sans incident.*
The ceremony took place without incident.

(2) *Se passer de* = "To do without."

E.g.: *Je ne peux pas me passer de tabac.*
I can't do without tobacco.

PASSER + TIME EXPRESSION + À + INFINITIVE

(Idiomatic construction) = "To spend (time) + -ing."

E.g.: *Ils passent leur temps à jouer aux cartes.*
They spend their time playing cards.

J'ai passé trois jours à répéter.
I spent three days rehearsing.

PASSIVE VOICE

The passive voice *(la voix passive)* indicates that the subject undergoes the action of the verb.

E.g.: *La voiture est conduite par l'homme.*

   The car is driven by the man.

Any active "transitive verb + direct object" construction can be turned into a passive construction, with the direct object becoming the subject and the subject becoming the "agent" (or "doer") of the passive verb.

E.g.: ACTIVE: *Nous écrivons le livre.*

   We are writing the book.

   PASSIVE: *Le livre est écrit par nous.*

   The book is (being) written by us.

CONSTRUCTION:

The passive voice is constructed by using the verb *être* + the past participle of the verb in question. The *être* part is conjugated in whatever tense is needed.

E.g.: *Le criminel est arrêté (a été arrêté, sera arrêté, etc.) par la police.*

   The criminal is (has been, will be, etc.) arrested by the police.

REMEMBER: Since the passive voice is always constructed with *être*, the past participle of the verb will always agree with the subject.

CONJUGATION OF A VERB IN THE PASSIVE VOICE: ***être interrogé***

INDICATIF:

PRÉSENT: *suis interrogé(e), es interrogé(e), est interrogé(e), sommes interrogé(e)s, êtes interrogé(e)s, sont interrogé(e)s.*

IMPARFAIT: *étais interrogé(e), étais interrogé(e), était interrogé(e), étions interrogé(e)s, étiez interrogé(e)s, étaient interrogé(e)s.*

PASSÉ SIMPLE: *fus interrogé(e), fus interrogé(e), fut interrogé(e), fûmes interrogé(e)s, fûtes interrogé(e)s, furent interrogé(e)s.*

FUTUR: *serai interrogé(e), seras interrogé(e), sera interrogé(e), serons interrogé(e)s, serez interrogé(e)s, seront interrogé(e)s.*

PASSÉ COMPOSÉ: *ai été interrogé(e), as été interrogé(e), a été interrogé(e), avons été interrogé(e)s, avez été interrogé(e)s, ont été interrogé(e)s.*

PLUS-QUE-PARFAIT: *avais été interrogé(e), avais été interrogé(e), avait été interrogé(e), avions été interrogé(e)s, aviez été interrogé(e)s, avaient été interrogé(e)s.*

PASSÉ ANTÉRIEUR: *eus été interrogé(e), eus été interrogé(e), eut été interrogé(e), eûmes été interrogé(e)s, eûtes été interrogé(e)s, eurent été interrogé(e)s.*

FUTUR ANTÉRIEUR: *aurai été interrogé(e) auras été interrogé(e), aura été interrogé(e), aurons été interrogé(e)s, aurez été interrogé(e)s, auront été interrogé(e)s.*

CONDITIONNEL:

PRÉSENT: *serais interrogé(e), serais interrogé(e), serait interrogé(e), serions interrogé(e)s, seriez interrogé(e)s, seraient interrogé(e)s.*

PASSÉ: *aurais été interrogé(e), aurais été interrogé(e), aurait été interrogé(e), aurions été interrogé(e)s, auriez été interrogé(e)s, auraient été interrogé(e)s.*

IMPÉRATIF:

PRÉSENT: *sois interrogé(e), soyons interrogé(e)s, soyez interrogé(e)s.*

PASSÉ: *aie été interrogé(e), ayons été interrogé(e)s, ayez été interrogé(e)s.*

SUBJONCTIF:

PRÉSENT: *sois interrogé(e), sois interrogé(e), soit interrogé(e), soyons interrogé(e)s, soyez interrogé(e)s, soient interrogé(e)s.*

IMPARFAIT: *fusse interogé(e), fusses interrogé(e), fût interrogé(e), fussions interrogé(e)s, fussiez interrogé(e)s, fussent interrogé(e)s.*

PASSÉ: *aie été interrogé(e), aies été interrogé(e), ait été interrogé(e), ayons été interrogé(e)s, ayez été interrogé(e)s, aient été interrogé(e)s, aient été interrogé(e)s.*

PLUS-QUE-PARFAIT: *eusse été interrogé(e), eusses été interrogé(e), eût été interrogé(e), eussions été interrogé(e)s, eussiez été interrogé(e)s, eussent été interrogé(e)s.*

INFINITIF:
PRÉSENT: _être interrogé(e)(s)._
PASSÉ: _avoir été interrogé(e)(s)._
PARTICIPE:
PRÉSENT: _étant interrogé(e)(s)._
PASSÉ: _été interrogé(e)(s); ayant été interrogé(e)(s)._

PAST PARTICIPLES, AGREEMENT OF

RULE 1: The past participle of verbs conjugated with _avoir_ agrees with the preceding direct object. That is, it does not agree unless the direct object is placed before the verb.
E.g.: _Les filles que j'ai vues._
    The girls (whom) I saw.
BUT: _J'ai vu les filles._
    I saw the girls.
NOTE:
When the pronoun _en_ is used, there is no agreement.
E.g.: _Des livres, il en a acheté plusieurs._
    (As for) books, he has bought several.
RULE 2: The same rule applies for the past participle of reflexive and reciprocal verbs (both of which are conjugated with _être_): The past participle agrees with the preceding direct object. That is, it does not agree unless the direct object is placed before the verb.
E.g.: _Elle s'est lavée._   _Ils se sont rencontrés._
    She washed (herself).   They met (each other).
NOTES:
(1) The direct object can be (a) a personal pronoun or (b) a relative pronoun (whose number and gender are found by looking at its antecedent).
    E.g.: (a) _Les fleurs, je les ai achetées hier._
            (As for) the flowers, I bought them yesterday.
        (b) _Les fleurs que j'ai achetées hier sentent bon._
            The flowers (that) I bought yesterday smell good.
(2) With reflexive and reciprocal verbs, the reflexive pronoun will be either (a) a direct object, with which there is agreement, or (b) an indirect object, with which there is no agreement.
    E.g.: (a) _Elle s'est lavée._
            She washed (herself).
    BUT: (b) _Elle s'est lavé les cheveux._
            She washed her hair.
            (In this sentence the direct object is after the verb.)
RULE 3: The past participle of verbs conjugated with _être_ agrees with the subject.
E.g.: _Elle est arrivée._
    She arrived.
REMEMBER: The verbs conjugated with _être_ are the "DR. & MRS. VANDERTRAMP" verbs.
NOTES:
(1) The past participles of verbs in the passive voice always agree with the subject (since the passive forms are always constructed with _être_).
    E.g.: _Elle a été accusée._   _Nous aurons été vaccinés._
        She was accused.   We will have been vaccinated.
(2) There is never any agreement when the pronoun _en_ is used.
    E.g.: _Des fleurs, elle en a acheté._
        (As for) flowers, she has bought some.
(3) A past participle used alone, with no auxiliary verb, agrees in number and gender with the word to which it refers. (In this case it is an adjective.)
    E.g.: _Ce sont des enfants abandonnés._
        They are abandoned children.

        Les fleurs coupées ne durent pas longtemps.
        Cut flowers do not last long.

See also **PAST PARTICIPLES, AGREEMENT OF (WITH VERBS OF PERCEPTION)**

PAST PARTICIPLES, AGREEMENT OF (WITH VERBS OF PERCEPTION)

With the verbs *écouter, entendre, regarder, sentir,* and *voir,* the past participle agrees with the preceding direct object only if the verb actually refers to this direct object.

E.g.:   *Les femmes que j'ai entendues chanter.*
The women (whom) I heard singing.
(What did I hear? The women, who were singing.)

If the object of the verb is the infinitive that follows, there is no agreement.

E.g.:   *Les airs que j'ai entendu jouer.*
The tunes (that) I heard playing (being played).
(What did I hear? Someone playing. Playing what? The tunes.)

PAST PERFECT

See ***PLUS-QUE-PARFAIT***
See also ***PASSÉ ANTÉRIEUR***

PAST TENSES

There are eleven past tenses:

(1) Imperfect *(imparfait).*
(2) *Passé composé.*
(3) *Passé simple.*
(4) *Passé antérieur.*
(5) *Passé surcomposé.*
(6) Pluperfect *(plus-que-parfait).*
(7) Future perfect *(futur antérieur).*
(8) Past conditional *(conditionnel passé).*
(9) Imperfect subjunctive *(subjonctif imparfait).*
(10) Past subjunctive *(subjonctif passé).*
(11) Pluperfect subjunctive *(subjonctif plus-que-parfait).*

For a description of each one, see the appropriate heading.

PEINDRE

(To paint)
PRÉS: *peins, peins, peint, peign-ons, -ez, -ent.*
IMPARF.: *peign-ais, -ais, -ait, -ions, -iez, -aient.*
PASSÉ SIMPLE: *peign-is, -is, -it, -îmes, -îtes, -irent.*
FUT.: *peindr-ai, -as, -a, -ons, -ez, -ont.*
CONDIT.: *peindr-ais, -ais, -ait, -ions, -iez, -aient.*
IMPÉR.: *peins, peignons, peignez.*
SUBJ. PRÉS.: *peign-e, -es, -e, -ions, -iez, -ent.*
SUBJ. IMPARF.: *peign-isse, -isses, -ît, -issions, -issiez, -issent.*
P. PRÉS.: *peignant.*
P. PASSÉ: *peint.*

PENDANT vs. *POUR* + TIME EXPRESSION

(Prepositions)

(1) *Pendant* is used to indicate duration.
E.g.:   *J'ai étudié pendant quatre heures hier soir.*
I studied for four hours last night.

(2) *Pour* is used after the verbs *aller, partir,* and *venir* to state the duration of situations that will prevail in the future.
E.g.:   *Elle ira en Espagne pour un mois.*   *Nous partons pour un an.*
She will go to Spain for a month.   We are leaving for a year.

PENDRE

(To hang)
Conjugated like **RENDRE**

PENSER

(To think)
NOTES:
(1) In the affirmative, *penser* takes the indicative.
   E.g.: *Je pense qu'elle dit la vérité.*
      I think she is saying the truth.
(2) In the negative, *ne pas penser* takes the subjunctive.
   E.g.: *Je ne pense pas qu'elle dise la vérité.*
      I don't think she is saying the truth.
See also **PENSER À vs. PENSER DE**

PENSER À vs. PENSER DE

(1) *Penser à* = "To think about."
   E.g.: *Ils pensent à leurs parents.*
      They are thinking about their parents.
This verb does not take an indirect object, but the preposition *à* + object of the preposition.
Therefore, if a pronoun follows the verb, it is the object of a preposition pronoun (not the indirect object pronoun).
   E.g.: *Ils pensent <u>à eux</u>.* (for persons)
      They are thinking about them.
   BUT: *Ils y pensent.* (for things)
      They are thinking about it.
See **Y**
(2) *Penser de* = "To think of, to have an opinion about."
   E.g.: *Que penses-tu d'elle?* (for persons)
      What do you think of her?

   Que penses-tu de ce film?
      What do you think of this film?

   Qu'en penses-tu? (for things)
      What do you think of it?

PEOPLE

(Noun)
(1) "People in general (an indefinite number)" = *gens* (masculine plural).
   E.g.: *Ces gens sont malheureux.*
      These people are unhappy.
(2) "People (a definite number)" = *personnes* (feminine plural).
   E.g.: *Il y a 23 personnes ici.*
      There are 23 people here.
(3) "The people (of a nation)" = *Le peuple.*
   E.g.: *Le peuple des États-Unis jouit de la liberté.*
      The people of the United States enjoy freedom.
   (Note that in French the verb is singular since the subject is singular.)
(4) "The people (as a social class)" = *Le peuple.*
   E.g.: *Le peuple s'est révolté contre l'aristocratie.*
      The people rebelled against the aristocracy.
   (Again, note that the verb is in the singular because the subject is singular.)

PER

(Preposition indicating distribution or measure) = *Par.*
E.g.: *Il gagne 2.000 francs par jour.*   *Ils reçoivent cent francs par enfant.*
He earns 2,000 francs per day.   They receive one hundred francs per child.
BUT: *Trois francs <u>au</u>* (or *du*) *kilomètre.*
Three francs per kilometer.

PERCEPTION, VERBS OF

Verbs of perception *(Écouter, entendre, regarder, sentir, voir),* when followed by a verb, take the infinitive.
E.g.: *Nous entendons Caroline <u>chanter</u>.*   *Il a senti le lion <u>approcher</u>.*
We hear Caroline sing.   He smelled the lion approaching.

NOTE:
If the direct object is a personal pronoun, this pronoun comes before the verb of perception (except if the verb is an affirmative command).
E.g.: *Nous l'écoutons chanter.*
We listen to him (her) singing.

Il l'a senti approcher.
He smelled it approaching.

Regarde-le danser.
Look at him dance.

See **PAST PARTICIPLES, AGREEMENT OF (WITH VERBS OF PERCEPTION)**

PERDRE

(To lose)
Conjugated like **RENDRE**

PERMETTRE

(To allow, to permit)
Conjugated like **METTRE**

PERSON (GRAMMATICAL)

The person *(la personne)* is the form of the conjugation that indicates the person(s) who is (are) speaking, to whom one is speaking, or about whom one is speaking.
E.g.: *Je travaille.*   I work.
    Tu travailles.   You work.
    Il (elle, on) travaille.   He (she, one) works.
    Nous travaillons.   We work.
    Vous travaillez.   You work.
    Ils (elles) travaillent.   They work.

PERSONAL PRONOUNS
See **PRONOUNS, PERSONAL**

PERSONNE

(1) (Feminine noun) *Une personne* = "A person, somebody."
    E.g.: *Il y a une personne que je ne connais pas.*
        There is a person I do not know.
(2) (Indefinite pronoun) *Personne* = "Nobody." Always used with *ne* except when there is no verb.
    E.g.: *Personne ne me comprend.*   *Vois-tu quelqu'un? Non, personne.*
        Nobody understands me.   Do you see anybody? No, nobody.
See **NE . . . PERSONNE**
See also **GENS**

PESER

(To weigh)

The *e* of the stem changes to *è* before a silent syllable. Therefore, the following forms are slightly irregular:

PRÉS.: *je pèse, tu pèses, il pèse, (nous pesons, vous pesez), ils pèsent.*

FUT.: *je pèserai, tu pèseras, il pèsera, nous pèserons, vous pèserez, ils pèseront*

CONDIT.: *je pèserais, tu pèserais, il pèserait, nous pèserions, vous pèseriez, ils pèseraient.*

SUBJ. PRÉS.: *que je pèse, que tu pèses, qu'il pèse, (que nous pesions, que vous pesiez), qu'ils pèsent.*

PEU

(1) (Adverb) *Peu* = "Little, not much."

E.g.: *Ils voyagent peu.*
They don't travel much.

(2) (Adverbial expression) *Un peu* = "A little."

E.g.: *Essayez de manger un peu.*
Try to eat a little.

(3) (Adverbial expression of quantity) *Peu de* = "Little, not much, few, not many."

E.g.: *Nous avons eu peu de pluie pendant nos vacances.*
We had little rain during our vacation.

(4) (Adverbial expression of quantity) *Un peu de* = "A little (bit) of."

E.g.: *J'ai un peu d'argent à la banque.*
I have a little money in the bank.

PEUR

See **AVOIR PEUR**

PEUT-ÊTRE

(Adverb) = "Perhaps, maybe."

Like all adverbs, it goes after the verb it modifies. However, for emphasis it may be placed at the beginning of the sentence, in which case it is followed by inversion.

E.g.: *Il a peut-être eu un accident.*
He has perhaps had an accident.

Peut-être a-t-il eu un accident.
Perhaps he has had an accident.

NOTE:

To avoid inversion, use *Peut-être que.*

E.g.: *Peut-être que vous avez raison.*
Perhaps you are right.

Peut-être qu'il a eu un accident.
Perhaps he has had an accident.

PLACE

(Noun) = *Un lieu, un endroit.*

E.g.: *Je ne connais pas cet endroit (ce lieu).*
I don't know this place.

For the expression "To take place," see **AVOIR LIEU**

PLACE

(1) "(Public) square."

E.g.: *La place de la Concorde se trouve à Paris.*
The Place de la Concorde is in Paris.

(2) "Place."

    E.g.: *Il faut remettre les choses à leur place.*
        You must put things back in their place.

(3) "Space."

    E.g.: *Je n'ai pas pu trouver de place pour stationner.*
        I could not find a parking space.

(4) "Seat."

    E.g.: *C'est une voiture à six places.*   *J'ai réservé trois places.*
        It's a car with seats for six people.   I have reserved three seats.

PLAINDRE

(To pity)

Conjugated like **CRAINDRE**

The reflexive form *Se plaindre (de)* = "To complain (about)."

E.g.: *Cet enfant se plaint toujours de sa sœur.*
     This child is always complaining about his sister.

PLAIRE

(To please, to be pleasing)

PRÉS.: *plais, plais, plaît, plaisons, plaisez, plaisent.*
IMPART.: *plais-ais, -ais, -ait, -ions, -iez, -aient.*
PASSÉ SIMPLE: *pl-us, -us, -ut, -ûmes, -ûtes, -urent.*
FUT.: *plair-ai, -as, -a, -ons, -ez, -ont.*
CONDIT.: *plair-ais, -ais, -ait, -ions, -iez, -aient.*
IMPÉR.: *plais, plaisons, plaisez.*
SUBJ. PRÉS.: *plais-e, -es, -e, -ions, -iez, -ent.*
SUBJ. IMPARF.: *pl-usse, -usses, -ût, -ussions, -ussiez, -ussent.*
P. PRÉS.: *plaisant.*
P. PASSÉ: *plu(e).*

NOTE:

Plaire takes an indirect object and has the meaning "To be pleasing to." In this sense it is frequently used as the equivalent of "To like." The construction is different from the English equivalent, however:

E.g.: Teresa likes the book.
     Le livre plaît à Thérèse.

     I don't like that man at all.
     Cet homme ne me plaît pas du tout.

     Do you like it?
     Est-ce que ça vous plaît?

to PLAY (GAME or INSTRUMENT)

See **JOUER À vs. JOUER DE**

PLEASE

(1) "Please!" = *S'il vous plaît!* (informal = *S'il te plaît!*)

    E.g.: *Passe-moi le sel, s'il te plaît.*
        Please pass me the salt.

(2) "To please someone" = *Faire plaisir à quelqu'un.*

    E.g.: *Cela me fait plaisir de voir cela.*
        It pleases me to see that.

See **FAIRE PLAISIR (À)**

PLEUVOIR

(To rain) (Impersonal verb)
PRÉS.: *il pleut.*
IMPARF.: *il pleuvait.*
PASSÉ SIMPLE: *il plut.*
FUT.: *il pleuvra.*
CONDIT.: *il pleuvrait.*
SUBJ. PRÉS.: *qu'il pleuve.*
SUBJ. IMPARF.: *il plût.*
P. PRÉS.: *pleuvant.*
PASSÉ: *plu.*

PLUPART

(Feminine noun) = "The greater number, most."
E.g.: *La plupart des gens n'aiment pas la grammaire.*
     Most people do not like grammar.
La plupart takes the preposition *de* before a noun but the prepositional construction *d'entre* before a pronoun. The noun or pronoun is always in the plural, except in the expression *La plupart du temps* (= "Most of the time").
E.g.: *La plupart des étudiants n'aiment pas la grammaire.*
     Most students do not like grammar.
BUT: *La plupart d'entre eux n'aiment pas la grammaire.*
     Most of them do not like grammar.

PLUPERFECT

See **PLUS-QUE-PARFAIT**

PLURAL

"Plural" *(le pluriel)* always expresses the idea of more than one item. For example, "books" is plural (as contrasted with "book," which is singular).
See **SINGULAR**

PLURAL OF ADJECTIVES

See **ADJECTIVES, PLURAL OF**

PLURAL OF NOUNS

See **NOUNS, PLURAL OF**

PLUSIEURS

(1) (Indefinite adjective) *Plusieurs* (= "Several").
    This has only one form, used for both the masculine and the feminine.
    E.g.: *J'ai invité plusieurs amis.*   *Elle a plusieurs amies.*
        I have invited several friends.   She has several (girl) friends.
(2) (Indefinite pronoun) *Plusieurs* (= "Several people").
    This also has only one form.
    E.g.: *Plusieurs pensent qu'il a raison.*   *Des amis, j'en ai plusieurs.*
        Several (people) think he is right.   (As for) friends, I have several.
NOTE:
When it is followed by a personal pronoun, *plusieurs* takes the prepositional construction *d'entre*.
E.g.: *Plusieurs d'entre nous.*   *Plusieurs d'entre eux.*
     Several of us.   Several of them.

PLUS, MOINS + NUMBERS

(Adverbs)
Before numbers, *plus* and *moins* take the preposition *de*.
E.g.: *J'ai plus de vingt cousins.*   *Elle a moins de cent francs.*
       I have more than twenty cousins.   She has less than a hundred francs.

PLUS . . . PLUS, MOINS . . . MOINS

(Idiomatic constructions) = "The more . . . , the more," "the less . . . , the less."
E.g.: *Plus il mange, plus il grossit.*
       The more he eats, the more he gains weight.

       Moins elle travaille, moins elle gagne d'argent.
       The less she works, the less money she earns.

PLUS-QUE-PARFAIT (PLUPERFECT)

This tense describes an action ended in the past before another action in the past. It corresponds grammatically to the past perfect in English but is used somewhat differently.
FORMATION:
Imperfect of the auxiliary verb + past participle.
E.g.: *J'avais mangé.*   *Elle était descendue.*
       I had eaten.   She had come down.
USAGE:
The pluperfect in French is used in the same way as the past perfect in English:
(1) After *quand, lorsque, aussitôt que, dès que,* and *après que* to describe a habitual action when the main verb is in the imperfect.
    E.g.: *Il regardait toujours la télévision quand il avait fini ses devoirs.*
          He would [used to] always watch TV when he had finished his homework.
(2) After *si* indicating a past unrealized hypothesis.
    E.g.: *Si tu m'avais appelé, je serais venu.*
          If you had called me, I would have come.
(3) In indirect discourse in the past to convey the past.
    E.g.: *Elle a dit qu'elle avait fini le travail à sept heures.*
          She said (that) she had finished the job at seven o'clock.
NOTE:
In English, the use of the pluperfect is often overlooked.
E.g.: He said he saw him = He said he had seen him.
       He claimed he didn't do it = He claimed he hadn't done it.
Such negligence is not allowed in French. The *plus-que-parfait* must be used:
E.g.: *Il a dit qu'il l'avait vu.*   *Il a prétendu qu'il ne l'avait pas fait.*
       He said (that) he had seen him.   He claimed (that) he had not done it.
For the pluperfect subjunctive, see **SUBJUNCTIVE MOOD**

POSITION OF OBJECT PRONOUNS

See **PRONOUNS, OBJECT OF VERB**

POSSESSION

Possession can be expressed by "*Être à* + emphatic pronoun."
E.g.: *Ce livre est à moi.*
       This book is mine.
See **ADJECTIVES, POSSESSIVE**
See also **PRONOUNS, POSSESSIVE** and **to BELONG TO**

POSSESSIVE ADJECTIVES

See **ADJECTIVES, POSSESSIVE**

POSSESSIVE PRONOUNS
See **PRONOUNS, POSSESSIVE**

POSSIBLY

(Adverb) = *Peut-être* (followed by inversion if it comes at the beginning of the sentence) or "*Il se peut que* + subjunctive."

E.g.: *Peut-être arriveront-ils demain.*
  Possibly they will arrive tomorrow.

  Ils arriveront peut-être demain.
  Perhaps they will arrive tomorrow.

  Il se peut qu'ils viennent avec nous.
  They might come with us.

See **PEUT-ÊTRE**

POUR

(Preposition)

Use to indicate (a) direction: "for," "to"; (b) time: "for," "by"; (c) intention, destination: "for"; (d) approbation: "for," "in favor of"; (e) point of view: "in (one's) view"; (f) cause: "for"; (g) "in exchange for, in place of"; and (h) purpose: "to," "in order to."

E.g.: (a) *Ils sont partis pour la France.*
  They left for France.
  On s'en va pour l'Amérique la semaine prochaine.
  We're off to America next week.

(b) *Il me l'a promis pour demain.*
  He promised it to me for tomorrow.

(c) *J'ai un cadeau pour toi.*
  I have a gift for you.

(d) *Moi, je suis pour l'avortement sur demande.*
  I'm in favor of abortion on demand.

(e) *Pour eux, c'est impossible.*
  In their view it's impossible.

(f) *Fermé pour réparations.*
  Closed for repairs.

(g) *Il y est allé pour moi.*
  He went there in my place.

(h) *Il travaille pour gagner sa vie.*
  He works (in order) to earn his living.

REMEMBER: When "to" in English means "in order to," use *pour*.

E.g.: *Elle a téléphoné pour demander ton adresse.*
  She called to ask for your address.

See **POUR QUE + SUBJUNCTIVE**

POUR AINSI DIRE

(Idiomatic expression) = "So to speak."

E.g.: *Il est si puissant qu'il est comme un tsar, pour ainsi dire.*
  He is so powerful that he is like a czar, so to speak.

POUR vs. PENDANT + TIME EXPRESSION
See **PENDANT vs. POUR + TIME EXPRESSION**

POUR QUE + SUBJUNCTIVE

(Conjunctional expression) = "So that, in order that."

E.g.: *Ils iront en France pour que leurs enfants apprennent le français.*

They will go to France so that their children may learn French.

NOTE:

If the two verbs have the same subject, use "*Pour* + infinitive," not "*Pour que* + subjunctive."

E.g.: *Il ira en France pour apprendre le français.*

He will go to France to learn French.

See **POUR and SO THAT**

POUVOIR

(To be able)

PRÉS.: *peux, peux, peut, pouvons, pouvez, peuvent.*

IMPARF.: *pouv-ais, -ais, -ait, -ions, -iez, -aient.*

PASSÉ SIMPLE: *pus, pus, put, pûmes, pûtes, purent.*

FUT.: *pourr-ai, -as, -a, -ons, -ez, -ont.*

CONDIT.: *pourr-ais, -ais, -ait, -ions, -iez, -aient.*

SUBJ. PRÉS.: *puiss-e, -es, -e, -ions, -iez, -ent.*

SUBJ. IMPARF.: *pusse, pusses, pût, pussions, pussiez, pussent.*

P. PRÉS.: *pouvant.*

P. PASSÉ: *pu.*

NOTE:

Pouvoir refers to physical ability. Do not confuse it with *savoir*, which refers to mental ability or knowledge.

E.g.: *Il ne peut pas écrire parce qu'il s'est coupé le doigt.*

He can't (is not able to) write because he cut his finger.

BUT: *Il ne sait pas écrire, car il n'est jamais allé à l'école.*

He can't (does not know how to) write because he has never gone to school.

PREDICATE

The predicate *(l'attribut)* is the part of a sentence that expresses what is said about the subject. It must be linked to the subject by means of the verb *être* or a verb such as *devenir, paraître,* or *sembler.*

E.g.: *Elle veut devenir <u>la plus grande artiste de son époque</u>.*

She wants to become <u>the greatest artist of her time</u>.

to PREFER + VERB

(1) If both verbs have the same subject: "*Préférer* + infinitive."

E.g.: *Nous préférons dormir.*

We prefer to sleep.

(2) If the two verbs have different subjects: "*Préférer que* + subjunctive."

E.g.: *Nous préférons qu'elle dorme.*

We prefer that she sleep.

PRÉFÉRER

(To prefer)

The e of the stem changes to è before a silent syllable that comes at the end of the verb.

Therefore, the following forms are slightly irregular:

PRÉS.: *je préfère, tu préfères, il préfère, (nous préférons, vous préférez), ils préfèrent.*

SUBJ. PRÉS.: *que je préfère, que tu préfères, qu'il préfère, (que nous préférions, que vous préfériez), qu'ils préfèrent.*

PRENDRE

(To take)
PRÉS.: *prends, prends, prend, prenons, prenez, prennent.*
IMPARF.: *pren-ais, -ais, -ait, -ions, -iez, -aient.*
PASSÉ SIMPLE: *pris, pris, prit, prîmes, prîtes, prirent.*
FUT.: *prendr-ai, -as, -a, -ons, -ez, -ont.*
CONDIT.: *prendr-ais, -ais, -ait, -ions, -iez, -aient.*
IMPÉR.: *prends, prenons, prenez.*
SUBJ. PRÉS.: *prenne, prennes, prenne, prenions, preniez, prennent.*
SUBJ. IMPARF.: *prisse, prisses, prît, prissions, prissiez, prissent.*
P. PRÉS.: *prenant.*
P. PASSÉ: *pris(e).*

PRENDRE FIN

(Idiomatic construction) = "To come to an end."
E.g.: *La crise économique a pris fin en 1987.*
    The depression came to an end in 1987.

PRENDRE FROID

(Idiomatic construction) = "To catch a cold."
E.g.: *Elle a pris froid quand elle est sortie.*
    She caught a cold when she went out.

PRENDRE PEUR

(Idiomatic construction) = "To be afraid."
E.g.: *Il a pris peur en voyant arriver le cheval.*
    He was afraid when he saw the horse coming.

to PREPARE vs. PREPARE FOR vs. PREPARE TO

(1) "To prepare something" = *Préparer.*
    E.g.: *Je prépare le repas pour ce soir.*
        I am preparing the meal for tonight.
(2) "To prepare (oneself) for" = *Se préparer pour.*
    E.g.: *Je me prépare pour l'examen.*
        I am preparing for the examination.
(3) "To prepare to + verb" = "*Se préparer à* + infinitive."
    E.g.: *Je me prépare à partir.*
        I am getting ready to leave.

PREPOSITION

A preposition *(une préposition)* is an invariable word that serves to establish a link with another word (called the *object of the preposition*). Examples of prepositions: *à, avec, chez, de, devant, par, pour, sans, sur.*

E.g.: *Elle va à Paris.*   *Je parle de ma sœur.*
    She goes to Paris.   I am talking about my sister.
    Il travaille avec moi.   *Le livre est sur la table.*
    He works with me.   The book is on the table.

When the object of a preposition is a verb, it is always in the infinitive (except with *en*, which is followed by the present participle).
E.g.: *Je travaille pour gagner de l'argent.*
    I work in order to earn some money.
See **EN**
See also **GERUND**

SPECIAL CASE:

The preposition *après* is followed by the past infinitive.

E.g.: *Après avoir mangé.*

   After eating (= After having eaten).

   Après être arrivé.

   After arriving (= After having arrived).

NOTE:

The preposition must be repeated before each new object.

E.g.: *Il écrit à Marie et à Nicole.*

   He writes to Mary and Helen.

   Nous allons en France et en Italie.

   We are going to France and Italy.

   J'ai envie d'acheter ce livre et de le lire.

   I feel like buying this book and reading it.

PREPOSITIONAL PRONOUNS
See **PRONOUNS, OBJECT OF PREPOSITION**

PREPOSITIONS + GEOGRAPHICAL NAMES
See **GEOGRAPHICAL NAMES, PREPOSITIONS WITH**

PREPOSITIONS + INFINITIVE

When a verb introduces an infinitive, it does so in one of three ways: without any preposition, with the preposition *à*, or with the preposition *de*.

(1) SOME COMMON VERBS THAT TAKE NO PREPOSITION:

Aimer	Entendre	Pouvoir
Aimer mieux	Espérer	Regarder
Aller	Faire	Savoir
Compter	Falloir	Sembler
Désirer	Laisser	Valoir mieux
Détester	Oser	Venir
Devoir	Paraître	Voir
Écouter	Préférer	Vouloir

(2) SOME COMMON VERBS THAT TAKE THE PREPOSITION *à*:

Aider (qqn) à	Enseigner (à qqn) à	S'amuser à
Aimer à	Hésiter à	S'attendre à
Apprendre (à qqn) à	Inviter (qqn) à	Se décider à
Arriver à	Jouer à	S'ennuyer à
Avoir à	Obliger (qqn) à	S'habituer à
Chercher à	Parvenir à	S'intéresser à
Commencer à	Passer (du temps) à	Se mettre à
Consentir à	Renoncer à	Se plaire à
Consister à	Réussir à	Se préparer à
Continuer à	S'accoutumer à	Tenir à
Encourager (qqn) à		

(3) SOME COMMON VERBS THAT TAKE THE PREPOSITION *de*:

Achever de	*Excuser de*	*Refuser de*
Arrêter de	*Féliciter (qqn) de*	*Regretter de*
Attendre de	*Finir de*	*Remercier (qqn) de*
Avertir (qqn) de	*Interdire (à qqn) de*	*Reprocher (à qqn) de*
Blâmer (qqn) de	*Jurer de*	*Résoudre de*
Cesser de	*Manquer de*	*Risquer de*
Choisir de	*Menacer de*	*S'arrêter de*
Commander (à qqn) de	*Mériter de*	*Se dépêcher de*
Conseiller (à qqn) de	*Négliger de*	*S'étonner de*
Craindre de	*Offrir de*	*S'excuser de*
Décider de	*Ordonner (à qqn) de*	*Se garder de*
Défendre (à qqn) de	*Oublier de*	*Se plaindre de*
Demander (à qqn) de	*Pardonner (à qqn) de*	*Se souvenir de*
Dire (à qqn) de	*Permettre (à qqn) de*	*Souffrir de*
Empêcher (qqn) de	*Persuader (qqn) de*	*Supplier (qqn) de*
Entreprendre de	*Prier (qqn) de*	*Tâcher de*
Essayer de	*Promettre (à qqn) de*	*Tenter de*
Éviter de	*Punir (qqn) de*	*Venir de*

See **VERBS + PREPOSITION + INFINITIVE**

PREPOSITIONS + NAMES OF COUNTRIES
See **GEOGRAPHICAL NAMES, PREPOSITIONS WITH**

PREPOSITIONS + PLACE NAMES
See **GEOGRAPHICAL NAMES, PREPOSITIONS WITH**

PREPOSITIONS + SEASONS

En été.	*En automne.*	*En hiver.*	BUT: *Au printemps.*
In the fall.	In the summer.	In the winter.	In the spring.

PRESENT PARTICIPLE
See **PARTICIPLE, PRESENT**

PRESENT TENSE
The present tense *(le présent)* describes an action taking place at the present moment.
E.g.: *Elle parle maintenant.*
     She is speaking now.
As in English, it is also used:
(1) To describe an action that will take place in the near future.
     E.g.: *Je pars demain.*
          I am leaving tomorrow.
(2) To describe a future action after a simple condition with *si.*
     E.g.: *Si tu vas à Paris, j'irai avec toi.*
          If you go to Paris, I shall go with you.
Note that whereas in English there are three forms of the present, there is only one in French.
English:
Simple present: I work.
Progressive present: I am working.
Emphatic present: I do work.
French:
Je travaille.

PRÉTENDRE

(To claim, to assert)
Conjugated like **RENDRE**
NOTE:
It does not mean "To pretend."
"To pretend, to feign" = "*Faire semblant* (*de* + infinitive)."
E.g.: *Il fait semblant d'être malade.*
      He is pretending to be sick.

PRÉVENIR

(To warn)
Conjugated like **TENIR**

PRÉVOIR

(To foresee)
Conjugated like **VOIR**

PRICE

The price *(le prix)* of something is expressed by using the definite article + unit of measurement.
E.g.: *Cent francs le litre.*
      One hundred francs a liter.
      Trois francs le kilo.
      Three francs a kilogram.
      Quinze francs le mètre.
      Fifteen francs a meter.

PROBABILITY

The concept of probability can be rendered in four ways:
(1) The adverbs *probablement* and *peut-être.*
    E.g.: *Elle est probablement fatiguée.*
        She is probably tired.
(2) "*Devoir* + infinitive."
    E.g.: *Elle doit être fatiguée.*   *J'ai dû me tromper.*
        She must be tired.   I must have made a mistake.
See **DEVOIR**
(3) Expressions such as "*Il est possible que* + subjunctive" and "*Il se peut que* + subjunctive."
    E.g.: *Il est possible (Il se peut) qu'elle ne vienne pas.*
        It is possible that she will not come.
See **SUBJUNCTIVE MOOD**
(4) The conditional mood.
    E.g.: *Elle serait partie en vacances.*
        She is probably away on vacation.
See **CONDITIONAL MOOD**

PRODUIRE

(To produce)
Conjugated like **CONDUIRE**

PROGRESSIVE PRESENT

There is no progressive present form in French. Simply use the normal present tense.
E.g.: I am working. = *Je travaille.*
Do not say *"Je suis travaillant"*! To emphasize the progressive nature of the action, use *"En train de + infinitive."*
E.g.: *Je suis en train de travailler.*
    I'm (busy) working.
See **EN TRAIN DE + INFINITIVE**

PROGRESSIVE PAST

There is no progressive past in French. Simply use the imperfect tense to indicate an action or situation that was going on.
E.g.: He was singing. = *Il chantait.*
Do not say *"Il était chantant"*! To emphasize the progressive nature of the action, use *"En train de + infinitive."*
E.g.: *Il était en train de chanter.*
    He was singing.
See **EN TRAIN DE + INFINITIVE**

PROMETTRE

(To promise)
Conjugated like **METTRE**

PRONOUN

A pronoun *(un pronom)* is a word used as a substitute for a noun (sometimes an idea or a clause) expressed elsewhere in the context.
E.g.: *Voici de l'argent; dépensez-le comme vous voudrez.*
    Here is some money; spend it as you wish.

PRONOUNS, DEMONSTRATIVE

These pronouns *(les pronoms démonstratifs)* replace the noun while pointing to it and distinguishing it from others.
FORMS:

	Singular			Plural	
	Masc.	**Fem.**	**Neut.**	**Masc.**	**Fem.**
Simple forms:	*celui*	*celle*	*ce*	*ceux*	*celles*
Compound forms:	*celui-ci* *celui-là*	*celle-ci* *celle-là*	*ceci* *cela (ça)*	*ceux-ci* *ceux-là*	*celles-ci* *celles-là*

USAGE:
Celui, celle, ceux, celles are used:
(1) Before a participle.
    E.g.: *Ce livre et celui <u>écrit</u> par Camus.*
        This book and that (= the one) written by Camus.
(2) Before a preposition and its object.
    E.g.: *Mon livre et celui <u>de</u> Camus.*
        My book and Camus' (= the one of Camus or the one by Camus).

(3) Before a relative pronoun.

> E.g.: *Mon livre et celui que Camus a écrit.*
>
> My book and the one that Camus wrote.

Ce is used:

(1) Before a relative pronoun.

> E.g.: *Ce que je vois.*   *Ce dont il parle.*
>
> What I see.   What he is talking about.

(2) As the subject of the verb *être* when this verb is followed by (a) a noun, (b) a pronoun, or (c) an adjective (but only if this adjective refers to a general concept or idea).

> E.g.: (a) *C'est un garçon.*
>
>   It's a boy.
>
> (b) *C'est moi.*
>
>   It's me.
>
> (c) *C'est bizarre.*
>
>   It's strange.

Ceci, celui-ci, celle(s)-ci, ceux-ci, etc., are used in opposition to *cela, celui-là, celle(s)-là, ceux-là,* etc.

> E.g.: *Ceci est bon, cela est mauvais.*
>
> This is good; that is bad.
>
> *Voici deux maisons; préfères-tu celle-ci ou celle-là?*
>
> Here are two houses; do you prefer this one or that one?

NOTE:

These expressions are also used to convey "the former" and "the latter." Note that the order is the opposite of the English construction. *Celui-ci* corresponds to "the latter," and *celui-là* corresponds to "the former."

> E.g.: *Washington et Lafayette étaient de grands hommes; celui-ci était français, celui-là était américain.*
>
> Washington and Lafayette were great men; the former was American, the latter French.

See **FORMER . . . LATTER**

PRONOUNS, DOUBLE OBJECT

When two object pronouns are used in the same sentence, their order is as follows:

(a) BEFORE THE VERB (i.e., normal position):

me				
te	*le*	*lui*		
se	*la*	*leur*	*y*	*en*
nous	*les*			
vous				

(b) AFTER THE VERB (i.e., with an affirmative command):

	moi (m')		
le	*toi (t')*		
la	*lui*	*y*	*en*
les	*nous*		
	vous		
	leur		

> E.g.: (a) *Tu as donné les fleurs à Marie. → Tu les lui as données.*
>
>   You gave Mary the flowers. → You gave them to her.
>
>   *N'écrivez pas la lettre au garçon. → Ne la lui écrivez pas!*
>
>   Don't write the letter to the boy! → Don't write it to him!
>
> (b) *Donne le livre à l'enfant! → Donne-le-lui!*
>
>   Give the book to the child! → Give it to him!

PRONOUNS, EMPHATIC

These pronouns (also called disjunctive, stressed, or independent pronouns) are used to add stress or emphasis.

FORMS:

Moi, toi, lui, elle, nous, vous, eux, elles.

E.g.: *Moi, je suis français; eux, ils sont asiatiques.*

I am French; *they* are Asians.

Nous, on reste à la maison.

(As for) us, we are staying home. (OR *We* are staying home.)

See **DISJUNCTIVE PRONOUNS**

PRONOUNS, INDEFINITE

These pronouns *(les pronoms indéfinis)* replace indefinite or unspecified persons or things that may or may not be otherwise mentioned in the sentence.

(1) *Aucun(e)* = "No, not any." Used only as a direct object. Used with *ne,* which is placed immediately before the verb.

E.g.: *Des livres, il n'en a aucun.*

(As for) books, he does not have any.

When used without a verb, *ne* is omitted.

E.g.: *Avez-vous des ennemis? Non, aucun.*

Do you have any enemies? No, none.

(2) *Autrui* = "Others." Used only for persons.

E.g.: *Il faut penser à autrui.*

One must think of others.

(3) *Chacun(e)* = "Each (one)."

E.g.: *Chacun(e) a reçu un livre.*

Each (one) received a book.

(4) *On* = "One, someone, anyone, we, you, they, people." Also frequently conveyed by the passive voice in English.

E.g.: *On frappe à la porte.*   *On va en ville.*

Someone is knocking at the door.   We're going downtown.

On doit manger pour vivre.   *On parle français ici.*

One must eat to live.   French is spoken here.

(5) *Personne* = "Nobody." Used with *be,* which is placed immediately before the verb.

E.g.: *Personne n'est venu.*   *Je ne vois personne.*

Nobody came.   I do not see anybody.

When used without a verb, *ne* is omitted.

E.g.: *Qui as-tu vu? Personne.*

Whom did you see? Nobody.

(6) *Plusieurs* = "Several."

E.g.: *Des cousins, j'en ai plusieurs.*

(As for) cousins, I have several.

(7) *Quelqu'un* = "Somebody."

E.g.: *Quelqu'un frappe à la porte.*

Somebody is knocking at the door.

(8) *Rien* = "Nothing." Used with *ne,* which is placed immediately before the verb.

E.g.: *Rien ne l'intéresse.*   *Il ne sait rien.*

Nothing interests him.   He doesn't know anything.

When used without a verb, *ne* is omitted.

E.g.: *Que fais-tu? Rien.*

What are you doing? Nothing.

(9) *Tous, toutes* = "All (of them)."

E.g.: *Tous sont arrivés.*   *Je les aime toutes.*

All have arrived.   I like them all.

(10) *Tout* = "Everything."
   E.g.: *Tout l'intéresse.*   *Elle aime tout.*
          Everything interests him.   She likes everything.
See the appropriate heading for more information about each indefinite pronoun.

PRONOUNS, INDEPENDENT
See **PRONOUNS, EMPHATIC**

PRONOUNS, INTERROGATIVE

Interrogative pronouns *(les pronoms interrogatifs)* are used to ask a question concerning a person or a thing. (Be careful because their forms are easily confused with those of the relative pronouns.)

	Persons	**Things**
Subject:	qui qui est-ce qui	qu'est-ce qui
Direct object:	qui qui est-ce que	que qu'est-ce que
Object of preposition:	qui	quoi
For choosing among options:	lequel, laquelle, lesquels, lesquelles	

USAGE:
(1) The short forms *(qui, que)* are followed by inversion.
   E.g.: *Qui êtes-vous?*
          Who are you?
          Que dit-elle?
          What does she say?
          Que fait Pierre? (NOT *"Que Pierre fait-il?"*)
          What is Peter doing?
(2) The long forms *(qui est-ce qui, qu'est-ce qui, qui est-ce que, qu'est-ce que)* are followed by the normal word order.
   E.g.: *Qui est-ce qui parle?*
          Who is speaking?
          Qu'est-ce qu'il dit?
          What is he saying?
          Qui est-ce que vous connaissez?
          Whom do you know?
(3) *Lequel, laquelle, lesquels, lesquelles* are used in making a choice among various options.
   E.g.: *De toutes ces autos, laquelle préférez-vous?*
          Of all these cars, which one do you prefer?
See **INTERROGATIVE SENTENCES**

PRONOUNS, MULTIPLE
See **PRONOUNS, DOUBLE OBJECT**

PRONOUNS, OBJECT OF PREPOSITION

The forms of the prepositional pronouns are *moi, toi, lui, elle, nous, vous, eux, elles.*
REMEMBER:
(1) Some verbs take a preposition in English but not in French.
   E.g.: To wait for   = "*Attendre* + direct object"
          To listen to = "*Écouter* + direct object"
          To look for   = "*Chercher* + direct object"
          To look at   = "*Regarder* + direct object"
See **DIRECT OBJECT vs. INDIRECT OBJECT**

(2) Some verbs take an indirect object in French whereas the English equivalent does not make it clear whether the object is direct or indirect.
E.g.: *Écrire à quelqu'un.* = To write (to) somebody.
Téléphoner à quelqu'un. = To call (or telephone) somebody.
These verbs do not take the pronoun object of a preposition but rather an indirect object pronoun.
E.g.: *J'ai écrit à mes parents.* → *Je leur ai écrit.*
I wrote (to) my parents. → I wrote (to) them.

PRONOUNS, OBJECT OF VERB

POSITION IN THE SENTENCE:
Object pronouns are placed BEFORE the verb of which they are the object except when the verb is in the affirmative imperative, in which case the object pronouns are placed AFTER the verb and are linked to it by hyphens.

E.g.: *Je le regarde.*	*Nous les avons mangés.*
I look at him.	We have eaten them.
BUT: *Regarde-la!*	*Mangez-les!*
Look at her!	Eat them!

For the order of multiple pronouns, see **PRONOUNS, DOUBLE OBJECT**

PRONOUNS, PERSONAL

(Les pronoms personnels) The term "personal pronouns" is really a misnomer because they are used not only for persons but also for things and even, in some cases, for adjectives and ideas.
FORMS:

Subject:
je, tu, il, elle, on, nous, vous, ils, elles

Direct object:
me (*moi* after the imperative), *te* (*toi* after the imperative), *le, la, nous, vous, les*

Indirect object:
me, te, lui, se, nous, vous, leur

Object of preposition:
moi, toi, lui, elle, soi, nous, vous, eux, elles

Reflexive:
me, te, se, nous, vous, se.

Emphatic:
moi, toi, lui, elle, soi, nous, vous, eux, elles.

PRONOUNS, POSSESSIVE

(Les pronoms possessifs) these pronouns replace the noun while indicating its possessor.
FORMS:

If the noun belongs to ONE OWNER:

Masc. sing. noun:	*le mien*	*le tien*	*le sien*
Masc. plur. nouns:	*les miens*	*les tiens*	*les siens*
Fem. sing. noun:	*la mienne*	*la tienne*	*la sienne*
Fem. plur. nouns:	*les miennes*	*les tiennes*	*les siennes*

If the noun belongs to SEVERAL OWNERS:

Masc. sing. noun:	*le nôtre*	*le vôtre*	*le leur*
Masc. or fem. plur. nouns:	*les nôtres*	*les vôtres*	*les leurs*
Fem. sing. noun:	*la nôtre*	*la vôtre*	*la leur*
Masc. or fem. plur. nouns:	*les nôtres*	*les vôtres*	*les leurs*

NOTE:

With the verb *être*, possession is generally expressed by "*Être à* + noun (or emphatic pronoun)."

E.g.: *Cette maison est à M. Dupont.*

This house belongs to Mr. Dupont.

E.g.: *Ces lunettes sont à mon frère.*

These glasses belong to my brother.

E.g.: *Ce livre est à toi.*

This book is yours.

See **POSSESSION**

PRONOUNS, RECIPROCAL

(Les pronoms réciproques) These pronouns express the concept that the subjects perform the action of the verb reciprocally, that is, to (on, for, at) each other.

FORMS:

nous, vous, se.

E.g.: *Nous nous verrons demain.*

We shall see each other tomorrow.

See **VERBS, RECIPROCAL**

PRONOUNS, REFLEXIVE

(Les pronoms réfléchis) These pronouns reflect the action of the verb onto the subject. They are used with (and are a part of) reflexive verbs.

FORMS:

me, te, se, nous,vous, se.

See **VERBS, REFLEXIVE**

PRONOUNS, RELATIVE

(Les pronoms relatifs) These pronouns connect a relative clause to the noun or pronoun that they stand for.

E.g.: *Le livre que j'ai acheté.*

The book that I have bought.

(*que* stands for "le livre;" *j'ai acheté* relates to it.)

The noun or pronoun that the relative pronoun stands for is called the *antecedent.*

NOTE:

Although relative pronouns are frequently omitted in English, they must always be expressed in French.

E.g.: The book I bought

= The book that I bought

Le livre que j'ai acheté.

FORMS:

Simple Forms		
	Persons	Things
Subject:	*qui*	*qui*
Direct object:	*que (qu')*	*que (qu')*
Object of preposition:	*qui*	*quoi*

Compound Forms				
	Singular		Plural	
	Masc.	Fem.	Masc.	Fem.
	lequel	*laquelle*	*lesquels*	*lesquelles*
With *de*	*duquel*	*de laquelle*	*desquels*	*desquelles*
With *à*	*auquel*	*à laquelle*	*auxquels*	*auxquelles*

Special Form
dont (= de qui, de quoi, duquel, de laquelle, desquels, desquelles)

USAGE:

(1) *Qui* is used:

    (a) As the subject (which can be a person or a thing).

        E.g.: *L'enfant qui est ici.*   *Le livre qui m'intéresse.*

            The child who is here.   The book that interests me.

    (b) As the object of a preposition (but only for persons).

        E.g.: *Le garçon avec qui je parle.*

            The boy with whom I speak.

(2) *Que* is used:

    As a direct object (a person or a thing).

    E.g.: *L'enfant que je vois.*   *La table que je vois.*

        The child (whom) I see.   The table (that) I see.

(3) *Quoi* is neuter. It is used as the object of a preposition (for things only.)

    E.g.: *Je ne sais pas de quoi il parle.*

        I don't know what he is talking about.

(4) *Lequel, laquelle, lesquels, lesquelles* are the objects of prepositions and generally refer to things.

    E.g.: *La chaise sur laquelle je suis assis.*

        The chair on which I am sitting.

        Les cahiers dans lesquels j'ai écrit.

        The notebooks in which I wrote.

(5) *Dont* is used for persons or things and incorporates the preposition *de*.

    E.g.: *La fille dont je parle.*

        The girl of whom I am speaking.

        L'homme dont je connais le frère.

        The man whose brother I know. (Note the different position in English and in French of the noun "brother").

NOTE:

Every relative pronoun must have an antecedent. If there is no expressed antecedent, the neuter relative pronoun *ce* must be used.

E.g.: *Je ne comprends pas ce qu'il dit.*   *Je ne sais pas ce dont elle a besoin.*

     I don't understand what he is saying.   I don't know what she needs.

PRONOUNS, STRESSED
See **PRONOUNS, EMPHATIC**

PRONOUNS, SUBJECT

They are used only as the subject of the verb.

FORMS:

je, tu, il, elle, on, nous, vous, ils, elles.

PRONUNCIATION

(La prononciation) Like English, French is not a phonetic language, which is to say that many words are spelled one way but pronounced another. Although rules of pronunciation have many exceptions, the following should be kept in mind:

(1) Final consonants are silent, except *c, f, l,* and *r*.

    E.g.: *Lon[g], garço[n], beaucou[p], marchan[d], cui[t], heureu[x], che[z].*

    BUT: *Sec, vif, appel, char.*

EXCEPTIONS:

    (a) The final consonant is not pronounced in *accro[c], ban[c], blan[c], cler[c], escro[c], estoma[c], flan[c], fran[c], por[c], taba[c], tron[c].*

    (b) The final *r* is not pronounced in most words with an *-er* ending:

        E.g.: *Alle[r], dange[r], étrange[r], lége[r].*

        BUT: *Hier* and *fier* are pronounced *[ièrr]* and *[fièrr].*

    (c) The *f* is not pronounced in *cle[f]* and *che[f]-d'œuvre.*

(d) The *l* is not pronounced in *fusi[l]*, *genti[l]*, and *persi[l]*.

(e) The *s* is pronounced in *hélas, lis, mœurs,* and *plus* (when it means "more").

(2) The *-tion* ending is pronounced *-ssion.*

(3) The letter *e* followed by any two consonants is pronounced *è.*

E.g.: *Ils prennent* = *"Ils prènn."*   *Ils jettent* = *"Ils jètt."*
      Descendre = *"Déscendr."*   *Expert* = *"èxpèrr."*

There are many more exceptions, which can be learned only through exposure to the spoken language.

See **ALPHABET**

PROTÉGER

(To protect)

The *e* of the stem changes to *è* before a silent syllable at the end of the verb. Therefore, the following forms are slightly irregular:

PRÉS.: *je protège, tu protèges, il protège, (nous protégeons, vous protégez), ils protègent.*

SUBJ. PRÉS.: *que je protège, que tu protèges, qu'il protège, (que nous protégions, que vous protégiez), qu'ils protègent.*

PROXIMATE FUTURE

(Le futur proche) This corresponds to the English construction "To be going to + verb." The French equivalent construction is "*Aller* + infinitive."

E.g.: *Nous allons visiter Paris.*

   We are going to visit Paris.

PUIS

(Adverb) = "(And) then (in a succession or an enumeration)."

E.g.: *Je me suis levée, je me suis habillée, puis j'ai déjeuné.*

   I got up, got dressed, and then had breakfast.

PUISQUE

(Conjunction) = "Since, seeing that."

E.g.: *Puisque vous êtes malade, restez au lit.*

   Since you are ill, stay in bed.

PUNCTUATION

(La ponctuation) Punctuation rules are somewhat different in French than in English. French tends to use more punctuation marks.

GENERAL RULES:

(1) Clauses introduced by conjunctions other than *et, ou,* and *ni* are generally set off with commas.

E.g.: *Il est fatigué, donc il va se coucher.*

   He is tired, so he is going to bed.

(2) Clauses starting with *quand* or *si* and placed at the beginning of the sentence are set off with a comma.

E.g.: *Quand tu arriveras ici, je partirai.*

   When you arrive here, I shall leave.

   Si tu es fatigué, couche-toi.

   If you are tired, go to bed.

(3) Quotation marks are different from those used in English and are used differently. They look like this « » and are used mainly with single, isolated statements or thoughts.

E.g.: *Il a dit:* « *Allons au cinéma* ».

   He said, "Let's go to the movies."

For continuing dialogue, a dash (—) at the start of a new line is used to indicate each speaker.

E.g.: —*Allons au cinéma, dit Marie.*

   —*Non, je préfère le théâtre, répondit Jacqueline.*

   "Let's go to the movies," said Mary.

   "No, I prefer the theater," answered Jacqueline.

NOTE:

In this book American-style double quotation marks are used for the English-language portions of the text.

Note the use of inversion after the quotation: *dit-il* (he said), *demanda-t-elle* (she asked), *demanda Pierre* (Peter asked).

(4) No punctuation is used in writing dates in French.

E.g.: *le 5 janvier 1990*
       January 5, 1990

PUNCTUATION MARKS

Punctuation marks *(les signes de ponctuation)* used in French are in almost all cases identical to those used in English:

Period = *Le point* .

Comma = *La virgule* ,

Semicolon = *Le point-virgule* ;

Colon = *Les deux points* :

Question mark = *Le point d'interrogation* ?

Exclamation point = *Le point d'exclamation* !

Suspension points = *Les points de suspension* . . .

Parentheses = *Les parenthèses* ( )

Quotation marks = *Les guillemets* « »

Dash = *Le tiret* —

Hyphen = *Le trait d'union* -

Asterisk = *L'astérisque* *

Q

QUAND MÊME

(Adverbial expression) = "In spite of everything, after all, anyway."

E.g.: *Elle a trois enfants mais elle travaille quand même comme ingénieur.*
    She has three children, but she works as an engineer anyway.

QUAND, TENSES WITH

(Conjunction) = "When + indicative."

E.g.: *Elles ont vu le film quand elles étaient à Dijon.*
    They saw the movie when they were in Dijon.

REMEMBER: When the sentence is in a future context, use the future tense in the subordinate clause as well as in the main clause. (This is in contrast to English, where the present is used in the subordinate clause.)

E.g.: *Elles verront le film quand elles <u>seront</u> à Dijon.*
    They will see the film when they <u>are</u> in Dijon.

QUANT À

(Prepositional construction) = "As for, as regards."

E.g.: *Quant à moi, je resterai ici.*
    As for me, I shall stay here.

QUANTITY, EXPRESSIONS OF

(Adverbs) *Assez, beaucoup, peu, trop, un peu, tant, tellement*, etc.
They take the preposition *de* (without any article) before the noun.
E.g.: *J'ai assez d'argent.*
    I have enough money.

    Tu as beaucoup de livres.
    You have a lot of books.

    Il a tant de charme.
    He has so much charm.

QUE

(1) Relative pronoun (direct object) used for persons or things.
    E.g.: *Le garçon que je vois.*   *Les livres que tu lis.*
            The boy (whom) I see.   The books (that) you are reading.
(2) Interrogative pronoun (object) used for things.
    E.g.: *Que mangent-ils?*
            What are they eating?
(3) Conjunction used:
    (a) To introduce a subordinate clause.
        E.g.: *Je sais que tu vas partir en voyage.*
               I know that you are going to leave on a trip.
    (b) To avoid repetition of *quand, comme*, etc., in certain subordinate clauses:
        E.g.: *Si tu la vois et qu'elle est triste, console-la.*
               If you see her and she is sad, cheer her up.
    (c) To introduce a clause in the subjunctive expressing a wish, desire, resignation, etc.:
        E.g.: *Que la lumière soit!*
               Let there be light!
    (d) To introduce the second term of a comparison (= "than"):
        E.g.: *Tu es plus grand que moi.*
               You are taller than I.
(4) Adverb used before an adjective, an adverb, or a noun to express an exclamation:
    Qu'elle est intelligente!   *Que de problèmes vous avez!*
    How intelligent she is!   You have so many problems!

QUELQUE CHOSE

(Indefinite pronoun) = "Something."
E.g.: *Quelque chose est arrivé.*
    Something has happened.

    Voici quelque chose qui vous intéressera.
    Here is something that will interest you.
When followed by an adjective, *quelque chose* takes the preposition *de*.
E.g.: *Voici quelque chose d'intéressant.*
    Here's something interesting.
See **SOMETHING + ADJECTIVE**

QUELQUE CHOSE À + INFINITIVE

"Something to + verb."
E.g.: *Elle a quelque chose à dire.*
    She has something to say.

QUELQUE . . . QUE

(Indefinite expression) = "However + adjective or adverb + subjunctive."
E.g.: *Quelque compliqué que soit le problème, je trouverai la solution.*
    However difficult the problem may be, I'll find the solution.
See **SUBJUNCTIVE MOOD**

QUELQUEFOIS

(Adverb) = "Sometimes, occasionally, at times."

E.g.: *Il dort quelquefois toute la matinée.*
  Sometimes he sleeps all morning long.

See **SOMETIMES**

QUELQUES, QUELQUES-UN(E)S

(1) (Adjective) *Quelques* = "A few."

  E.g.: *Attendez quelques minutes.*
    Wait a few minutes.

(2) (Pronoun) *Quelques-un(e)s* = "A few."

  E.g.: *Des dictionnaires? J'en ai quelques-uns.*
    Dictionaries? I have a few.

  Des cassettes! J'en ai quelques-unes.
    Cassettes! I have a few.

NOTE:

When *quelques-un(e)s* is followed by a pronoun, add the preposition *d'entre:* "*Quelques-un(e)s d'entre* + pronoun."

E.g.: *Quelques-uns d'entre eux sont allés en voyage.*
  A few of them went on a trip.

  Quelques-unes d'entre elles savent chanter.
  A few of them can sing.

QUELQU'UN

(Indefinite pronoun) = "Somebody." *Quelqu'un* is always masculine singular.

E.g.: *Quelqu'un arrive.*   *Je connais quelqu'un à Paris.*
  Somebody is arriving.   I know somebody in Paris.

NOTE:

When followed by an adjective, *quelqu'un* takes the preposition *de.*

E.g.: *Quelqu'un d'autre.*   *J'ai rencontré quelqu'un d'intéressant.*
  Somebody else.   I met someone interesting.

See **SOMEBODY**

QUEL(S) QUE, QUELLE(S) QUE

(Indefinite adjectival construction) = "Whatever, whichever, whoever + subjunctive."

E.g.: *Remplissez ce formulaire, quelle que soit votre nationalité.*
  Fill out this form whatever your nationality.

See **WHATEVER** and **WHICHEVER**

QU'EST-CE QUE?

(1) Long form of the direct object interrogative pronoun. Used for things only.

  E.g.: *Qu'est-ce que tu dis?*
    What do you say?

See **PRONOUNS, INTERROGATIVE**

(2) Interrogative construction used before a noun to ask for a definition or an explanation. It means "What is . . . ?"

  E.g.: *Qu'est-ce qu'un piolet?*
    What is an ice axe?

QU'EST-CE QUE C'EST?

This interrogative construction is used in asking for an explanation or a definition = "What is . . . ?" "What is that?"

E.g.: *Un anévrisme? Qu'est-ce que c'est?*
  An aneurysm? What is that?

NOTE:
When followed by a noun or a pronoun, add *que* to form the interrogative: *Qu'est-ce-que c'est que . . . ?*
E.g.: *Qu'est-ce que c'est qu'un anévrisme?*
    What is an aneurysm?
See **PRONOUNS, INTERROGATIVE**

QU'EST-CE QUI?

Long form of the subject interrogative pronoun. Used for things only.
E.g.: *Qu'est-ce qui fait ce bruit?*
    What is making this noise?
See **PRONOUNS, INTERROGATIVE**

QUESTIONS, WORD ORDER IN

(1) In conversational style, use "*Est-ce que* + normal affirmative word order."
   E.g.: *Est-ce que tu viens?*   *Qui est-ce qui a dit cela?*
       Are you coming?   Who said that?

       Est-ce que Jean boit du café?   *Combien est-ce que ça coûte?*
       Does John drink coffee?   How much does it cost?

(2) In written or more formal style, use inversion: Place the subject after the verb (unless, of course, the interrogative word is itself the subject).
   E.g.: *Viens-tu?*   *Que font les enfants?*
       Are you coming?   What are the children doing?

       Qui a dit cela?   *Combien cela coûte-t-il?*
       Who said that?   How much does it cost?

NOTES:
(1) After the interrogatives *Pourquoi* and *Quand*, the noun subject may not come immediately after the verb. It must come before the verb, and the corresponding subject pronoun must be added after the verb.
   E.g.: *Pourquoi Pierre a-t-il dit cela?*   *Quand Pierre viendra-t-il?*
       Why did Peter say that?   When will Peter come?

(2) If the verb has a direct object, the noun subject may not come immediately after the verb. It must come before the verb, and the corresponding subject pronoun must be added after the verb.
   E.g.: *Où Robert a-t-il mis le livre?*   *Comment Marie a-t-elle fait cela?*
       Where did Robert put the book?   How did Mary do that?

QUI

(1) The relative pronoun, used:
   (a) As the subject, for persons or things.
       E.g.: *L'homme qui parle est mon père.*
         The man who is speaking is my father.

         L'avion qui arrive de Paris est en retard.
         The plane that is arriving from Paris is late.
   (b) As the object of a preposition, for persons only.
       E.g.: *La femme avec qui je parle.*
         The woman with whom I am speaking.
(2) The interrogative pronoun, used:
   (a) As the subject, for persons only.
       E.g.: *Qui parle?*
         Who is speaking?
   (b) As the direct object, for persons only.
       E.g.: *Qui aimez-vous?*
         Whom do you love?

(c) As the object of a preposition, for persons only.

E.g.: *Avec qui travailles-tu?*

With whom do you work?

QUI EST-CE QUE?

Long form of the direct object interrogative pronoun. Used for persons only.

E.g.: *Qui est-ce que vous aimez?*

Whom do you love?

See **PRONOUNS, INTERROGATIVE**

QUI EST-CE QUI?

Long form of the subject interrogative pronoun. Used for persons only.

E.g.: *Qui est-ce qui parle?*

Who is speaking?

See **PRONOUNS, INTERROGATIVE**

QUI QUE + SUBJUNCTIVE

(Relative pronoun subject with no antecedent) = "Whoever . . ."

E.g.: *Qui que vous soyez, vous devez obéir.*

Whoever you may be, you must obey.

QUICONQUE

Relative pronoun that refers to no antecedent. It means "He or she, whoever he or she may be."
It takes the third person singular and is usually the subject of the verb.

E.g.: *Quiconque veut me suivre peut m'accompagner.*

Whoever wants to follow me may accompany me.

QUITE A LOT OF

(Idiomatic expression) "*Pas mal de* + noun."

E.g.: *Ils ont pas mal de travail.*

They have quite a lot of of work.

See *PAS MAL (DE)*

QUITTER vs. LAISSER, PARTIR, S'EN ALLER, SORTIR

See *LAISSER vs. PARTIR, QUITTER, S'EN ALLER, SORTIR*

QUOI

(1) Relative pronoun with no specific antecedent. Used as the object of a preposition.

E.g.: *Je ne sais pas avec quoi il écrit.*

I don't know with what he writes.

(2) Interrogative pronoun, object of a preposition. Used for things only.

E.g.: *Avec quoi écrivez-vous?*

With what do you write?

See **PRONOUNS, INTERROGATIVE**

See also **PRONOUNS, RELATIVE**

QUOI QUE + SUBJUNCTIVE

Relative pronoun with its neuter antecedent. It means "Whatever" and takes the subjunctive.

E.g.: *Quoi que vous pensiez.*

Whatever you may think.

Do not confuse with the conjunction *Quoique*, which means "Although" and also takes the subjunctive.

See **SUBJUNCTIVE MOOD** and *QUOIQUE*

QUOIQUE

(Conjunction) "*Quoique* + subjunctive" = "Though, although, even though."
E.g.: *Il ira en France quoique sa femme soit malade.*
   He will go to France even though his wife is ill.
Do not confuse with *Quoi que.*
See **SUBJUNCTIVE MOOD** and *QUOI QUE*

R

RAISON

See *AVOIR RAISON*

to **REALIZE**

(Idiomatic construction) = "*Se rendre compte de* + noun or pronoun" OR "*Se rendre compte que* + indicative."
E.g.: *Il ne se rend pas compte du problème.*
   He doesn't realize the problem.
   Il ne se rend pas compte qu'il y a un problème.
   He doesn't realize that there is a problem.
NOTE:
When "To realize" means "To accomplish, to fulfill" translate it as *Réaliser.*
E.g.: *Elle a réalisé son rêve quand elle a visité la Grèce.*
   She realized her dream when she visited Greece.
See *SE RENDRE COMPTE DE* vs. *SE RENDRE COMPTE QUE*

to **RECALL**

See **to** *REMEMBER*

RECENT PAST

The recent past *(le passé récent)* expresses the fact that an action was recently completed: "To have just + past participle" = "*Venir de* + infinitive."
E.g.: *Nous venons d'apprendre la nouvelle.*
   We have just learned the news.
NOTE:
Since this construction describes a state of affairs or a state of being (and not an action), when it is in the past, it must always be in the imperfect.
E.g.: *Je venais d'entrer quand tu m'as vu.*   *Nous venions d'apprendre la nouvelle.*
   I had just entered when you saw me.   We had just learned the news.
See *VENIR DE* + **INFINITIVE**

RECEVOIR

(To receive)
PRÉS.: *reçois, reçois, reçoit, recevons, recevez, reçoivent.*
IMPARF.: *recev-ais, -ais, -ait, -ions, -iez, -aient.*
PASSÉ SIMPLE: *reç-us, -us, -ut, -ûmes, -ûtes, -urent.*
FUT.: *recevr-ai, -as, -a, -ons, -ez, -ont.*
CONDIT.: *recevr-ais, -ais, -ait, -ions, -iez, -aient.*
IMPÉR.: *reçois, recevons, recevez.*
SUBJ. PRÉS.: *reçoive, reçoives, reçoive, recevions, receviez, reçoivent.*
SUBJ. IMPARF.: *reç-usse, -usses, -ût, -ussions, -ussiez, -ussent.*
P. PRÉS.: *recevant.*
P. PASSÉ: *reçu(e).*

RECIPROCAL VERBS
See **VERBS, RECIPROCAL**

REFLEXIVE VERBS
See **VERBS, REFLEXIVE**

REGARDER vs. VOIR

(1) *Regarder* = "To look at, to watch." It is transitive and therefore takes a direct object.
E.g.: *Ils regardent le match de football.*
They are watching the soccer game
Elle regarde le tableau de Monet.
She is looking at the painting by Monet.
(2) *Voir* = "To see." It is also transitive.
E.g.: *Ils ont vu l'accident.*
They saw the accident.

REGULAR VERBS

FIRST CONJUGATION: **"-er"**
E.g.: *AIMER* (To love, to like)
PRÉS.: *aim-e, -es, -e, -ons, -ez, -ent.*
IMPARF.: *aim-ais, -ais, -ait, -ions, -iez, -aient.*
PASSÉ SIMPLE: *aim-ai, -as, -a, -âmes, -âtes, -èrent.*
FUT.: *aimer-ai, -as, -a, -ons, -ez, -ont.*
CONDIT.: *aimer-ais, -ais, -ait, -ions, -iez, -aient.*
IMPÉR.: *aime, aimons, aimez.*
SUBJ. PRÉS.: *aim-e, -es, -e, -ions, -iez, -ent.*
SUBJ. IMPARF.: *aim-asse, -asses, -ât, -assions, -assiez, -assent.*
P. PRÉS.: *aimant.*
P. PASSÉ: *aimé(e).*
SECOND CONJUGATION: **"-ir"**
(A) E.g.: *FINIR* (To finish)
PRÉS.: *fin-is, -is, -it, -issons, -issez, -issent.*
IMPARF.: *finiss-ais, -ais, -ait, -ions, -iez, -aient.*
PASSÉ SIMPLE: *fin-is, -is, -it, -îmes, -îtes, -irent.*
FUT.: *finir-ai, -as, -a, -ons, -ez, -ont.*
CONDIT.: *finir-ais, -ais, -ait, -ions, -iez, -aient.*
IMPÉR.: *finis, finissons, finissez.*
SUBJ. PRÉS.: *finiss-e, -es, -e, -ions, -iez, -ent.*
SUBJ. IMPARF.: *fin-isse, -isses, -ît, -issions, -issiez, -issent.*
P. PRÉS.: *finissant.*
P. PASSÉ: *fini(e).*
See **"-IR" VERBS CONJUGATED LIKE FINIR**
(B) E.g.: *SENTIR* (To feel)
PRÉS.: *sen-s, -s, -t, -tons, -tez, -tent.*
IMPARF.: *sent-ais, -ais, -ait, -ions, -iez, -aient.*
PASSÉ SIMPLE: *sent-is, -is, -it, -îmes, -îtes, -irent.*
FUT.: *sentir-ai, -as, -a, -ons, -ez, -ont.*
CONDIT.: *sentir-ais, -ais, -ait, -ions, -iez, -aient.*
IMPÉR.: *sens, sentons, sentez.*
SUBJ. PRÉS.: *sent-e, -es, -e, -ions, -iez, -ent.*
SUBJ. IMPARF.: *sent-isse, -isses, -ît, -issions, -issiez, -issent.*
P. PRÉS.: *sentant.*
P. PASSÉ: *senti(e).*

THIRD CONJUGATION: **"-re"**
E.g.: *RENDRE* (To return, to give back)
PRÉS.: *rend-s, -s, - , -ons, -ez, -ent.*
IMPARF.: *rend-ais, -ais, -ait, -ions, -iez, -aient.*
PASSÉ SIMPLE: *rend-is, -is, -it, -îmes, -îtes, -irent.*
FUT.: *rendr-ai, -as, -a, -ons, -ez, -ont.*
CONDIT.: *rendr-ais, -ais, -ait, -ions, -iez, -aient.*
SUBJ. PRÉS.: *rend-e, -es, -e, -ions, -iez, -ent.*
SUBJ. IMPARF.: *rend-isse, -isses, -ît, -issions, -issiez, -issent.*
P. PRÉS.: *rendant.*
P. PASSÉ: *rendu(e).*
FOURTH CONJUGATION: **"-oir"**
E.g.: *POURVOIR* (To provide)
PRÉS.: *pourvoi-s, -s, -t, pourvoyons, pourvoyez, pourvoient.*
IMPARF.: *pourvoy-ais, -ais, -ait, -ions, -iez, -aient.*
PASSÉ SIMPLE: *pourv-us, -us, -ut, -ûmes, -ûtes, -urent.*
FUT.: *pourvoir-ai, -as, -a, -ons, -ez, -ont.*
CONDIT.: *pourvoir-ais, -ais, -ait, -ions, -iez, -aient.*
SUBJ. PRÉS.: *pourvoi-e, -es, -e, -ions, -iez, -ent.*
P. PRÉS.: *pourvoyant.*
P. PASSÉ: *pourvu(e).*

RELATIVE PRONOUNS
See **PRONOUNS, RELATIVE**

to REMEMBER

There are two French equivalents. Note the difference in their usage.
(1) *Se rappeler* is transitive and therefore takes a direct object.
    E.g.: *Tu te rappelles ton voyage en Suisse?*
        Do you remember your trip to Switzerland?
(2) *Se souvenir de* takes the object of the preposition.
    E.g.: *Tu te souviens de ton voyage en Suisse?*
        Do you remember your trip to Switzerland?

RENDRE + ADJECTIVE

(Transitive verb) With an adjective, *Rendre* means "To make (someone or something) + adjective" in the sense of changing from one state to another.
E.g.: *Caroline me rend heureux.*   *La nourriture m'a rendu malade.*
     Caroline makes me happy.   The food made me sick.

RENDRE COMPTE
See *SE RENDRE COMPTE DE* vs. *SE RENDRE COMPTE QUE*

RENDRE VISITE À

(Idiomatic construction) = "To visit (someone)."
E.g.: *Elle a rendu visite à sa cousine à l'hôpital.*
     She visited her cousin in the hospital.
NOTE:
"To visit (a place)" = *Visiter.*
E.g.: *J'ai visité le musée du Louvre.*
     I visited the Louvre museum.

RENTRER

(To go back in, to come back in, to go home, to come home, to bring in, to take in)
(1) If *Rentrer* takes no direct object, it is intransitive (i.e., conjugated with *être*).
   E.g.: *Ils sont rentrés à minuit.*
      They came home at midnight.
(2) If *Rentrer* has a direct object, it is transitive (i.e., conjugated with *avoir*).
   E.g.: *Ils ont rentré leurs voitures au garage.*
      They brought their cars into the garage.

REPEATED ACTIONS

See **IMPERFECT TENSE**

RÉPÉTER

(To repeat)
The é of the stem changes to è before a silent syllable that comes at the end of the verb.
Therefore, the following forms are slightly irregular:
PRÉS.: *je répète, tu répètes, il répète, (nous répétons, vous répétez), ils répètent.*
SUBJ. PRÉS.: *que je répète, que tu répètes, qu'il répète, (que nous répétions, que vous répétiez), qu'ils répètent.*

REQUESTS

There are two ways to make polite requests.
(1) "*Puis-je* + infinitive."
   E.g.: *Puis-je quitter la table?*
      May I leave the table?
(2) The conditional mood of a verb such as *Aimer* or *Pouvoir*.
   E.g.: *J'aimerais vous poser une question.*   *Pourriez-vous m'aider?*
      I should like to ask you a question.   Could you help me?

to RESIST

(Verb) = *Résister.*
This verb is intransitive in French. It takes an indirect object.
E.g.: *Nous résisterons à l'ennemi.*   *Nous lui avons résisté.*
   We shall resist the ennemi.   We resisted him (her.)

RÉSOUDRE

(To resolve)
PRÉS.: *résous, résous, résout, résolv-ons, -ez, -ent.*
IMPARF.: *résolv-ais, -ais, -ait, -ions, -iez, -aient.*
PASSÉ SIMPLE: *résol-us, -us, -ut, -ûmes, -ûtes, -urent.*
FUT.: *résoudr-ai, -as, -a, -ons, -ez, -ont.*
CONDIT.: *résoudr-ais, -ais, -ait, -ions, -iez, -aient.*
IMPÉR.: *résous, résolvons, résolvez.*
SUBJ. PRÉS.: *résolv-e, -es, -e, -ions, -iez, -ent.*
SUBJ. IMPARF.: *résol-usse, -usses, -ût, -ussions, -ussiez, -ussent.*
P. PRÉS.: *résolvant.*
P. PASSÉ: *résolu(e).*

RESSENTIR

(To feel, to experience)
Conjugated like **MENTIR**
NOTE:
It does not meant "To resent." "To resent" = "*Être indigné de.*"
E.g.: *Je suis indigné de votre attitude.*
   I resent your attitude.

to REST

(Verb) = *Se reposer.*
E.g.: *Nous nous reposons chaque après-midi.*
     We rest every afternoon.
Do not confuse with *Rester.*
See **RESTER**

RESTER

(1) (Intransitive verb) = "To stay, to remain."
    E.g.: *Elles sont restées en France toute l'année.*
        They stayed in France all year long.
(2) (Impersonal verb + indirect object) = "To be left, to remain."
    E.g.: *Il nous reste cinquante francs.*
        We have fifty francs left.

RETOURNER

(To return)
(1) (Intransitive verb) = "To go back."
    E.g.: *Elle est retournée chez elle.*
        She has gone back home.
(2) (Transitive verb) = "To return (something)."
    E.g.: *Elle a retourné les livres à la bibliothèque.*
        She returned the books to the library.

RIEN

See **NE . . . RIEN**

RIEN + ADJECTIVE

It requires the preposition *de* before an adjective: "*Rien de* + adjective."
E.g.: *Il n'y a rien de nouveau.*
    There is nothing new.

RIEN + VERB

The preposition *à* must be used: "*Rien à* + infinitive."
E.g.: *Elle n'a rien à dire.*
    She has nothing to say.

RIGHT

(1) (Adjective) Meaning the opposite of "Left" = *Droit(e).*
    E.g.: *Il écrit de la main droite, mais il mange de la main gauche.*
        He writes with his right hand, but he eats with his left hand.
(2) (Adjective) Meaning the opposite of "Wrong" = *Juste, exact.*
    E.g.: *Il n'a pas trouvé la réponse juste.*
        He did not get the right answer.
(3) (Idiomatic expression) "To be right" = *Avoir raison.*
    E.g.: *Tu as raison de ne pas partir tout de suite.*
        You are right not to leave immediately.
See **AVOIR RAISON**
(4) (Noun) Meaning "Entitlement" = *Le droit.*
    E.g.: *Vous n'avez pas le droit d'entrer par cette porte.*
        You do not have the right to enter through that door.

RIGHT AWAY

(Idiomatic expression) = *Tout de suite.*
E.g.: *Je vais le faire tout de suite.*
    I'll do it right away.

RIGHT NOW

(Idiomatic expression) = *En ce moment* or *À l'instant.*
E.g.: *En ce moment mes parents sont en France.*
    Right now my parents are in France.
    Elle veut lui téléphoner à l'instant.
    She wants to call him right now.

RIGHT THEN

(Idiomatic expression) = *À ce moment-là.*
E.g.: *À ce moment-là le téléphone a sonné.*
    Right then the telephone rang.

RIRE

(To laugh)
This verb is regular but note the *ii* in the imperfect and the present subjunctive.
IMPARF.: *je riais, tu riais, il riait, nous riions, vous riiez, ils riaient.*
SUBJ. PRÉS.: *que je rie, que tu ries, qu'il rie, que nous riions, que vous riiez, qu'ils rient.*
NOTE:
Rire is followed by the preposition *de.*
E.g.: *Ne ris pas de ses fautes.*
    Don't laugh at his mistakes.

ROMPRE

(To break)
PRÉS.: *romp-s, -s, -t, -ons, -ez, -ent.*
IMPARF.: *romp-ais, -ais, -ait, -ions, -iez, -aient.*
PASSÉ SIMPLE: *romp-is, -is, -it, -îmes, -îtes, -irent.*
FUTUR.: *rompr-ai, -as, -a, -ons, -ez, -ont.*
CONDIT.: *rompr-ais, -ais, -ait, -ions, -iez, -aient.*
IMPÉR.: *romps, rompons, rompez.*
SUBJ. PRÉS.: *romp-e, -es, -e, -ions, -iez, -ent.*
SUBJ. IMPARF.: *romp-isse, -isses, -ît, -issions, -issiez, -issent.*
P. PRÉS.: *rompant.*
P. PASSÉ: *rompu(e).*

S

SANS vs. *SANS QUE*

(1) (Preposition) *Sans* = "Without."
    E.g.: *Elle est partie sans dire au revoir.*
        She left without saying goodbye.
        Il est sorti sans parapluie.
        He went out without an umbrella.

(2) (Conjunction) *Sans que* = "Without + verb."
   E.g.: *Il ira en France sans que sa femme le sache.*
      He will go to France without his wife knowing it.
If the main verb and the subordinate verb have the same subject, do not use the subjunctive. Use "*Sans* + infinitive."
   E.g.: *Il ira en France sans passer par Londres.*
      He will go to France without going via London.

SANS DOUTE

(Adverb) = "Doubtless, no doubt." When it is at the beginning of a sentence, it requires inversion.
   E.g.: *Il a sans doute raison.*
      No doubt he is right.
   BUT: *Sans doute a-t-il raison.*
      No doubt he is right.

SANS FAUTE

(Adverbial expression) = "Without fail."
   E.g.: *Je vous appellerai lundi sans faute.*
      I'll call you Monday without fail.

SANS PLUS

(Adverbial expression) = "No more."
   E.g.: *Nous leur disons bonjour, sans plus.*
      We say hello to them, no more.

S'ASSEOIR

(To sit down)
This verb has two conjugations, both of which are in common use.
PRÉS.: *m'assois, t'assois, s'assoit, nous assoyons, vous assoyez, s'assoient* OR *m'assieds, t'assieds, s'assied, nous asseyons, vous asseyez, s'asseyent.*
IMPARF.: *m'assoyais, t'assoyais, s'assoyait, nous assoyions, vous assoyiez, s'assoyaient* OR *m'asseyais, t'asseyais, s'asseyait, nous asseyions, vous asseyiez, s'asseyaient.*
PASSÉ SIMPLE: *m'assis, t'assis, s'assit, nous assîmes, vous assîtes, s'assirent.*
FUT.: *m'assoirai, t'assoiras, s'assoira, nous assoirons, vous assoirez, s'assoiront* OR *m'assiérai, t'assiéras, s'assiéra, nous assiérons, vous assiérez, s'assiéront.*
CONDIT.: *m'assoirais, t'assoirais, s'assoirait, nous assoirions, vous assoiriez, s'assoiraient* OR *m'assiérais, t'assiérais, s'assiérait, nous assiérions, vous assiériez, s'assiéraient.*
IMPÉR.: *assois-toi, assoyons-nous, assoyez-vous* OR *assieds-toi, asseyons-nous, asseyez-vous.*
SUBJ. PRÉS.: *m'assoie, t'assoies, s'assoie, nous assoyions, vous assoyiez, s'assoient* OR *m'asseye, t'asseyes, s'asseye, nous asseyions, vous asseyiez, s'asseyent.*
SUBJ. IMPARF.: *m'assisse, t'assisses, s'assît, nous assissions, vous assissiez, s'assissent.*
P. PRÉS.: *s'asseyant or s'assoyant.*
P. PASSÉ: *assis(e).*

S'ASSEOIR vs. ÊTRE ASSIS

(1) *S'asseoir* = The action of sitting.
   E.g.: *Elle entre, elle s'assied et elle commence à parler.*
      She comes in, sits down, and begins to speak.
(2) *Être assis* = The state of being seated.
   E.g.: *Elle est assise devant la télévision.*
      She is sitting (seated) in front of the TV set.

S'ATTENDRE À

(Idiomatic construction) = "To expect."
E.g.: *Je m'attendais à ton coup de téléphone.*
     I was expecting your telephone call.

SAVOIR

(To know)
PRÉS.: *sais, sais, sait, savons, savez, savent.*
IMPARF.: *sav-ais, -ais, -ait, -ions, -iez, -aient.*
PASSÉ SIMPLE: *sus, sus, sut, sûmes, sûtes, surent.*
FUT.: *saur-ai, -as, -a, -ons, -ez, -ont.*
CONDIT.: *saur-ais, -ais, -ait, -ions, -iez, -aient.*
IMPÉR.: *sache, sachons, sachez.*
SUBJ. PRÉS.: *sach-e, -es, -e, -ions, -iez, -ent.*
SUBJ. IMPARF.: *susse, susses, sût, sussions, sussiez, sussent.*
P. PRÉS.: *sachant.*
P. PASSÉ: *su(e).*
NOTES:
(1) Do not confuse *Savoir* and *Connaître.*
    Savoir means "to know a fact or something learned, to know how."
    Connaître means "To be acquainted with."
    E.g.: *Je sais conduire.*   *Il sait jouer du violon.*
         I know how to drive.   He can play the violin.
    BUT: *Elle connaît mon cousin.*
         She knows my cousin.
(2) Do not confuse *Savoir* and *pouvoir.*
    Savoir means "to have the knowledge needed for."
    Pouvoir means "To have the physical or mental ability to."
    E.g.: *Je sais conduire un voiture.*
         I can (know how to) drive a car.
    BUT: *Je ne peux pas conduire, car je n'ai pas mes lunettes.*
         I can't drive because I don't have my glasses.

SE DÉBROUILLER

(Idiomatic expression) = "to manage, to sort out, to come out of a difficulty."
E.g.: *Je me débrouillerai pour quitter le bureau à trois heures.*
     I'll find a way to leave the office at three o'clock.

SE DEMANDER

(Reflexive verb with idiomatic meaning) = "To wonder."
E.g.: *Je me demande quand elle arrivera.*
     I wonder when she will arrive.

SE FAIRE À

(Idiomatic construction) = "To get used to."
E.g.: *Elle ne peut pas se faire au climat.*
     She cannot get used to the climate.
See **USED TO (meaning ACCUSTOMED TO)**

SE PASSER vs. SE PASSER DE

(Reflexive verbs)
(1) *Se passer* = "To take place, to happen."
    E.g.: *L'histoire se passe à Paris en 1932.*
        The story takes place in Paris in 1932.

        Qu'est-ce qui se passe?
        What's happening? (What's going on?)
(2) "*Se passer de* + object of preposition" = "To do without, to dispense with."
    E.g.: *En Amérique on ne peut pas se passer d'automobile.*
        In America you can't do without a car.
See **to DO WITHOUT**

SE PRÉPARER vs. PRÉPARER

(1) *Se préparer* = "To prepare (oneself) for."
    E.g.: *Nous nous préparons pour la course de bicyclette.*
        We are preparing (ourselves) for the bicycle race.
(2) *Préparer* = "To prepare (something)."
    E.g.: *J'ai préparé la chambre pour les invités.*
        I prepared the room for the guests.
See **to PREPARE vs. PREPARE FOR vs. PREPARE TO**

SE PROMENER

(Reflective verb) = "To go for a walk, to take a walk."
Conjugated like **MENER**

SE RAPPELER

(Reflexive verb) = "To remember." This verb is transitive and therefore takes a direct object.
E.g.: *Il se rappelle très bien Mlle Delacre.*
     He remembers Miss Delacre very well.

SE RENDRE

(Reflexive verb) It has two different meanings:
(1) "To go."
    E.g.: *Il s'est rendu à Bordeaux en auto.*
        He went to Bordeaux by car.
(2) "To surrender."
     E.g.: *Tout le régiment s'est rendu aux forces ennemies.*
        The whole regiment surrendered to the enemy forces.
NOTE:
The noun *Un rendez-vous* ("A date, an appointment") comes from this verb, of which it is the second person plural imperative form.

SE RENDRE COMPTE DE vs. SE RENDRE COMPTE QUE

(Idiomatic expression)
(1) "*Se rendre compte de* + noun or pronoun" = "To realize."
    E.g.: *Ils se rendent compte de la difficulté.*
        They realize the difficulty.
(2) "*Se rendre compte que* + indicative" = "To realize that."
    E.g.: *Ils se rendent compte que c'est difficile.*
        They realize that it is difficult.
See **to REALIZE**

SE SENTIR

(Reflexive verb) = "To feel (in a certain state of health)."
E.g.: *Je me sens malade.*
    I feel sick.

SE SERVIR DE

(Idiomatic expression) = "to use, to make use of."
E.g.: *Je me sers d'une fourchette pour manger.*
    I use a fork to eat.

SE SOUVENIR DE

(Reflexive verb) = "To remember" (conjugated with *être*).
Conjugated like **TENIR**
E.g.: *Elle ne se souvient pas de moi.*
    She does not remember me.

SE TAIRE

(To be silent, to keep quiet)
PRÉS.: *me tais, te tais, se tait, nous taisons, vous taisez, se taisent.*
IMPARF.: *me tais-ais, -ais, -ait, -ions, -iez, -aient.*
PASSÉ SIMPLE: *me tus, tus, tut, tûmes, tûtes, turent.*
FUT.: *me tair-ai, -as, -a, -ons, -ez, -ont.*
CONDIT.: *me tair-ais, -ais, -ait, -ions, -iez, -aient.*
IMPÉR.: *tais-toi, taisons-nous, taisez-vous.*
SUBJ. PRÉS.: *me tais-e, -es, -e, -ions, -iez, -ent.*
SUBJ. IMPARF.: *me tusse, tusses, tût, tussions, tussiez, tussent.*
P. PRÉS.: *taisant.*
P. PASSÉ.: *tu(e).*

SE VÊTIR

(To get dressed)
PRÉS.: *me vêts, te vêts, se vêt, nous vêtons, vous vêtez, se vêtent.*
IMPARF.: *me vêt-ais, -ais, -ait, -ions, -iez, -aient.*
PASSÉ SIMPLE: *me vêt-is, -is, -it, -îmes, -îtes, -irent.*
FUT.: *me vêtir-ai, -as, -a, -ons, -ez, -ont.*
CONDIT.: *me vêtir-ais, -ais, -ait, -ions, -iez, -aient.*
IMPÉR.: *vêts-toi, vêtons-nous, vêtez-vous.*
SUBJ. PRÉS.: *me vêt-e, -es, -e, -ions, -iez, -ent.*
SUBJ. IMPARF.: *me vêt-isse, -isses, -ît, -issions, -issiez, -issent.*
P. PRÉS.: *vêtant.*
P. PASSÉ: *vêtu(e).*

SEASONS, PREPOSITIONS WITH
See **PREPOSITIONS + SEASONS**

SEE YOU SOON

(Idiomatic expression) = *À bientôt.*

to SEEM + ADJECTIVE

"*Avoir l'air* + adjective."
E.g.: *Elles ont l'air fatiguées.*
    They seem tired.

NOTE:
The adjective may agree with the subject or with *L'air*; that is, it may remain in the masculine singular: *Elles ont l'air fatigué.*
See **AVOIR L'AIR (DE)**

to SEEM TO + VERB

"*Avoir l'air de* + infinitive."
E.g.: *Vous avez l'air de comprendre.*
     You seem to understand.
See **AVOIR L'AIR (DE)**

SELF

(Reflexive pronoun) "Myself, yourself, etc."
FORMS:
moi-même, toi-même, lui-même, elle-même, nous-mêmes, vous-mêmes, eux-mêmes, elles-mêmes; soi-même (used only with *celui qui, chacun, on, quiconque,* and *tout le monde*).
USAGE:
These forms are used for emphasis only. They are not needed in the normal construction of reflexive verbs.
E.g.: *Je me suis coupé les cheveux.*
     I cut my hair.
BUT for emphasis:
     Je me suis coupé les cheveux moi-même.
     I cut my hair myself.

     On doit se servir soi-même dans ce magasin.
     You have to help yourself in this store.
See **SOI vs. LUI or ELLE**

SELON

(Preposition) = "According to."
E.g.: *L'évangile selon saint Mathieu.*
     The Gospel according to St. Matthew.

     Selon lui, il n'y aura pas de révolution.
     According to him, there will be no revolution.

SEMBLANT

See **FAIRE SEMBLANT DE**

SEMER

(To sow, to scatter)
The e of the stem changes to è before a silent syllable. Therefore, the following forms are slightly irregular:
PRÉS.: *je sème, tu sèmes, il sèmes, (nous semons, vous semez), ils sèment.*
FUT.: *je sèmerai, tu sèmeras, il sèmera, nous sèmerons, vous sèmerez, ils sèmeront.*
CONDIT.: *je sèmerais, tu sèmerais, il sèmerait, nous sèmerions, vous sèmeriez, ils sèmeraient.*
SUBJ. PRÉS.: *que je sème, que tu sèmes, qu'il sème (que nous semions, que vous semiez), qu'ils sèment.*

S'EN ALLER vs. LAISSER, PARTIR, QUITTER, SORTIR

See **LAISSER vs. PARTIR, QUITTER, S'EN ALLER, SORTIR**

S'EN FAIRE

(Idiomatic construction) = "To worry."
E.g.: *Ne vous en faites pas.*
    Don't worry.

to SEND FOR

(Idiomatic expression) = *Faire venir*
E.g.: *Nous avons fait venir un spécialiste.*
    We sent for a specialist.

S'ENFUIR

(To flee)
PRÉS.: *m'enfuis, t'enfuis, s'enfuit, nous enfuyons, vous enfuyez, s'enfuient.*
IMPARF.: *m'enfuy-ais, -ais, -ait, -ions, -iez, -aient.*
PASSÉ SIMPLE: *m'enf-uis, -uis, -uit, -uîmes, -uîtes, -uirent.*
FUT.: *m'enfuir-ai, -as, -a, -ons, -ez, -ont.*
CONDIT.: *m'enfuir-ais, -ais, -ait, -ions, -iez, -aient.*
IMPÉR.: *enfuis-toi, enfuyons-nous, enfuyez-vous.*
SUBJ. PRÉS.: *m'enfuie, t'enfuies, s'enfuie, nous enfuyions, vous enfuyiez, s'enfuient.*
SUBJ. IMPARF.: *m'enfu-isse, -isses, -ît, -issions, -issiez, -issent.*
P. PRÉS.: *s'enfuyant.*
P. PASSé: *enfui(e).*

SENTIR

(To smell, to feel)
PRÉS.: *sens, sens, sent, sentons, sentez, sentent.*
IMPARF.: *sent-ais, -ais, -ait, -ions, -iez, -aient.*
PASSÉ SIMPLE: *sent-is, -is, -it, -îmes, -îtes, -irent.*
FUT.: *sentir-ai, -as, -a, -ons, -ez, -ont.*
CONDIT.: *sentir-ais, -ais, -ait, -ions, -iez, -aient.*
IMPÉR.: *sens, sentons, sentez.*
SUBJ. PRÉS.: *sent-e, -es, -e, -ions, -iez, -ent.*
SUBJ. IMPARF.: *sent-isse, -isses, -ît, -issions, -issiez, -issent.*
P. PRÉS.: *sentant.*
P. PASSÉ: *senti(e).*
See **SE SENTIR**

SERVIR

(To serve)
PRÉS.: *sers, sers, sert, servons, servez, servent.*
IMPARF.: *serv-ais, -ais, -ait, -ions, -iez, -aient.*
PASSÉ SIMPLE: *serv-is, -is, -it, -îmes, -îtes, -irent.*
FUT.: *servir-ai, -as, -a, -ons, -ez, -ont.*
CONDIT.: *servir-ais, -ais, -ait, -ions, -iez, -aient.*
IMPÉR.: *sers, servons, servez.*
SUBJ. PRÉS.: *serv-e, -es, -e, -ions, -iez, -ent.*
SUBJ. IMPARF.: *serv-isse, -isses, -ît, -issions, -issiez, -issent.*
P. PRÉS.: *servant.*
P. PASSÉ: *servi(e).*
See **SERVIR À; SERVIR DE;** and **SE SERVIR DE**

SERVIR À

(Idiomatic construction) = "To be useful for, to be used for."
E.g.: *Cet outil sert à réparer les pneus crevés.*
    This tool is used for repairing punctured tires.

SERVIR DE

(Idiomatic construction) = "To be used as."
E.g.: *Cette pièce nous sert de chambre d'amis.*
    This room is used as a guest room.

SEVERAL

(Indefinite adjective) = *Plusieurs.* It has the same form in the masculine and the feminine.
E.g.: *Ils ont plusieurs amis.*
    They have several friends.

SHALL and WILL

"Shall" and "will" are used to form the future in English. The corresponding construction in French is simply the future tense.
E.g.: *J'irai chez moi.*   *Ils arriveront.*
    I shall go home.   They will arrive.
NOTE:
If "Shall" and "Will" are used to express determination or intention, use "*Vouloir* + infinitive."
E.g.: *Il ne veut pas obéir.*
    He simply *will* not obey.

SHOULD

See *DEVOIR*

SHOULD (meaning IF)

This English construction corresponds to the French "*Si* + present indicative."
E.g.: Should you see them, tell them to call us.
    Si vous les voyez, dites-leur de nous téléphoner.

SI

(1) (Conjunction) = "If."
See *SI* CLAUSES.
Si also means "Whether" to introduce certain subordinate clauses.
E.g.: *Je ne sais pas s'il viendra ou non.*
    I don't know whether he will come or not.
NOTE:
Si contracts to *s'* only before *il* and *ils.*
(2) (Adverb) = "So, so much."
    E.g.: *Elle est si douée.*
        She is so gifted.
(3) (Adverb) An affirmation in response to a negative question.
    E.g.: *Vous n'avez pas faim? Si, au contraire, j'ai très faim.*
        Aren't you hungry? Yes, on the contrary, I am very hungry.

SI BIEN QUE

(Conjunctional construction) = "Consequently; with the result that."
E.g.: *Elle a gagné beaucoup d'argent, si bien qu'elle ne doit plus travailler.*
    She earned a lot of money, so she doesn't have to work anymore.

SI CE N'EST

(Idiomatic expression) = "Except."
E.g.: *Je ne l'ai jamais rencontrée, si ce n'est en passant.*
I've never met her, except in passing.

SI CLAUSES

A clause introduced by *Si* expresses a supposition. That clause, the subordinate clause, describes the condition, and the main clause describes the result of this condition.
There are three kinds of *si* clauses: possible, contrary to fact in the present, and contrary to fact in the past.
(1) THE SUPPOSITION IS POSSIBLE:

Condition Clause	Result Clause
Si + present indicative	(a) present indicative
	(b) future
	(c) imperative

E.g.: (a) *S'il fait froid, je reste chez moi.*
If it's cold, I stay home.
(b) *S'il fait froid, je resterai chez moi.*
If it's cold, I shall stay home.
(c) *S'il fait froid, restez chez vous!*
If it's cold, stay home!

(2) THE SUPPOSITION IS CONTRARY TO FACT IN THE PRESENT:

Condition Clause	Result Clause
Si + imperfect	Present conditional

E.g.: *S'il faisait froid, je resterais chez moi.*
If it were cold, I would stay home.

(3) THE SUPPOSITION IS CONTRARY TO FACT IN THE PAST:

Condition Clause	Result Clause
Si + pluperfect	Past conditional

E.g.: *S'il avait fait froid, je serais restée chez moi.*
If it had been cold, I would have stayed home.

NOTE: "*Si* + imperfect" can also be used to express a suggestion:
E.g.: *Si tu venais avec nous!*
Why don't you come with use?
See **SUGGESTING**

SI OUI and SINON

(Idiomatic constructions) = "If so" and "If not."
E.g.: *Êtes-vous Français? Si oui, vous n'avez pas besoin de visa. Sinon, allez au bureau numéro quinze.*
Are you French? If so, you don't need a visa. If not, go to office number fifteen.

SILENT "E"

The final *e* of many French words is not pronounced in normal speech.
E.g.: *Une belle femme* is pronounced as only three syllables.
Note, however, that within a word, an unaccented *e* followed by two consonants is usually pronounced *è*.
E.g.: *celle* ["*selle*"]; *domestique* ["*domèstique*"]; *raquette* ["*raquètte*"].

SINCE

(1) (Conjunction) Meaning "Because" = *Puisque* or *Comme.*
> E.g.: *Puisque vous ne parlez pas français, n'allez pas en France.*
> *Comme vous ne parlez pas français, n'allez pas en France.*
> Since you don't speak French, don't go to France.

(2) (Conjunction) "Since + time expression" = *Depuis que.*
> E.g.: *Il pleut depuis que nous sommes arrivés.*
> It's been raining since we arrived.

(3) (Preposition) = *Depuis.*
> E.g.: *Elle est ici depuis midi.*
> She has been here since noon.

See **DEPUIS + TIME EXPRESSION**

SINGULAR

"Singular" *(le singulier)* expresses that there is only one. For example, "book" is singular (as opposed to "books," which is plural).
See **PLURAL**

S'INQUIÉTER

(Reflexive verb) = "To worry."
> E.g.: *Ne vous inquiétez pas, il n'y a pas de danger.*
> Don't worry, there is no danger.

"To worry" meaning "to cause worry to someone else" = *Inquiéter.*
> E.g.: *La situation politique inquiète le président.*
> The political situation worries the president.

S'INTÉRESSER À

(Reflexive construction) = "To be interested in."
> E.g.: *Il s'intéresse à l'histoire ancienne.*
> He is interested in ancient history.

SIZES AND MEASUREMENTS

(1) *La longueur* = The length
La largeur = The width
La hauteur = The height
La profondeur = The depth
> E.g.: *Quelle est la hauteur de la tour Eiffel?*
> What is the height of the Eiffel Tower?
>
> *Elle a 300 mètres de hauteur (de haut).*
> It is 300 meters in height (high).
>
> *La salle a 5 mètres de longueur (de long).*
> The room is 5 meters in length (long).

(2) Measurements (of clothing, etc.) = *"La taille."*
> E.g.: *Quelle est votre taille?*
> What is your size?
>
> *Combien faites-vous? Je fais du 38.*
> What's your size? Size 38.

(3) Height, weight (of persons) = *"La taille, le poids."*

E.g.: *Quelle est votre taille?*

What is your height? (How tall are you?)

Je mesure 1 mètre 80 centimètres. (Je fais 1 mètre 80.)

I'm 1 meter 80 (centimeters) tall.

Combien pesez-vous?

How much do you weight?

Je pèse 65 kilos.

I weigh 65 kilograms.

See **METRIC SYSTEM**

SO + ADJECTIVE or ADVERB

"Si + adjective or adverb."

E.g.: *Il est si intelligent!*   *Elle parle si vite!*

He is so intelligent?   She speaks so fast!

See ***TANT; TELLEMENT;*** and **SO MANY or SO MUCH + NOUN**

SO MANY or SO MUCH + NOUN

(1) (Adverb) = *Tant, tellement.*

E.g.: *Elles parlent tant (tellement).*

They talk so much.

(2) (Expression of quantity) = *"Tant de* + noun" or *"Tellement de* + noun."

E.g.: *J'ai tant de travail!*   *Elle a tellement d'amis!*

I have so much work!   She has so many friends!

SO THAT

(Conjunctional construction)

(1) Expressing intention = *"Pour que* + subjunctive" or *"Afin que* + subjunctive" or *"De sorte que* + subjunctive."

E.g.: *Ils travaillent pour que leurs enfants soient heureux.*

They work so that their children might be happy.

See **SUBJUNCTIVE MOOD**

(2) Expressing consequence: *"Si bien que* + indicative."

E.g.: *Elle a beaucoup voyagé, si bien qu'elle est très bien informée.*

She has traveled a lot, so she is well informed.

S'OCCUPER DE

(Reflexive verb) It has two different meanings:

(1) "To take care of."

E.g.: *La mère s'occupe de son bébé toute la journée.*

The mother takes care of her baby all day long.

(2) "To deal with."

E.g.: *Je m'occuperai de votre demande demain matin.*

I'll deal with your request tomorrow morning.

SOI vs. LUI or ELLE

(Personal pronouns, third person)

(1) *Soi* (oneself) refers to an indefinite subject, such as *chacun, celui qui, on, tout le monde,* or *quiconque.*

E.g.: *Chacun pour soi.*

Each one for himself.

On ne voyait pas devant soi à cause du brouillard.

You couldn't see in front of you because of the fog.

(2) *Lui* or *elle* refers to a definite subject.

    E.g.: *Jacques a vu le loup devant lui.*

        James saw the wolf in front of him.

        Marguerite a emmené Jacques avec elle.

        Margaret took James (along) with her.

See **SELF**

SOIF

See **AVOIR SOIF**

SOIR vs. SOIRÉE

Both words mean "Evening."

(1) *Le soir* generally indicates the moment in time.

    E.g.: *Un cours du soir.*   *Le soir tombe vite.*

        An evening class.   Night falls rapidly.

(2) *La soirée* generally stresses the duration of time.

    E.g.: *Il passe la soirée à regarder la télévision.*

        He spends the evening watching television.

(3) *La soirée* also means an evening performance or reception.

    E.g.: *La pièce se joue en matinée à 15 heures et en soirée à 20 heures.*

        There is a matinee performance of the play at 3:00 P.M. and an evening performance at 8:00 P.M.

SOIT . . . SOIT

(Conjunction) = "Either . . . or."

It expresses an idea of choice between two nouns, pronouns, adjectives, or adverbs.

    E.g.: *Prenez soit le trait soit l'avion.*

        Take either the train or the plane.

        Faites le soit demain soit après-demain.

        Do it either tomorrow or the day after tomorrow.

See **EITHER . . . OR**

SOME

(Adjective) = *Du, de l', de la, des.*

See **ARTICLES, PARTITIVE**

SOMEONE + ADJECTIVE

"*Quelqu'un de* + adjective." The adjective is always in the masculine singular form

E.g.: *Quelqu'un de nouveau.*

    Somebody new.

See **QUELQU'UN**

SOMEONE (WHO, WHOM, WHOSE)

(Relative pronoun and its antecedent) = *Quelqu'un (qui, que, dont).*

E.g.: *Quelqu'un qui ne sait pas conduire.*

    Someone who can't drive.

    Quelqu'un que je ne connais pas.

    Someone whom I don't know.

SOMETHING + ADJECTIVE

"*Quelque chose de* + adjective." The adjective is always in the masculine singular form.

E.g.: *Quelque chose d'intéressant.*

    Something interesting.

See **QUELQUE CHOSE**

SOMETIMES

(Adverb) = *Quelquefois* or *Parfois* or *De temps en temps.*
E.g.: *Quelquefois je me lève tôt.*
    Sometimes I get up early.

   Parfois je me lève tôt.
    Sometimes I get up early.

   De temps en temps, je me lève tôt.
    From time to time I get up early.
See **QUELQUEFOIS**

SOMEWHERE

(Adverb) = *Quelque part.*
E.g.: *Elle est allée quelque part en Afrique.*
    She went somewhere in Africa.
See **QUELQUE PART**

SOMEWHERE ELSE

(Adverb) = *Ailleurs.*
E.g.: *Ne restez pas ici; allez ailleurs.*
    Don't stay here; go somewhere else.

SORTIR

(To go out, to come out, to take out.)
PRÉS.: *sor-s, -s, -t, -tons, -tez, -tent.*
IMPARF.: *sort-ais, -ais, -ait, -ions, -iez, -aient.*
PASSÉ SIMPLE: *sort-is, -is, -it, -îmes, -îtes, -irent.*
FUT.: *sortir-ai, -as, -a, -ons, -ez, -ont.*
IMPÉR.: *sors, sortons, sortez.*
CONDIT.: *sortir-ais, -ais, -ait, -ions, -iez, -aient.*
SUBJ. PRÉS.: *sort-e, -es, -e, -ions, -iez, -ent.*
SUBJ. IMPARF.: *sort-isse, -isses, -ît, -issions, -issiez, -issent.*
P. PRÉS.: *sortant.*
P. PASSÉ: *sorti(e)*
NOTE:
This verb can be intransitive or transitive.
(1) If it has no direct object, it is conjugated with *Être.*
    E.g.: *Nous sommes sortis hier soir.*
        We went out last night.
(2) If it has a direct object, it is conjugated with *Avoir.*
    E.g.: *Nous avons sorti nos vêtements d'hiver.*
        We took out our winter clothes.

SORTIR vs. *LAISSER, PARTIR, QUITTER, S'EN ALLER*
See **LAISSER** vs. **PARTIR, QUITTER, S'EN ALLER, SORTIR**

SOUFFRIR

(To suffer)

PRÉS.: *souffr-e, -es, -e, -ons, -ez, -ent.*

IMPARF.: *souffr-ais, -ais, -ait, -ions, -iez, -aient.*

PASSÉ SIMPLE: *souffr-is, -is, -it, -îmes, -îtes, -irent.*

FUT.: *souffrir-ai, -as, -a, -ons, -ez, -ont.*

CONDIT.: *souffrir-ais, -ais, -ait, -ions, -iez, -aient.*

IMPÉR.: *souffre, souffrons, souffrez.*

SUBJ. PRÉS.: *souffr-e, -es, -e, -ions, -iez, -ent.*

SUBJ. IMPARF.: *souffr-isse, -isses, -ît, -issions, -issiez, -issent.*

P. PRÉS.: *souffrant.*

P. PASSÉ: *souffert(e).*

SPELLING CHANGES IN VERBS

See **CONJUGATION OF "-CER" VERBS; CONJUGATION OF "-ELER" VERBS; CONJUGATION OF "-ETER" VERBS; CONJUGATION OF "-GER" VERBS; CONJUGATION OF VERBS WITH "É" IN THE LAST SYLLABLE OF THE STEM; CONJUGATION OF "-YER" VERBS**

to SPEND

(1) "To spend money" = *Dépenser.*

    E.g.: *Nous avons dépensé tout notre argent.*

        We have spent all our money.

(2) "To spend time" = *Passer.*

    E.g.: *Nous avons passé trois semaines à Paris.*

        We spent three weeks in Paris.

NOTE:

"To spend time + present participle" = "*Passer son temps à* + infinitive."

E.g.: *Ils passent leur temps à regarder la télévision.*

    They spend their time watching television.

SPITE (IN SPITE OF)

See **DESPITE**

STEM

The stem *(la racine)* is the part of a word that expresses its core of meaning. It does not change or undergoes only minor changes. To the stem are added prefixes, suffixes, and endings.

E.g.: *Facile* - ment   *En* - *tour* - age   *Malad* - if
    (stem) (suffix)   (prefix) (stem) (suffix)   (stem) (suffix)

    Chant - er   *Fin* - issions   *Arriv* - aient
    (stem) (ending)   (stem) (ending)   (stem) (ending)

STILL

(1) (Adverb) Meaning "Up to this time" = *Encore* or *Toujours.*

    E.g.: *Elle est encore (toujours) en Europe.*

        She is still in Europe.

(2) (Adverb) Meaning "Nevertheless, nonetheless" = *Quand même.*

    E.g.: *Ça coûte terriblement cher, mais je vais quand même l'acheter.*

        It's terribly expensive, but still, I'm going to buy it.

See **QUAND MÊME**

(3) (Adjective) Meaning "Motionless" = *Immobile* or *Tranquille* or *Sans bouger.*

E.g.: *Restez tranquille!*

    Sit still!

STRESSED PRONOUNS
See **PRONOUNS, EMPHATIC**

SUBJECT

The subject *(le sujet)* is the word or group of words about which the verb expresses an action or a state.
E.g.: *Les livres sont sur la table.*
   The books are on the table.

SUBJECT PRONOUNS
See **PRONOUNS, SUBJECT**

SUBJUNCTIVE, AVOIDING THE

(1) If the subject is the same in the main clause and the relative clause, use the infinitive in the subordinate clause.
   E.g.: *Je suis contente d'être ici.*
      I am glad to be here.
(2) Verbs of command, permission, or refusal generally take "*à* + indirect object + *de* + infinitive."
   E.g.: *Il refuse à son fils de prendre la voiture.*
      He refuses his son permission to take the car.
See **SUBJUNCTIVE MOOD**
See also **VERBS + PREPOSITION + INFINITIVE**

SUBJUNCTIVE MOOD

The subjunctive *(le subjonctif)* presents the action of the verb as contingent or dependent on some emotion (desire, wish, will power, doubt, etc.). It is also used in a number of other situations, as explained under "Usage."
E.g.: *Je veux que cet homme fasse le travail.*
   (I want that this man do the work)
   = I want this man to do the work.
   Il faut que cet homme fasse le travail.
   It is necessary that this man do the work.
   Je doute que cet homme fasse le travail.
   I doubt that this man does the work.
TENSES:
There are four tenses in the subjunctive mood:
(1) The *PRÉSENT:*
FORMATION:
Replace the *-ent* of the third person plural of the present indicative by *-e, -es, -e, -ions, -iez, -ent.*
E.g.: *Il faut que je finisse.*
   It is necessary that I finish (I absolutely must finish.)
This tense is used also to indicate a future action that must be expressed in the subjunctive. (There is no future tense in the subjunctive.)
E.g.: *Il faut qu'elle vienne demain.*
   She must come tomorrow.
(2) The *IMPARFAIT* (used only in the literary style):
FORMATION:
Use the stem of the *passé simple* and change the endings as follows:

PASSÉ SIMPLE ENDINGS	→ IMPERFECT SUBJUNCTIVE ENDINGS
-ai, -as, -a, -âmes, -âtes, -èrent	→ *-asse, -asses, -ât, -assions, -assiez, -assent*
-is, -is, -it, -îmes, -îtes, -irent	→ *-isse, -isses, -ît, -issions, -issiez, -issent*
-us, -us, -ut, -ûmes, -ûtes, -urent	→ *-usse, -usses, -ût, -ussions, -ussiez, -ussent*

E.g.: *Il fallait qu'il vînt.*
   It was necessary that he come.

(3) The *PASSÉ:*
FORMATION:
Present subjunctive of the auxiliary verb + past participle.
E.g.: *Elle est contente que tu sois venu.*
      She is glad that you have come.
(4) The *PLUS-QUE-PARFAIT* (used only in the literary style);
FORMATION:
Imperfect subjunctive of the auxiliary verb + past participle.
E.g.: *Elle était contente qu'il fût arrivé.*
      She was glad that he had arrived.

NOTE:
The subjunctive mood is most often encountered in a subordinate clause introduced by *que*. But this does not mean that *que* is always followed by a subjunctive. It is incorrect to think, "This takes the subjunctive because there is a *que*"! The reason for the presence of the subjunctive will always be that the clause is contingent on an emotion (desire, wish, willpower, doubt, etc.) or a specific construction that requires the subjunctive (see "Usage").

USAGE:
The subjunctive mood is used in a subordinate clause in the following instances:
(1) When the main verb expresses an emotion (sorrow, joy, fear, surprise, anger, etc.).

    SOME COMMON EXPRESSIONS OF EMOTION THAT REQUIRE THE SUBJUNCTIVE:
    Avoir crainte, avoir peur
    Craindre, regretter
    Être bouleversé, choqué, content, désolé, enchanté, étonné, fâché, furieux, heureux,
    malheureux, mécontent, ravi, stupéfait, surpris, triste
    Se fâcher, se réjouir
    E.g.: *Je regrette que tu sois malade.*   *Nous craignons qu'ils fassent une erreur.*
        I am sorry that you are sick.   We fear that they might make a mistake.

        Il est content que vous ayez raison.   *Elle est étonnée que tu saches cela.*
        He is glad that you are right.   She is surprised that you know that.
(2) When the main verb expresses desire, will, or a wish.

    SOME COMMON EXPRESSIONS OF DESIRE, WILL, OR WISH THAT REQUIRE THE
    SUBJUNCTIVE:
    Aimer bien, commander, consentir, défendre, demander, désirer, empêcher, exiger, interdire,
    ordonner, permettre, préférer, souhaiter, vouloir
    E.g.:   *Nous voulons qu'elle vienne.*   *Elle défend qu'on soit en retard.*
          We want her to come.   She forbids us to be late.
(3) When the main verb is an impersonal expression of necessity, uncertainty, or possibility.

    SOME COMMON IMPERSONAL EXPRESSIONS OF EMOTION, NECESSITY,
      UNCERTAINTY, OR POSSIBILITY THAT REQUIRE THE SUBJUNCTIVE:

Il est bon que	*Il est possible que*
Il est désirable que	*Il est préférable que*
Il est (c'est) dommage que	*Il est regrettable que*
Il est important que	*Il est temps que*
Il est impossible que	*Il est urgent que*
Il est indispensable que	*Il est utile que*
Il est juste que	*Il faut que*
Il est nécessaire que	*Il se peut que*
Il est peu probable que	*Il vaut mieux que*

        E.g.: *Il faut que vous disiez la vérité.*
            You must speak the truth.

           Il est peu probable qu'elle puisse venir.
           It is unlikely that she might be able to come.

           Il est possible que vous ayez le temps.
           It is possible that you might have time.

(4) When the main clause contains a superlative or an expression having superlative value.

E.g.: *C'est le meilleur médecin que je connaisse.*

He is the best doctor (that) I know.

Il n'y a personne qui puisse nous aider.

There is nobody who can help us.

Voici le premier homme qui soit capable de faire cela.

Here is the first man who is able to do that.

(5) When the subordinate clause is introduced by certain conjunctions, namely:

(a) *à condition que* = Provided that
(b) *afin que* = So that
(c) *à moins que* = Unless
(d) *avant que* = Before
(e) *bien que* = Although
(f) *de crainte que* = For fear that, lest
(g) *de peur que* = For fear that, lest
(h) *de sorte que* = So that
(i) *en attendant que* = While waiting for
(j) *jusqu'à ce que* = Until
(k) *malgré que* = Although, despite the fact that
(l) *pour que* = So that
(m) *pourvu que* = Provided that
(n) *quoique* = Although
(o) *sans que* = Without

E.g.: (a) *J'irai à condition qu'il fasse beau.*

I shall go provided that it is nice (weather).

(b) *Il se lèvera afin que nous puissions partir tôt.*

He will get up so that we might leave early.

(c) *Je partirai à moins qu'il fasse mauvais.*

I shall leave unless it is bad weather.

(d) *Elle arrivera avant qu'il fasse nuit.*

She will arrive before it is dark.

(e) *Nous resterons bien qu'il fasse mauvais.*

We shall stay though the weather is bad.

(f) *Elle est partie de crainte qu'on ne la voie.*

She left for fear that someone might see her.

(g) *Elle est partie de peur qu'on ne la voie.*

She left for fear that someone might see her.

(h) *Vous partirez de sorte qu'il ne vous voie pas.*

You will leave so that he doesn't see you.

(i) *On restera ici en attendant qu'il vienne.*

We shall stay here while waiting for him to come.

(j) *Nous resterons ici jusqu'à ce qu'il vienne.*

We shall stay here until he comes.

(k) *Il est parti malgré que vous l'attendiez.*

He left despite the fact that you were waiting for him.

(l) *Elles sont venues pour que nous leur parlions.*

They came so that we might speak to them.

(m) *Je t'accompagnerai pourvu que je sois libre.*

I'll accompany you, provided that I am free.

(n) *Elles viennent quoique leur mère leur défende de sortir.*

They are coming even though their mother forbids them to go out.

(o) *Nous partons sans qu'on puisse nous voir.*

We leave without anyone being able to see us.

(6) When the main clause contains a relative pronoun whose antecedent is indefinite or uncertain.

E.g.: *Connaissez-vous quelqu'un qui sache le chinois?*
Do you know someone who knows Chinese?

Je cherche un livre qui puisse m'intéresser.
I'm looking for a book that might interest me.

(7) When the main clause contains certain indefinite relative pronouns, namely:

(a) *Qui que* = Whoever
(b) *Quoi que* = Whatever
(c) *Quel (quelle, quels, quelles) que* = Whatever
(d) *Quelque . . . que* = However . . .

E.g.: (a) *Qui que vous soyez, entrez.*
Whoever you may be, come in.

(b) *Quoi que vous fassiez, ce sera bien.*
Whatever you do, it will be fine.

(c) *Quels que soient vos motifs, ils sont bons.*
Whatever your motives might be, they are good.

(d) *Quelque difficile que cela soit, faites-le.*
However difficult it may be, do it.

NOTE:

If the two clauses have the same subject, use the infinitive.

E.g.: NOT: *Il va en France pour qu'il voie ses parents.*
BUT: *Il va en France pour voir ses parents.*
He goes to France to see his parents.

AGREEMENT OF TENSES IN THE SUBJUNCTIVE:

(1) NORMAL CONVERSATIONAL USAGE:

(a) If the action in the subjunctive takes place at the same time as or in the future in relation to the main verb, use the present subjunctive.

E.g.: *Il est triste qu'elle soit malade.*
He is sad that she is sick.

Je veux que tu viennes demain.
I want you to come tomorrow.

(b) If the action in the subjunctive took place before that of the main verb, use the past subjunctive.

E.g.: *Je regrette qu'elle ait eu un accident.*
I am sorry that she had an accident.

Bien qu'elle ait perdu son billet, on lui a permis d'entrer.
Although she had lost her ticket, they let her in.

(2) LITERARY USAGE:

The main verb will normally be in a past tense (e.g.: *imparfait, passé simple*) or the conditional.

(a) If the action of the subjunctive took place at the same time as the main verb, use the imperfect subjunctive.

E.g.: *Elle craignait qu'il fût malade.*
She feared that he was sick.

Ils sortirent sans qu'on leur donnât la permission.
They went out without anyone having given them permission.

(b) If the action of the subjunctive took place before that of the main verb, use the pluperfect subjunctive.

E.g.: *Elle craignait qu'il se fût cassé la jambe.*
She was afraid that he had broken his leg.

Ils partirent bien qu'on leur eût donné l'ordre de rester.
They left even though they had been ordered to stay.

SUBJUNCTIVE vs. INDICATIVE
See **INDICATIVE vs. SUBJUNCTIVE**
See also **SUBJUNCTIVE MOOD**

SUBJUNCTIVE vs. INFINITIVE

(1) When the subject of the subordinate clause is different from the subject of the main clause, use the subjunctive in the subordinate clause.

E.g.: *Je ne veux pas que tu ailles là-bas.*

I don't want you to go there.

(2) When the subject of the subordinate clause is the same as the subject of the main clause, use the infinitive in the subordinate clause.

E.g.: *J'irai en France à condition de ne pas y aller seul.*

I shall go to France provided that I not go alone.

NOTE:

In this case, the conjunction will be replaced by the corresponding preposition.

CONJUNCTION + SUBJUNCTIVE	PREPOSITION + INFINITIVE
À condition que	→ *À condition de*
À moins que	→ *À moins de*
Afin que	→ *Afin de*
Avant que	→ *Avant de*
De crainte que	→ *De crainte de*
De peur que	→ *De peur de*
En attendant que	→ *En attendant de*
Pour que	→ *Pour*
Sans que	→ *Sans*

NOTE:

The conjunctions *bien que, de sorte que, jusqu'à ce que*, and *malgré que* have no corresponding preposition that can be used with an infinitive.

SUBORDINATE CLAUSE

The subordinate clause *(la proposition subordonnée)* is dependent on another clause, called the main clause *(la proposition principale)*.

E.g.: *Il a dit que le président était ici.*

He said that the president was here.

to SUCCEED

(1) Meaning "To be successful" = *Réussir.*

E.g.: *J'ai réussi à obtenir un emploi.*

I succeeded in obtaining a job.

(2) Meaning "To follow" = "*Succéder à* + indirect object."

E.g.: *Louis XIV a succédé à Louis XIII.*

Louis XIV succeeded Louis XIII.

SUCH

(Adjective) = *Tel, telle, tels, telles.*

E.g.: *Je n'ai jamais vu une telle catastrophe.*

I have never seen such a catastrophe.

NOTE:

In the singular, the indefinite article must be used before *Tel*. In the plural, *de* (not *des*) must be used.

E.g.: *Ils ont fait de telles recettes à Noël.*

They did such good business at Christmastime.

See **TEL(S), TELLE(S)**

SUCH AS

Tel que, telle que, tels que, telles que.

E.g.: *On enseigne des langues telles que l'anglais, le français, etc.*

They teach such languages as English and French.

See **TEL(S) QUE, TELLE(S) QUE**

SUFFIRE

(To suffice)

PRÉS.: *suff-is, -is, -it, -isons, -isez, -isent.*

IMPARF.: *suffis-ais, -ais, -ait, -ions, -iez, -aient.*

PASSÉ SIMPLE: *suff-is, -is, -it, -îmes, -îtes, -irent.*

FUT.: *suffir-ai, -as, -a, -ons, -ez, -ont.*

CONDIT.: *suffir-ais, -ais, -ait, -ions, -iez, -aient.*

IMPÉR.: *suffis, suffisons, suffisez.*

SUBJ. PRÉS.: *suffis-e, -es, -e, -ions, -iez, -ent.*

SUBJ. IMPARF.: *suff-isse, -isses, -ît, -issions, -issiez, -issent.*

P. PRÉS.: *suffisant.*

P. PASSÉ: *suffi(e).*

SUGGESTING

To offer a suggestion, use one of the following expressions.

(1) "*Proposer de* + noun or infinitive," or "*Proposer que* + subjunctive."

E.g.: *Il propose de nous rendre visite la semaine prochaine.*

He suggests that he might visit us next week.

Il propose que nous allions chez lui.

He suggests that we go to his house.

(2) "*Suggérer* + noun," "*Suggérer de* + infinitive," or "*Suggérer que* + subjunctive."

E.g.: *Je suggère une promenade dans le parc.*

I suggest a walk in the park.

Il a suggéré d'aller au théâtre.

He suggested going to the theater.

Je suggère que vous achetiez un billet de loterie.

I suggest that you buy a lottery ticket.

(3) *Devoir* in the conditional mood.

E.g.: *Tu devrais aller te coucher.*

You ought to go to bed.

See **DEVOIR**

to SUIT (meaning to FIT)

(Verb) = "*Aller à* + indirect object."

E.g.: *Cette robe va très bien à Caroline.*

This dress suits Caroline very well.

Ces chaussures ne lui vont pas du tout.

These shoes don't fit him (her) at all.

SUIVRE

(To follow)
PRÉS.: *suis, suis, suit, suivons, suivez, suivent.*
IMPARF.: *suiv-ais, -ais, -ait, -ions, -iez, -aient.*
PASSÉ SIMPLE: *suiv-is, -is, -it, -îmes, -îtes, -irent.*
FUT.: *suivr-ai, -as, -a, -ons, -ez, -ont.*
CONDIT.: *suivr-ais, -ais, -ait, -ions, -iez, -aient.*
IMPÉR.: *suis, suivons, suivez.*
SUBJ. PRÉS.: *suiv-e, -es, -e, -ions, -iez, -ent.*
SUBJ. IMPARF.: *suiv-isse, -isses, -ît, -issions, -issiez, -issent.*
P. PRÉS.: *suivant.*
P. PASSÉ.: *suivi(e).*

SUPERLATIVE + IN

The preposition *de* must be used for the complement of the superlative expression. (Do not use *dans*.)
E.g.: *Le meilleur élève de la classe.*
The best student in the class.

SUPERLATIVE + SUBJUNCTIVE

See **SUBJUNCTIVE MOOD**

SUPERLATIVE OF ADJECTIVES

See **ADJECTIVES, SUPERLATIVE OF**

SUPERLATIVE OF ADVERBS

See **ADVERBS, COMPARATIVE AND SUPERLATIVE OF**

SUPPOSED TO (meaning OUGHT)

(Idiomatic construction) = "*Être censé* + infinitive."
E.g.: *Elle est censée me téléphoner cet après-midi.*
She is supposed to call me this afternoon.
See also **DEVOIR**

SYLLABICATION

A syllable *(une syllabe)* is a sound or group of sounds forming a unit of the spoken language. For example, in English the word "figure" consists of two sounds or syllables:
fig - ure
(Most dictionaries indicate the division of words into syllables.)
The rules for division into syllables in French are not always the same as in English. The French word *figure*, for example, consists of three syllables:
fi - gu - re
In French, syllables tend to end on a vowel rather than a consonant, as is often the case in English.
Knowing how to divide words into syllables is important for the correct splitting of words at the end of a line.
BASIC RULES OF SYLLABICATION:
(1) Do not split one-syllable words.
(2) Make the division between consonants, but never separate *bl, br, ch, cl, cr, dr, gl, gr, pl, pr, th, tr,* or *vr.*

(3) If there are double consonants, split between the consonants. Here are a few examples of how words should be split in French:

Ad - mi - nis - tra - tion   Man - gi - ons
Char - la - tan   Nè - gre
Fré - quem - ment   Par - fois
In - té - res - sant   Ré - gner
Lo - cu - tion   Vien - drai

T

-T-

When the subject pronouns *il, ils, elle,* or *elles* come after the verb and the verb ends with a silent *e* or an *a,* it is necessary to add *-t-* between the verb and the subject. This is to make the pronunciation easier and clearer.

E.g.: *Alla-t-il à Paris?*   *Que demande-t-il?*
      Did he go to Paris?   What is he asking?

to TAKE

(1) Meaning "To pick up, to remove" = *Prendre.*
    E.g.: *Elle a pris le livre qui était sur la table.*
          She took the book that was on the table.
(2) Meaning "To take food" = *Prendre.*
    E.g.: *Nous prendrons le déjeuner à une heure.*
          We'll have lunch at one o'clock.
(3) Meaning "To tolerate" = *Accepter.*
    E.g.: *Il n'acceptera pas un refus.*
          He won't take no for an answer.
(4) Meaning "To lead (a person)" = *Emmener.*
    E.g.: *Il m'a emmenée au cinéma.*
          He took me to the movies.
(5) Meaning "To take along" = *Emporter.*
    E.g.: *Elle n'a pas emporté son parapluie.*
          She didn't take her umbrella.
(6) Meaning "To take a course, a class" = *Suivre.*
    E.g.: *J'ai suivi un cours de dactylographie.*
          I took a typing course.
(7) Meaning "To take an examination" = *Se présenter à.*
    E.g.: *Elle s'est présentée au baccalauréat.*
          She took the high school graduation examination.

to TAKE PLACE

See *AVOIR LIEU*

to TALK TO vs. to TALK ABOUT

(1) "To talk to" = "*Parler à* + indirect object."
    E.g.: *Nous parlons à̲ Marie.*   *Nous lui parlons.*
          We are speaking to Mary.   We are speaking to her (him).

(2) "To talk about" = "*Parler de* + object of the preposition."
    E.g.: *Elle parle de Jacques.*
           She is talking about James.

           Elle parle de lui.
           She is talking about him.

           Elle en parle.
           She is talking about it.
See **PARLER**

TANDIS QUE

(Conjunctional construction) = "While, whereas."
(1) Indicating simultaneity of two actions.
    E.g.: *Tandis que je lisais, elle écrivait des lettres.*
           While I was reading, she was writing letters.
(2) Indicating opposition or contrast between two actions or situations.
    E.g.: *L'air de la campagne est pur, tandis que l'air des villes est pollué.*
           Country air is pure, whereas city air is polluted.
See **WHILE + VERB (-ING)**

TANT

Adverb) = "As much, as many, so much, so many."
E.g.: *Il n'a pas tant de travail que moi.*   *Elle a tant d'amis!*
       He doesn't have as much work as I.   She has so many friends!

TANT BIEN QUE MAL

(Idiomatic expression) = "After a fashion, so-so."
E.g.: *J'ai réussi à réparer le moteur, tant bien que mal.*
       I managed to fix the motor, after a fashion.

TANT QU'À FAIRE

(Idiomatic expression) = "Might as well."
E.g.: *Tant qu'à faire, emportons aussi une radio.*
       We might as well take along a radio.

TANT QUE

(Conjunctional construction) = "As long as."
E.g.: *Tant qu'il y aura des hommes, il y aura des guerres.*
       As long as there are men, there will be wars.
Note that both verbs are in the same tense.

TEINDRE

(To dye)
PRÉS.: *teins, teins, teint, teign-ons, -ez, -ent.*
IMPARF.: *teign-ais, -ais, -ait, -ions, -iez, -aient.*
PASSÉ SIMPLE: *teign-is, -is, -it, -îmes, -îtes, -irent.*
FUT.: *teindr-ai, -as, -a, -ons, -ez, -ont.*
CONDIT.: *teindr-ais, -ais, -ait, -ions, -iez, -aient.*
IMPÉR.: *teins, teignons, teignez.*
SUBJ. PRÉS.: *teign-e, -es, -e, -ions, -iez, -ent.*
SUBJ. IMPARF.: *teign-isse, -isses, -ît, -issions, -issiez, -issent.*
P. PRÉS.: *teignant.*
P. PASSÉ: *teint(e).*

TELLEMENT

(Adverb) = "So, so much, so many."

E.g.: *Elles étaient tellement contentes qu'elles nous ont téléphoné tout de suite.*
They were so happy that they called us right away.

Il y avait tellement de gens que je n'ai pas pu pas entrer.
There were so many people that I was not able to go in.

See **TANT** and **SI**

TEL(S), TELLE(S)

(Adjective) = "Such."

E.g.: *Une telle paresse est impardonnable.*
Such laziness is unforgivable.

See **TEL(S) QUEL(S), TELLE(S), QUELLE(S)**

TEL(S) QUE, TELLE(S) QUE

(Idiomatic construction) = "Such as." It is used to introduce examples illustrating a previous statement.

E.g.: *Certaines pièces de Molière, telles que « l'Avare » et « le Misanthrope » sont bien connues du public américain.*
Some of Moliere's plays, such as *The Miser* and *The Misanthrope*, are well known to the American public.

See **SUCH AS**

TEL(S) QUEL(S), TELLE(S) QUELLE(S)

(Idiomatic construction) = "As is, as it stands."

E.g.: *La maison est à vendre telle quelle.*
The house is for sale as is.

TEMPERATURE

(1) When talking about the climate, the weather = *La température.*

E.g.: *La température moyenne en été est de trente degrés (Celsius).*
The average temperature in the summer is eight-six degrees (Fahrenheit).

(2) When talking about a medical condition = *La fièvre.*

E.g.: *L'enfant a de la fièvre.*
The child is running a temperature.

NOTE:

In France, as in most parts of the world, the Celsius temperature scale is used. The conversion formulas are:

$C = 5/9 (F - 32)$

$F = 9/5 (C + 32)$

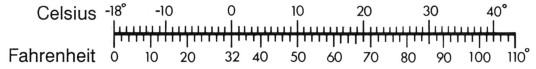

TEMPS vs. HEURE

(1) *Le temps* = "Time" or "Weather," depending on the context.

E.g.: *Il a passé beaucoup de temps sur ce livre.*
He spent a lot of time on this book.

Il fait mauvais temps.
The weather is bad.

(2) *L'heure* = "Time, o'clock."
    E.g.: *Quelle heure est-il? Il est cinq heures.*
        What time is it? It is five o'clock.
See **TIME EXPRESSIONS**

TENIR

(To hold)
PRÉS.: *tiens, tiens, tient, tenons, tenez, tiennent.*
IMPARF.: *ten-ais, -ais, -ait, -ions, -iez, -aient.*
PASSÉ SIMPLE: *tins, tins, tint, tînmes, tîntes, tinrent.*
FUT.: *tiendr-ai, -as, -a, -ons, -ez, -ont.*
CONDIT.: *tiendr-ais, -ais, -ait, -ions, -iez, -aient.*
IMPÉR.: *tiens, tenons, tenez.*
SUBJ. PRÉS.: *tienne, tiennes, tienne, tenions, teniez, tiennent.*
SUBJ. IMPARF.: *tinsse, tinsses, tînt, tinssions, tinssiez, tinssent.*
P. PRÉS.: *tenant.*
P. PASSÉ: *tenu(e).*

TENIR À vs. TENIR À CE QUE

(Idiomatic constructions)
(1) "*Tenir à* + infinitive" = "To be eager to + infinitive."
    E.g.: *Je tiens beaucoup à vous voir demain.*
        I am very eager to see you tomorrow.
(2) "*Tenir à ce que* + subjunctive" = "To be eager for (someone) to + infinitive."
    E.g.: *Elle tient à ce que tu ailles avec elle.*
        She is eager for you to go with her.
See **SUBJUNCTIVE MOOD**

TENSE

The tense *(le temps)* of a verb indicates at what moment the action takes place. This can be the present, the past, the future, the future in a past context, the past in a past context, etc.
See **IMPERFECT TENSE, FUTURE PERFECT, FUTURE TENSE, *PASSÉ ANTÉRIEUR*, *PASSÉ COMPOSÉ*, *PASSÉ SIMPLE*, *PASSÉ SURCOMPOSÉ*, *PLUS-QUE-PARFAIT*, PRESENT TENSE**

TENSES, AGREEMENT OF

See ***APRÈS* vs. *APRÈS QUE*; *DÈS QUE*, TENSES WITH; *LORSQUE*; PAST PARTICIPLES, AGREEMENT OF; *QUAND*, TENSES WITH; *SI* CLAUSES;** and **SUBJUNCTIVE MOOD**

THANKING

"Thank you" = *Merci.*
"To thank" =
(1) "*Remercier (qqn) pour* + noun."
    E.g.: *Je vous remercie pour ce beau cadeau.*
        (I) thank you for this beautiful gift.
(2) "*Remercier (qqn) de* + infinitive."
    E.g.: *Je vous remercie de m'avoir aidé.*
        (I) thank you for helping me.

THANKS TO

(Prepositional construction) = "*Grâce à* + noun or pronoun."
E.g.: *Grâce à cette invention on peut faire des photos en couleurs.*
    Thanks to this invention, people can take color photographs.

THAT

(1) (Demonstrative adjective) = *Ce, cet, cette, ces.*
See **ADJECTIVES, DEMONSTRATIVE**
(2) (Demonstrative pronoun) = *Cela, ça, ce.*
See **PRONOUNS, DEMONSTRATIVE**
(3) "That one" = *Celui-là, celle-là.*
See **PRONOUNS, DEMONSTRATIVE**
(4) Before a relative pronoun = *Celui, celle ceux, celles.*
See **PRONOUNS, DEMONSTRATIVE** and **THE ONE(S)**
(5) (Relative pronoun) = *Qui, que.*
See **PRONOUNS, RELATIVE**
(6) (Conjunction) = *Que.*
See **CONJUNCTIONS**

THE LESS . . . , THE LESS

(Idiomatic construction) = *Moins . . . moins.*
E.g.: *Moins tu étudies, moins tu comprends.*
   The less you study, the less you understand.
See ***MOINS . . . MOINS***

THE MORE . . . , THE MORE

(Idiomatic construction) = *Plus . . . plus.*
E.g.: *Plus on travaille, plus on gagne.*
   The more you work, the more you earn.
See ***PLUS . . . PLUS***

THE ONE(S)

"Demonstrative pronoun + relative pronoun."
E.g.: *Celui que j'aime coûte dix francs.*
   The one (that) I like costs ten francs.
REMEMBER that the demonstrative pronoun ("the one," "the ones," "that," "those") must agree in number and gender with the noun it replaces.
NOTE:
The relative pronoun ("that") may be omitted in English but must be expressed in French. It will change according to its function in the relative clause.
E.g.: *Ceux dont j'ai besoin coûtent dix francs.*
   Those (that) I need cost ten francs. (Referring to a masculine plural antecedent, e.g., *les livres.*)
   Celle dont j'ai besoin coûte dix francs.
   The one (that) I need costs ten francs. (Referring to a feminine singular antecedent, e.g., *la boîte.*)
See **PRONOUNS, DEMONSTRATIVE**

THEN

(Adverb)
(1) Meaning "At that time" = *Alors, à cette époque, à ce moment(-là).*
   E.g.: *Nous habitions Paris alors.*
      We lived in Paris then.
      À cette époque nous habitions Paris.
      At that time we lived in Paris.
      À ce moment-là nous habitions Paris.
      At that time we lived in Paris.

(2) Meaning "next, afterward" = *Ensuite* or *Puis.*
> E.g.: *Elle est allée en Suisse et ensuite (puis) elle a visité l'Allemagne.*
> She went to Switzerland and then visited Germany.

(3) Meaning "Therefore, consequently" = *Alors.*
> E.g.: *Tu veux faire le tour du monde? Alors, mets de l'argent de côté.*
> You want to go around the world? Then save some money.

THERE

(Adverb) = *Là, y.*
E.g.: *Nous serons bientôt là.*   *Nous y serons bientôt.*
     We shall soon be there.   We shall soon be there.

NOTE:
Y goes before the verb, wheras *là* goes after it.
See **Y**

THERE IS, THERE ARE

See **IL Y A**

to THINK ABOUT, to THINK OF

See **PENSER À vs. PENSER DE**

THIRSTY

See **AVOIR SOIF**

THIS

See **CE, CET, CETTE, CES**

THOSE (WHO, WHOM, WHICH)

See **THE ONE(S)**

TIME EXPRESSIONS

(1) "O'CLOCK:"
   (a) "It is . . ." = *Il est . . .*
      > E.g.: *Il est trois heures.*
      > It is three o'clock.
   (b) "Quarter past" = *. . . et quart.*
      > E.g.: *Il est dix heures et quart.*
      > It is a quarter past ten.
   (c) "Quarter of (to)" = *Moins le quart.*
      > E.g.: *Il est sept heures moins le quart.*
      > It is a quarter of (to) ten.
   (d) "Half past" = *. . . et demie.*
      > E.g.: *Il est cinq heures et demie.*
      > It is half past five.
   (e) "Noon" = *Midi.*
   (f) "Midnight" = *Minuit.*
   (g) "A.M." = *Du matin.*
      > E.g.: *Il est six heures et quart du matin.*
      > It is six fifteen A.M.
   (h) "P.M." = *De l'après-midi* or *Du soir.*
      > E.g.: *Il est quatre heures de l'après-midi.*
      > It is four P.M.
      >
      > *Il est sept heures du soir.*
      > It is seven P.M.

NOTES:
(1) *Demi* is the masculine after *Midi* and *Minuit.*
> E.g.: *Il est midi et demi.*   *Il est minuit et demi.*
>   It is half past noon.   It is half past midnight.

(2) The 24-hour clock is used for all official schedules and timetables.

E.g.: *Le train partira à 19h 43 (dix-neuf heures quarante-trois).*

The train will depart at 7:43 P.M.

The abbreviation for *heure* is "*h*," with no period.

(3) CALENDAR EXPRESSIONS:

"Today" = *Aujourd'hui.*

"Tomorrow" = *Demain.*

"Day after tomorrow" = *Après-demain.*

"Yesterday" = *Hier.*

"Day before yesterday" = *Avant-hier.*

"The following (next) day" = *Le lendemain.*

"Day before" = *La veille.*

"A week" = *Huit jours.*

"A week from today" = *(D')aujourd'hui en huit* or *Dans huit jours.*

"A week ago" = *Il y a huit jours.*

"Two weeks (a fortnight)" = *Quinze jours.*

"Two weeks from today" = *(D')aujourd'hui en quinze* or *Dans quinze jours.*

"In about two weeks" = *Dans une quinzaine (de jours).*

"Two weeks ago" = *Il y a quinze jours.*

"A year from now" = *D'ici un an* or *Dans un an.*

NOTES:

(1) *Dans* indicates a moment.

E.g.: *Je lirai le livre en une semaine.*

I shall read the book a week from now.

(2) *En* indicates duration.

E.g.: *Je lirai le livre en une semaine.*

I shall read the book in (over a span of) one week.

(3) "Time when" expressions take the relative pronoun *où* (rather than *quand*, as might be expected).

E.g.: *Le jour <u>où</u> il a eu son accident.*   *L'année <u>où</u> il est né.*

The day (when) he has his accident.   The year (when) he was born.

TIRED

(Idiomatic construction)

(1) Meaning "Physically tired" = *Être fatigué.*

E.g.: *Il est fatigué parce qu'il a couru 10 km.*

He is tired because he ran 10 km.

(2) Meaning "Sleepy" = *Avoir sommeil.*

E.g.: *J'ai sommeil parce qu'il est déjà minuit.*

I'm tired (sleepy) because it's already midnight.

TITLES, ARTICLES WITH PERSONAL

(1) When talking about someone, the definite article is used before a title.

E.g.: *Le docteur Lagrange est célèbre.*

Doctor Lagrange is famous.

(2) When addressing the person, no article is used. Note that you do not address people by their names in French.

E.g.: *Bonjour, docteur.*

Hello, Doctor Lagrange.

Likewise when writing letters, use only the title but no names.

E.g.: *(Cher) Monsieur,*   *(Chère) Madame,*   *Monsieur le Professeur,*

Dear Sir,   Dear Madam,   Dear Professor (name),

(Cher or *Chère* is used only if the addressee is a friend or is very well known to the writer.)

See **LETTER WRITING**

TO

(Preposition)
(1) Meaning "As far as, all the way to, up to" = *Jusqu'à.*
    E.g.: *Elle sait compter jusqu'à cent.*
        She can count up to a hundred.
See **JUSQUE, JUSQU'À**
(2) (Meaning "in order to" = *Pour.*
See **POUR**

TOMBER AMOUREUX (DE)

(Idiomatic expression) = "To fall in love (with)."
E.g.: *Elle est tombée amoureuse d'un homme beaucoup plus âgé qu'elle.*
    She has fallen in love with a man much older than herself.
See **ÊTRE AMOUREUX (DE)**

TOO + ADJECTIVE + TO + VERB

See **TROP + ADJECTIVE + POUR + INFINITIVE**

TOO MANY (MUCH) + NOUN

(Adverb of quantity) = "*Trop de* + plural noun."
E.g.: *Il a trop de choses à faire.*   *Il me donne trop de travail.*
    He has too many things to do.   He gives me too much work.
See **TROP DE + NOUN**

TORT

See **AVOIR TORT**

TOUJOURS

(Adverb)
(1) "Always."
    E.g.: *Il pense qu'il a toujours raison.*
        He thinks he is always right.
(2) "Still."
    E.g.: *Ils sont toujours à Paris.*
        They are still in Paris.

TOUR À TOUR

(Idiomatic expression) = "By turns, in turn."
E.g.: *Ils ont pompé tour à tour toute la nuit.*
    They took turns manning the pumps all night.

TOUS (TOUTES) LES + TIME EXPRESSION

(Idiomatic construction) = "Every . . ."
E.g.: *Ils vont en France tous les ans.*
    They go to France every year.

    Cela se passe toutes les dix minutes.
    It happens every ten minutes.

    Ils viennent tous les deux ans.
    They come every two years.

TOUT, TOUTE, TOUS, TOUTES

(1) (Adjectives) = "All, all the, the whole (of the)."

E.g.: *Tout le temps.*   *Tous les enfants.*
      All the time.   All the children.

      Tout le livre.   *Toutes les femmes.*
      The whole book.   All the women.

NOTE:

Tout and *Toute* can also mean "Each, every."

E.g.: *Tout homme est mortel.*
      Every man is mortal.

(2) (Pronouns) = "Everything, all, every one of them."

E.g.: *Elle a tout fait.*   *Ils sont tous arrivés.*
      She did everything.   All of them arrived.

(3) (Adverbs) = "Very much, completely, quite."

E.g.: *Ils sont tout étonnés.*
      They are completely surprised.

NOTES:

(1) Though an adverb, *Tout* changes to *Toute* before a feminine adjective.

E.g.: *Il est tout nu.*   *Elle est toute nue.*
      He is stark naked.   She is stark naked.

(2) *Tout* can be placed before "*en* + present participle" to add strength to the gerund expression.

E.g.: *Ils étudient tout en regardant la télévision.*
      They are studying, watching television all the while.

TOUT À COUP

(Adverbial expression) = "Suddenly, all of a sudden."

E.g.: *Tout à coup il s'est mis à pleurer.*
      All of a sudden he started to cry.

TOUT À FAIT

(Adverbial expression of intensity) = "Completely, quite."

E.g.: *Tu as tout à fait raté l'examen.*
      You completely failed the examination.

TOUT À L'HEURE

(Idiomatic expression) = "Later, in a little while" or "A little while ago."

E.g.: *Il reviendra tout à l'heure.*   *Ils sont partis tout à l'heure.*
      He will return in a little while.   They left a little while ago.

TOUT AU PLUS

(Idiomatic expression) = "At (the) most."

E.g.: *Nous serons absents tout au plus pendant une semaine.*
      We'll be absent for a week at the most.

TOUT DE MÊME

(Adverbial expression) = "All the same, anyway."

E.g.: *J'étais en retard mais je suis tout de même allé en classe.*
      I was late but I went to class all the same.

TOUT LE MONDE

(Idiomatic expression) = "Everybody."
E.g.: *Tout le monde est d'accord.*
    Everybody is in agreement.
NOTE:
This expression is singular.
See **MONDE**

TOWARD

(Preposition)
(1) Meaning "In the direction of" = *Vers.*
    E.g.: *Ils sont allés vers Lyon.*
        They went toward Lyon.
(2) Expressing feeling, emotion, attitude = *Envers.*
    E.g.: *Il a été cruel envers elle.*
        He was cruel toward her.
See **ENVERS** and **VERS**

TRADUIRE

(To translate)
Conjugated like **CONDUIRE**

TRAIT D'UNION

Le trait d'union ("hyphen") is used:
(1) In many compound nouns, pronouns, and adjectives:
    E.g.: *Les États-Unis, la Grande-Bretagne, grand-père, sourd-muet, moi-même, quelques-uns, extrême-oriental.*
(2) In numerals, between the tens and the units when *et* is not used.
    E.g.: *Trente-six, soixante-douze, dix-neuf.*
(3) Between the verb and the inverted subject or object pronouns:
    E.g.: *Dit-elle, Donnez-la moi.*
(4) To join *ci* and *là* to the words they qualify.
    E.g.: *Ces livres-ci, cette femme-là.*

TRANSITIVE VERBS
See **VERBS, TRANSITIVE**

TRANSPORTATION, MEANS OF

Prepositions with means of transportation:
(1) *En* if one travels inside the conveyance.
    E.g.: *On voyage en avion, en autobus, en bateau, en train, en voiture.*
        One travels by plane, by bus, by ship, by train, by car.
(2) *Dans le (la)* when referring to the conveyance.
    E.g.: *J'ai laissé ma valise dans le train.*
        I left my suitcase on the train.
(3) *À* if one travels on the conveyance.
    E.g.: *On voyage à cheval, à motocyclette, à pied, à vélo.*
        One travels on horseback, on a motorcycle, on foot, by bicycle.
NOTE:
Par avion = "By air mail."
See **to DRIVE TO; to FLY TO;** and **to WALK TO**

TRAVAILLER

(To work)
This verb is regular, but note the *lli* in the imperfect indicative and the imperfect subjunctive:
IMPARF.: *(je travaillais, tu travaillais, il travaillait), nous travaillions, vous travailliez, (ils travaillaient.)*
SUBJ. PRÉS.: *(que je travaille, que tu travailles, qu'il travaille), que nous travaillions, que vous travailliez, qu'ils travaillent.*

TRÉMA

Le tréma ("diaeresis") is a mark (¨) placed over a vowel to indicate that it is pronounced separately from the preceding vowel.
E.g.: *Naïf* is pronounced *"na-if,"* not *"nèf."*
Haïr is pronounced *"a-ir,"* not *"èrr."*

TRESSAILLIR

(To shudder, to be thrilled)
PRÉS.: *tressaill-e, -es, -e, -ons, -ez, -ent.*
IMPARF.: *tressaill-ais, -ais, -ait, -ions, -iez, -aient.*
PASSÉ SIMPLE: *tressaill-is, -is, -it, -îmes, -îtes, -irent.*
FUT.: *tressailler-ai, -as, -a, -ons, -ez, -ont.*
CONDIT.: *tressailler-ais, -ais, -ait, -ions, -iez, -aient.*
IMPÉR.: *tressaille, tressaillons, tressaillez.*
SUBJ. PRÉS.: *tressaill-e, -es, -e, -ions, -iez, -ent.*
SUBJ. IMPARF.: *tressaill-isse, -isses, -ît, -issions, -issiez, -issent.*
P. PRÉS.: *tressaillant.*
P. PASSÉ: *tressailli(e).*

TROP

(Adverb) = "Too, too much."
E.g.: *C'est trop grand.*   *Il boit trop.*
     It's too big.   He drinks too much.

TROP + ADJECTIVE + POUR + INFINITIVE

"Too + adjective + infinitive" requires the preposition *Pour.*
E.g.: *Elle est trop jeune pour aller avec nous.*
     She is too young to go with us.

TROP DE + NOUN

(Adverbial expression of quantity) = "Too much, too many."
E.g.: *Nous avons trop de travail.*   *Vous avez emporté trop de valises.*
     We have too much work.   You took too many suitcases with you.

TU vs. VOUS

Both *Tu* and *Vous* can be used to address one person.
(1) *Tu* is informal and is used when speaking to people one's own age and members of one's family.
     E.g.: *Salut, Marguerite! Comment vas-tu?*
        Hello, Margaret! How are you?
(2) *Vous* is formal and is used when speaking to people who are older or who hold a higher status and when speaking to a person one does not know.
     E.g.: *Bonjour, monsieur le professeur! Comment allez-vous?*
        Good morning, professor! How are you?

U

UN PEU

(Adverbial expression) = "A little bit, slightly."
E.g.: *Il lit un peu chaque jour.*   *C'est un peu abîmé.*
He reads a little bit each day.   It is slightly damaged.

UN PEU DE + NOUN

(Adverbial expression of quantity) = "A little, a bit of."
E.g.: *Donnez-moi un peu de vin.*
Give me a little wine.

UNCERTAINTY

The concept of uncertainty is conveyed by "*Douter que* + subjunctive," "*Ne pas être sûr que* + subjunctive," or "*Ne pas être certain que* + subjunctive."
E.g.: *Je ne suis pas sûr qu'elle sache la nouvelle.*
I am not sure that she knows the news.
See **DOUBT**
See also **SUBJUNCTIVE MOOD**

UNLESS

(Conjunction) = "*À moins que* + subjunctive."
E.g.: *Nous sortirons à moins qu'il ne pleuve.*
We shall go out unless it rains.
See *À MOINS DE* vs. *À MOINS QUE*
See also **SUBJUNCTIVE MOOD**

UNTIL vs. NOT UNTIL

(1) "Until:"
  (a) "*Jusqu'à* + noun."
    E.g.: *Nous resterons ici jusqu'à demain.*
    We shall stay here until tomorrow.
  (b) "*Jusqu'à ce que* + subjunctive."
    E.g.: *Nous resterons ici jusqu'à ce qu'il vienne.*
    We shall stay here until he arrives.
(2) "Not until:" When the main verb is in the negative, do not use *Jusqu'à.* Instead use one of the these three constructions:
  (a) "*Avant que* + subjunctive."
    E.g.: *Il ne partira pas avant que sa femme (ne) revienne.*
    He will not leave until his wife returns.
  (b) "*Ne . . . que* + indicative."
    E.g.: *Il n'est parti qu'après le déjeuner.*
    He didn't leave until after lunch.
  (c) "*À moins que* + subjunctive."
    E.g.: *Il ne le fera pas à moins que vous (ne) l'aidiez.*
    He won't do it until (= unless) you help him.

UPON + VERB (-ING)

(Idiomatic construction) = "*En* + present participle."
E.g.: *En entrant, elle a dit bonjour.*
     Upon entering, she said hello.
See **GERUND**

UPSIDE DOWN

(Idiomatic expression) = *À l'envers.*
E.g.: *Tu tiens le livre à l'envers.*
     You are holding the book upside down.

to USE

(Transitive verb) = *Utiliser* or *Employer.*
E.g.: *Elle utilise un crayon pour écrire.*
     She uses a pencil to write.
Do not confuse with *User*, which means "To wear out."
E.g.: *Son pantalon est usé.*
     His trousers are worn out.

USED TO (meaning ACCUSTOMED TO)

(1) "To be accustomed to" = "*Être habitué à* + noun" or "*Être habitué à* + infinitive."
     E.g.: *Je suis habitué à la chaleur.*
          I am used to the heat.

          Elle est habituée à se coucher tôt.
          She is used to going to bed early.
(2) "To become accustomed to" = "*S'habituer à*" or "*Se faire à.*"
     E.g.: *Je m'habitue à travailler la nuit.*
          I am getting used to working at night.
See *SE FAIRE À*

USED TO (meaning HABITUAL ACTION)

Habitual or repeated actions in the past are conveyed by the imperfect.
E.g.: *Je mangeais beaucoup.*
     I used to eat a lot.

     Ils allaient à la plage tous les jours.
     They used to go to the beach every day.
See **IMPERFECT TENSE**

VAINCRE

(To defeat, to vanquish)
PRÉS.: *vaincs, vaincs, vainc, vainqu-ons, -ez, -ent.*
IMPARF.: *vainqu-ais, -ais, -ait, -ions, -iez, -aient.*
PASSÉ SIMPLE: *vainqu-is, -is, -it, -îmes, -îtes, -irent.*
FUT.: *vaincr-ai, -as, -a, -ons, -ez, -ont.*
CONDIT.: *vaincr-ais, -ais, -ait, -ions, -iez, -aient.*
IMPÉR.: *vaincs, vainquons, vainquez.*
SUBJ. PRÉS.: *vainqu-e, -es, -e, -ions, -iez, -ent.*
SUBJ. IMPARF.: *vainqu-isse, -isses, -ît, -issions, -issiez, -issent.*
P. PRÉS.: *vainquant.*
P. PASSÉ: *vaincu(e).*

VALOIR

(To be worth)

PRÉS.: *vaux, vaux, vaut, valons, valez, valent.*
IMPARF.: *val-ais, -ais, -ait, -ions, -iez, -aient.*
PASSÉ SIMPLE: *val-us, -us, -ut, -ûmes, -ûtes, -urent.*
FUT.: *vaudr-ai, -as, -a, -ons, -ez, ont.*
CONDIT.: *vaudr-ais, -ais, -ait, -ions, -iez, -aient.*
IMPÉR.: *vaux, valons, valez,*
SUBJ. PRÉS.: *vaille, vailles, vaille, valions, valiez, vaillent.*
SUBJ. IMPARF.: *val-usse, -usses, -ût, -ussions, -ussiez, -ussent.*
P. PRÉS.: *valant.*
P. PASSÉ.: *valu(e).*
NOTES:
(1) Used impersonally, "*Valoir mieux* + infinitive" = "It is better to + verb."
    E.g.: *Il vaut mieux rester au lit quand on est malade.*
        It is better to stay in bed when one is sick.
(2) Used impersonally, "*Valoir mieux que* + subjunctive" = "It is better that + clause."
    E.g.: *Il vaut mieux que vous restiez ici.*
        It is better that you (should) stay here.

VALOIR LA PEINE (DE)

(Idiomatic expression) = "To be worthwhile."
E.g.: *Ça ne vaut pas la peine de lire ce livre.*
    It is not worthwhile reading this book.

VENDRE

(To sell)
Conjugated like **RENDRE**

VENIR

(To come)
(Conjugated with *être*)

PRÉS.: *viens, viens, vient, venons, venez, viennent.*
IMPARF.: *ven-ais, -ais, -ait, -ions, -iez, -aient.*
PASSÉ SIMPLE: *vins, vins, vint, vînmes, vîntes, vinrent.*
FUT.: *viendr-ai, -as, -a, -ons, -ez, -ont.*
CONDIT.: *viendr-ais, -ais, -ait, -ions, -iez, -aient.*
IMPÉR.: *viens, venons, venez.*
SUBJ. PRÉS.: *vienne, viennes, vienne, venions, veniez, viennent.*
SUBJ. IMPARF.: *vinsse, vinsses, vînt, vinssions, vinssiez, vinssent.*
P. PRÉS.: *venant.*
P. PASSÉ: *venu(e).*
See **VENIR DE** + **INFINITIVE**

VENIR DE + INFINITIVE

(Idiomatic construction) = "To have just + past participle." (This construction is called the "recent past").
E.g.: *Il vient d'arriver.*
    He has just arrived.
NOTE:
In a past context, this construction will always be in the imperfect because it describes a state of affairs, not an action.
E.g.: *Nous venions d'arriver quand le téléphone a sonné.*
    We had just arrived when the telephone rang.
See **JUST** and **RECENT PAST**

VERB

A verb *(un verbe)* is a word that expresses an action, a state of being, a transition from one state of being to another, or a link between the subject and the predicate.

E.g.: *Il parle.*   *Tu as un livre.*
     He speaks.   You have a book.

     Elle grandit.   *Hommes et femmes sont mortels.*
     She is growing.   Men and women are mortal.

VERBS + À + INFINITIVE
See **VERBS + PREPOSITION + INFINITIVE**

VERBS, AUXILIARY
See **AUXILIARY VERBS**

VERBS CONJUGATED WITH *"ÊTRE"*
See **VERBS, INTRANSITIVE**

VERBS + *DE* + INFINITIVE
See **VERBS + PREPOSITION + INFINITIVE**

VERBS FOLLOWED BY THE SUBJUNCTIVE
See **SUBJUNCTIVE MOOD**

VERBS, HELPING
See **AUXILIARY VERBS**

VERBS, IMPERSONAL

(Les verbes impersonnels) These are used only in the third person singular, with the subject pronoun *Il*, meaning "It."

E.g.: *Il pleut.*   *Il faut manger.*
     It is raining.   It is necessary to eat.

     Il fait froit.   *Il s'agit de votre salaire.*
     It is cold.   It's about your salary.

NOTE:
Many verbs can be used impersonally.

E.g.: *Il y a un livre* (or *des livres) sur la table.*
     There is a book (or books) on the table.

     Il est bon de se reposer.
     It is a good idea to rest.

     Il manque une page.
     There is a page missing.

     Il arrive des accidents.
     Accidents happen.

VERBS, INTRANSITIVE

(Les verbes intransitifs) These verbs do not (and cannot) take a direct object.

E.g.: *Je viens.*   *Elle arrive.*
     I am coming.   She arrives.

     Tu entres.   *Nous sommes tombés.*
     You enter.   We fell down.

NOTE:
Intransitive verbs are conjugated with *Être.*
See **"DR. & MRS. VANDERTRAMP" VERBS**

NOTE:
Some verbs are transitive in English but not in French, and vice versa:
(1) TRANSITIVE ENGLISH VERBS THAT ARE INTRANSITIVE IN FRENCH:
　　"To enter" = *Entrer <u>dans</u>.*
　　E.g.: *J'entre dans la maison.*
　　　　I enter the house.
　　"To leave" = *Partir <u>de</u>.*
　　E.g.: *Nous partons de la ville.*
　　　　We leave the city.
(2) TRANSITIVE FRENCH VERBS THAT ARE INTRANSITIVE IN ENGLISH:
　　Regarder = "To look <u>at</u>, to watch."
　　E.g.: *Elle regarde la photo.*
　　　　She is looking at the photograph.
　　Chercher = "To look <u>for</u>."
　　E.g.: *Il cherche sa clé.*
　　　　He is looking for his key.

VERBS OF PERCEPTION

Verbs of perception *(Écouter, Entendre, Regarder, Sentir, Voir)*, when followed by a verb, take the infinitive.
E.g.: *Nous entendons Caroline <u>chanter</u>.*　　*Il a senti le lion <u>approcher</u>.*
　　We hear Caroline sing.　　　　　　　　He smelled the lion approaching.
NOTE:
If the direct object is a personal pronoun, this pronoun comes before the verb of perception.
E.g.: *Nous l'écoutons chanter.*　　*Il l'a senti approcher.*
　　We listen to him (her) singing.　　He smelled it approaching.
See **PAST PARTICIPLES, AGREEMENT OF (WITH VERBS OF PERCEPTION)**

VERBS + PREPOSITION + INFINITIVE

These are the most common verbs that take *à, de,* or no preposition before an infinitive:

S'accoutumer à	*Défendre (à qqn) de*	*S'habituer à*
Achever de	*Demander (à qqn) de*	*Hésiter à*
Aider (qqn) à	*Se dépêcher de*	*Interdire (à qqn) de*
Aimer, aimer à, aimer mieux	*Désirer*	*S'intéresser à*
Aller	*Détester*	*Inviter (qqn) à*
S'amuser à	*Devoir*	*Jouer à*
Apprendre (à qqn) à	*Dire (à qqn) de*	*Jurer de*
S'arrêter de	*Écouter*	*Laisser*
Arriver à	*Empêcher (qqn) de*	*Manquer de*
Attendre de	*Encourager (qqn) à*	*Menacer de*
S'attendre à	*S'engager à*	*Mériter de*
Avertir (qqn) de	*S'ennuyer à*	*Se souvenir de*
Avoir à	*Enseigner (à qqn) à*	*Se mettre à*
Blâmer (qqn) de	*Entendre*	*Négliger de*
Cesser de	*S'entraîner à*	*Obliger (qqn) à*
Chercher à	*Entreprendre de*	*Offrir de*
Choisir de	*Essayer de*	*Ordonner (à qqn) de*
Commander (à qqn) de	*Espérer*	*Oser*
Commencer à	*S'étonner de*	*Oublier de*
Compter	*Éviter de*	*Pardonner (à qqn) de*
Conseiller (à qqn) de	*S'excuser de*	*Paraître*
Consentir à	*Faire*	*Parvenir à*
Consister à	*Falloir*	*Passer (du temps) à*
Continuer à	*Féliciter (qqn) de*	*Penser à*
Décider de	*Finir de*	*Permettre (à qqn) de*
Se décider à	*Se garder de*	*Persuader (qqn) de*

Se plaindre de	*Regarder*	*Souffrir de*
Se plaire à	*Regretter de*	*Supplier (qqn) de*
Préférer	*Remercier (qqn) de*	*Supporter de*
Se préparer à	*Renoncer à*	*Tâcher de*
Prier (qqn) de	*Reprocher (à qqn) de*	*Tenir à*
Promettre (à qqn) de	*Résoudre de*	*Tenter de*
Proposer de	*Se résoudre à*	*Valoir mieux*
Pouvoir	*Réussir à*	*Venir, venir de*
Punir (qqn) de	*Risquer de*	*Voir*
Rappeler (à qqn) de	*Savoir*	*Vouloir*
Refuser de	*Sembler*	

VERBS, RECIPROCAL

(Les verbes réciproques) These are always in a plural form and indicate that the action is performed reciprocally (i.e., to, for, at, or on each other). They are accompanied by the reciprocal pronouns (which are the same as the plural forms of the reflexive pronouns *nous vous, se*). For practical purposes, reciprocal verbs are indistinguishable from reflexive verbs.

E.g.: *Nous nous écrivons.*   *Elles se sont acheté des cadeaux.*
    We write to each other.   They bought each other presents.

See **VERBS, REFLEXIVE**

VERBS, REFLEXIVE

(Les verbes réfléchis) these are accompanied by the reflexive pronouns *me, te, se, nous, vous, se,* which refer to the subject of the verb. They can have various meanings:

(1) A reflexive meaning.
    E.g.: *Je me regarde dans le miroir.*
        I look at myself in the mirror.
(2) A reciprocal meaning.
    E.g.: *Nous nous regardons par la fenêtre.*
        We look at each other through the window.

See **VERBS, RECIPROCAL**

(3) A meaning with no reflexive or reciprocal concept.
    E.g.: *Elle se tait.*
        She keeps silent.
(4) A passive meaning.
    E.g.: *Le français se parle au Canada.*
        French is spoken in Canada.

NOTE:
The reflexive pronoun must be declined even when the verb is in the infinitive or the present participle.

E.g.: *Nous avons décidé de nous taire.*   *Vous êtes tombé en vous asseyant.*
    We decided to keep quiet.   You fell while sitting down.

SOME COMMON REFLEXIVE VERBS THAT ARE NOT REFLEXIVE IN ENGLISH:
S'asseoir = To sit down
Se coucher = To go to bed, to lie down
Se douter de = To suspect
Se laver = To wash (oneself)
Se lever = To get up, to stand up
Se moquer de = To make fun of
Se raser = To shave
Se sentir = To feel
Se taire = To remain silent
S'écrier = To exclaim
S'en aller = To go away
S'endormir = To fall asleep
S'enfuir = To flee
S'évanouir = To faint

CONJUGATION OF A REFLEXIVE VERB: *Se tromper.*
INDICATIF:
PRÉS.: *me trompe, te trompes, se trompe, nous trompons, vous trompez, se trompent.*
IMPARF.: *me trompais, te trompais, se trompait, nous trompions, vous trompiez, se trompaient.*
PASSÉ SIMPLE: *me trompai, te trompas, se trompa, nous trompâmes, vous trompâtes, se trompèrent.*
FUT.: *me tromperai, te tromperas, se trompera, nous tromperons, vous tromperez, se tromperont.*
PASSÉ COMPOSÉ: *me suis trompé(e), t'es trompé(e), s'est trompé(e), nous sommes trompé(e)s, vous êtes trompé(e)s, se sont trompé(e)s.*
PLUS-QUE-PARF.: *m'étais trompé(e), t'étais trompé(e), s'était trompé(e), nous étions trompé(e)s, vous étiez trompé(e)s, s'étaient trompé(e)s.*
PASSÉ ANT.: *me fus trompé(e), te fus trompé(e), se fut trompé(e), nous fûmes trompé(e)s, vous fûtes trompé(e)s, se furent trompé(e)s.*
FUT. ANT.: *me serai trompé(e), te seras trompé(e), se sera trompé(e), nous serons trompé(e)s, vous serez trompé(e)s, se seront trompé(e)s.*
CONDITIONNEL:
PRÉS.: *me tromperais, te tromperais, se tromperait, nous tromperions, vous tromperiez, se tromperaient.*
PASSÉ: *me serais trompé(e), te serais trompé(e), se serait trompé(e), nous serions trompé(e)s, vous seriez trompé(e)s, se seraient trompé(e)s.*
IMPÉRATIF: trompe-toi, trompons-nous, trompez-vous.
SUBJONCTIF:
PRÉS.: *me trompe, te trompes, se trompe, nous trompions, vous trompiez, se trompent.*
IMPARF.: *me trompasse, te trompasse, se trompât, nous trompassions, vous trompassiez, se trompassent.*
PASSÉ: *me sois trompé(e), te sois trompé(e), se soit trompé(e), nous soyons trompé(e)(s), vous soyez trompeé(e)(s), se soient tromp(é)(s).*
PLUS-QUE-PARF.: *me fusse trompé(e), te fusses trompé(e), se fût trompé(e), nous fussions trompé(e)(s), vous fussiez trompé(e)(s), se fussent trompé(e)(s).*
INFINITIF:
PRÉS.: *se tromper.*
PASSÉ: *s'être trompé(e)(s).*
PARTICIPE:
PRÉS.: *se trompant.*
PASSÉ: *trompé; s'étant trompé(e)(s).*

VERBS, TRANSITIVE

(Les verbes transitifs) These verbs can take a direct object. (Most verbs are of this type.)
E.g.: *Je mange le pain.*   *Vous avez vu le film.*
     I eat the bread.   You saw the film.
NOTE:
Some verbs are transitive in English but not in French, and vice versa:
(1) TRANSITIVE ENGLISH VERBS THAT ARE INTRANSITIVE IN FRENCH:
     "To enter" = *Entrer <u>dans</u>.*
     E.g.: *J'entre dans la maison.*
         I enter the house.
     "To leave" = *Partir <u>de</u>.*
     E.g.: *Nous partons de la ville.*
         We leave the city.
(2) TRANSITIVE FRENCH VERBS THAT ARE INTRANSITIVE IN ENGLISH:
     Regarder = "To look <u>at</u>, to watch."
     E.g.: *Elle regarde la photo.*
         She is looking at the photograph.
     Chercher = "To look <u>for</u>."
     E.g.: *Il cherche sa clé.*
         He is looking for his key.

VERS

(Preposition) = "Toward, about, around."
(1) Indicating direction:
    E.g.: *L'avion volait vers Paris quand l'accident a eu lieu.*
        The plane was flying toward Paris when the accident occurred.
(2) Indicating approximation:
    E.g.: *Il viendra vers midi.*
        He will come around noon.

VERY

(Adverb) = *Très, fort.*
E.g.: *Ceci est fort (très) compliqué.*
    This is very complicated.

VERY MUCH

(Adverb) = *Beaucoup.*
NOTE:
This word never takes a modifier. (Do not say *"Très beaucoup"*!)
E.g.: *Je l'aime beaucoup.*
    I love him (her) very much.

VEUILLEZ

(Imperative form of *Vouloir*, second person plural) This form is primarily used in polite expressions meaning "Please be so kind as to," "Would you kindly."
E.g.: *Veuillez attendre un instant.*
    (Would you) kindly wait a moment.
See **REQUESTS**

VIEUX, VIEIL, VIEILLE

(Adjective) *Vieux* changes to *Vieil* before a masculine singular noun beginning with a vowel or an unaspirated *h*.
E.g.: *Un vieux chien.*
    An old dog.
BUT: *Un vieil animal.*   *Un vieil homme.*
    An old animal.   An old man.
The feminine form of *Vieux* is *Vieille.*
E.g.: *Une vieille femme.*
    An old woman.

to VISIT

(1) "To visit a place (city, country, museum, etc.)" = "*Visiter* + direct object."
    E.g.: *Nous avons visité la Chine et le Japon.*
        We visited China and Japan.
(2) "To visit a person" = "*Rendre visite à* + indirect object."
    E.g.: *J'ai rendu visite à mes grands-parents.*
        I visited my grandparents.
        Je leur ai rendu visite.
        I visited them.

VISITER

See **to VISIT**

VIVRE

(To live)
PRÉS.: *vis, vis, vit, vivons, vivez, vivent.*
IMPARF.: *viv-ais, -ais, -ait, -ions, -iez, -aient.*
PASSÉ SIMPLE: *véc-us, véc-us, -ut, -ûmes, -ûtes, -urent.*
FUT.: *vivr-ai, -as, -a, -ons, -ez, -ont.*
CONDIT.: *vivr-ais, -ais, -ait, -ions, -iez, -aient.*
IMPÉR.: *vis, vivons, vivez.*
SUBJ. PRÉS.: *viv-e, -es, -e, -ions, -iez, -ent.*
SUBJ. IMPARF.: *véc-usse, -usses, -ût, -ussions, -ussiez, -ussent.*
P. PRÉS.: *vivant.*
P. PASSÉ: *vécu(e).*

VIVRE vs. DEMEURER, HABITER

See **DEMEURER vs. HABITER, VIVRE**

VOICI, VOILÀ

(Prepositions) *Voici* (= "Here is") and *Voilà* (= "There is") are expressions that point or designate. They place the stress on the "here" and "there."
E.g.: *Voici le musée et voilà le théâtre.*
    Here is the museum, and there is the theater.

    Où est le journal? Le voici.
    Where is the newspaper? Here it is.
NOTE:
Do not confuse *Voilà* with *Il y a. Il y a* is used when giving an explanation or stating the presence or existence of something.
E.g.: *Il y a une maison sur la colline.*
    There is a house on the hill.
See **IL Y A**

VOIR

(To see)
PRÉS.: *vois, vois, voit, voyons, voyez, voient.*
IMPARF.: *voy-ais, -ais, -ait, -ions, -iez, -aient.*
PASSÉ SIMPLE: *vis, vis, vit, vîmes, vîtes, virent.*
FUT.: *verr-ai, -as, -a, -ons, -ez, -ont.*
CONDIT.: *verr-ais, -ais, -ait, -ions, -iez, -aient.*
IMPÉR.: *vois, voyons, voyez.*
SUBJ. PRÉS.: *voie, voies, voie, voyions, voyiez, voient.*
SUBJ. IMPARF.: *visse, visses, vît, vissions, vissiez, vissent.*
P. PRÉS.: *voyant.*
P. PASSÉ: *vu(e).*

VOIR vs. REGARDER

(1) *Voir* = "To see."
    E.g.: *Je vois la tour Eiffel.*
        I see the Eiffel Tower.
(2) *Regarder* = "To look at, to watch" (a transitive verb that includes the preposition "At").
    E.g.: *Je regarde le paysage.*   *Elle regarde la télévision.*
        I look at the scenery.   She is watching television.

VOULOIR

(To want)
PRÉS.: *veux, veux, veut, voulons, voulez, veulent.*
IMPARF.: *voul-ais, -ais, -ait, -ions, -iez, -aient.*
PASSÉ SIMPLE: *voul-us, -us, -ut, -ûmes, -ûtes, -urent.*
FUT.: *voudr-ai, -as, -a, -ons, -ez, -ont.*
CONDIT.: *voudr-ais, -ais, -ait, -ions, -iez, -aient.*
IMPÉR.: *veuille, veuillons, veuillez.*
SUBJ. PRÉS.: *veuille, veuilles, veuille, voulions, vouliez, veuillent.*
SUBJ. IMPARF.: *voul-usse, -usses, -ût, -ussions, -ussiez, -ussent.*
P. PRÉS.: *voulant.*
P. PASSÉ: *voulu(e).*

VOUS vs. TU

See **TU vs. VOUS**

VOWEL

Vowels *(les voyelles)* are the letters *a, e, i, o. u,* and *y.* They represent sounds produced without any interference in the flow of breath during speech.

W

to WAIT FOR

(Transitive verb)
(1) "*Attendre* + direct object."
    E.g.: *J'attends Bernadette.*
          I am waiting for Bernadette.
NOTE:
The preposition "For" is included in the verb.
(2) "*Attendre que* + subjunctive."
    E.g.: *J'attends que Bernard vienne ici.*
          I am waiting for Bernard to come here.
See **SUBJUNCTIVE MOOD**

to WALK TO

"To walk" = *Marcher.*
NOTE:
"To walk (as opposed to ride or drive)" = *Aller à pied.*
E.g.: *Elle va au bureau à pied.*
     She walks to the office.
See **TRANSPORTATION, MEANS OF**
See also **to DRIVE TO** and **to FLY TO**

to WANT TO + VERB

(1) If both verbs have the same subject: "*Vouloir* + infinitive."
    E.g.: *Elle veut aller à Paris.*
          She wants to go to Paris.
(2) If the two verbs have different subjects: "*Vouloir que* + subjunctive."
    E.g.: *Elle veut que j'aille à Paris.*
          She wants me to go to Paris.
See **SUBJUNCTIVE MOOD**
See also **DESIRE**

WHAT

(1) (Interrogative adjective) = *Quel, quelle, quels, quelles.*
See **ADJECTIVES, INTERROGATIVE**

(2) (Interrogative pronoun) = (subject) *Qu'est-ce qui,* (object) *Qu'est-ce que,* (object of preposition) *Quoi.*
See **PRONOUNS, INTERROGATIVE**

(3) (Relative pronoun) Meaning "That which" = (subject) *Ce qui,* (object) *Ce que.*
See **PRONOUNS, RELATIVE**

(4) (Exclamatory pronoun) = *Quel, quelle, quels, quelles.*
See **WHAT (A) . . . !**

WHAT (A) . . . !

(Exclamation) Use the exclamatory (or interrogative) adjectives *Quel(s), quelle(s)* with no article.
E.g.: *Quelle idée formidable!*
      What a wonderful idea!

      Quelles belles journées nous venons de passer!
      What beautiful days we have just had!
See **EXCLAMATIONS**

WHAT IS . . .?

To ask for a definition or explanation, use:

(1) *Qu'est-ce que c'est?*
    E.g.: *Un laser! Qu'est-ce que c'est?*
          A laser! What is that?

(2) "*Qu'est-ce que c'est que* + noun or pronoun."
    E.g.? *Qu'est-ce que c'est qu'un laser?*
          What is a laser?
See *QU'EST-CE QUE C'EST?*

WHATEVER

(1) (Pronoun)
See *QUOI QUE* + **SUBJUNCTIVE**

(2) "Whatever + clause" = "*Quel(s), quelle(s) que* + subjunctive."
    E.g.: *Quelle que soit votre décision.*
          Whatever your decision may be.
See *QUEL(S) QUE, QUELLE(S) QUE* and **SUBJUNCTIVE MOOD**

(3) "Whatever + noun" = "*Quelque* + noun + *que* + subjunctive."
    E.g.: *Quelque excuse que vous ayez.*
          Whatever excuse you may have.
See *QUELQUE . . . QUE* and **SUBJUNCTIVE MOOD**

WHEN

(Conjunction) = *Quand* or *Lorsque.*
E.g.: *Quand (Lorsque) je voyage je prends beaucoup de photos.*
      When I travel, I take a lot of pictures.
See *APRÈS* vs. *APRÈS QUE*
See also *QUAND,* **TENSES WITH**

WHENEVER

(Conjunction)

(1) Meaning "Every time that" = *Chaque fois que.*
    E.g.: *Chaque fois que je parle français, je fais des fautes.*
          Whenever I speak French, I make mistakes.

(2) Meaning "At whatever time, no matter when" = *Peu importe quand.*
   E.g.: *Peu importe quand je la rencontre, elle est toujours seule.*
      Whenever I meet her, she is always alone.

WHEREAS

See *TANDIS QUE*

WHEREVER

(Conjunction)
(1) Meaning "No matter where" = "*Où que* + subjunctive."
   E.g.: *Où que vous soyez, écrivez-moi.*
      Wherever you may be, write to me.
(2) Meaning "Anywhere" = "*Où vous voulez.*"
   E.g.: *Asseyez-vous où vous voulez.*
      Sit wherever you like.
See **SUBJUNCTIVE MOOD**

WHETHER

See *SI*

WHICH

(1) (Interrogative adjective) = *Quel, quelle, quels, quelles.*
See **ADJECTIVES, INTERROGATIVE**
(2) (Interrogative pronoun) = *Lequel, laquelle, lesquels, lesquelles.*
See **PRONOUNS, INTERROGATIVE**
(3) Meaning "The one(s)" = *Celui, celle, ceux, celles.*
See **PRONOUNS, DEMONSTRATIVE**
(4) (Relative pronoun) = *Qui, que* (after preposition: *lequel, laquelle, lesquels, lesquelles*).
See **PRONOUNS, RELATIVE**

WHICH ONE, WHICH ONES

(Interrogative pronoun) = *Lequel, laquelle, lesquels, lesquelles.*
See **PRONOUNS, INTERROGATIVE**

WHICHEVER

(Adjective) = "*Quel que, quelle que, quels que, quelles que* + subjunctive."
E.g.: *Quelle que soit la robe que tu choisiras, je t'en ferai cadeau.*
   Whichever dress you choose, I shall give it to you as a present.
See *QUEL(S) . . . QUE, QUELLE(S) . . . QUE* and **SUBJUNCTIVE MOOD**

WHILE + VERB (-ING)

(1) Meaning "During the time that" = "*Pendant que* + indicative."
   E.g.: *Le téléphone a sonné pendant que vous dormiez.*
      The telephone rang while you were sleeping.
(2) Meaning "Whereas, by contrast" = "*Tandis que* + indicative."
   E.g.: *Nous allons en Italie, tandis que vous allez en Espagne.*
      We are going to Italy, while (whereas) you are going to Spain.
See *TANDIS QUE*
(3) Meaning "At the same time as" = "*En* + present participle."
   E.g.: *Il étudie en regardant la télévision.*
      He studies while watching television.
See **GERUND**

WHO, WHOM

(1) (Interrogative pronouns) = (subject) *(Qui est-ce) qui;* (object) *(Qui est-ce) que;* (after a preposition) *Qui.*
See PRONOUNS, INTERROGATIVE
(2) (Relative pronouns) – *Qui.*
See PRONOUNS, RELATIVE

WHOEVER, WHOMEVER

See *QUICONQUE*
See also *QUI QUE* + SUBJUNCTIVE

WHOSE

(1) (Relative pronoun) = *Dont.*
  E.g.: *La dame dont j'ai fait la connaissance est ingénieur.*
    The lady whose acquaintance I made is an engineer.
See DONT and PRONOUNS, RELATIVE
(2) (Interrogative pronoun) = *À qui?*
  E.g.: *À qui est ce livre?*
    Whose book is this?
See PRONOUNS, INTERROGATIVE

WILL and WOULD

(1) When "Will" and "Would" express the future and the conditional, respectively, they are translated by those tenses in French.
  E.g.: *Il ira chez lui la semaine prochaine.*   *Il irait chez lui s'il avait le temps.*
    He will go home next week.   He would go home if he had the time.
(2) When "Will" expresses will, it must be translated by a verb expressing this will or desire.
  E.g.: He just <u>will</u> not move
    Il refuse de bouger or *Il ne veut pas bouger.*
  And in the past:
  E.g.: He just <u>would</u> not go out
    Il a refusé de sortir or *Il n'a pas voulu sortir.*
NOTE:
In English, "Would" can mean a habitual or repeated action. It must be translated by the imperfect.
E.g.: When I was little, I would eat ice cream at every meal.
  Quand j'étais petit, je mangeais de la glace à chaque repas.
See FUTURE TENSE
See also CONDITIONAL MOOD and IMPERFECT TENSE

WITH

(Preposition) = *Avec.*
E.g.: *Je travaille avec mon frère.*
  I work with my brother.

WITHOUT

See **to DO WITHOUT**

WITHOUT + VERB (-ING)

(1) (Preposition) = "*Sans* + infinitive" if the two verbs have the same subject.
  E.g.: *Elle est partie sans dire au revoir.*
    She left without saying goodbye.

(2) (Conjunction) = "*Sans que* + subjunctive" if the subjects of the two clauses are different.

E.g.: *Elle est partie sans que je la voie.*

She left without my seeing her.

See **SANS vs. SANS QUE**

See also **SUBJUNCTIVE MOOD**

to WONDER

(Reflexive verb with idiomatic meaning) = *Se demander.*

E.g.: *Je me demande quand elle arrivera.*

I wonder when she will arrive.

See **SE DEMANDER**

WORD ORDER IN A SENTENCE

(1) In an affirmative sentence:

Subject - verb - object (or predicate).

E.g.: *Je mange la crème.*   *Elle est délicieuse.*

I eat the cream.   It is delicious.

(2) In interrogative sentences that do not begin with *Est-ce que*: Invert the subject:

Verb - subject - object (or predicate).

E.g.: *Mange-t-elle de la crème?*   *Est-elle délicieuse?*

Does she eat some cream?   Is it delicious?

NOTE:

When the subject is a noun, it stays before the verb, but the corresponding subject pronoun is added after the verb and hyphenated to it.

E.g.: *La crème est-elle délicieuse?*

Is the cream delicious?

For exceptions, see **INVERSION**

WORD ORDER IN A QUESTION

See **QUESTIONS, WORD ORDER IN**

to WORRY (ABOUT)

(1) Meaning "to be worried" = *S'inquiéter (de).*

E.g.: *Je m'inquiète quand tu rentres tard.*

I worry when you come home late.

Je m'inquiète de la situation politique.

I worry about the political situation.

(2) Meaning "To cause worry" = "*Inquiéter* + direct object."

E.g.: *La situation politique m'inquiète.*

The political situation worries me.

WORTHWHILE

(Idiomatic construction) = "*Valoir la peine de* + infinitive."

E.g.: *Ça ne vaut pas la peine de voir cette pièce.*

It is not worthwhile seeing that play.

WOULD

(1) If "Would" expresses the conditional mood in English, use the equivalent present tense of the conditional mood in French.

E.g.: I would eat (if I were hungry).

Je mangerais (si j'avais faim).

See **SI CLAUSES**

(2) If "Would" has the meaning "Was willing," use the verb *Vouloir* in the appropriate past tense.

E.g.: He <u>would</u> not eat (although he was hungry).

Il ne voulait pas manger, bien qu'il eût faim.

(3) If "Would" indicates a polite request, use the conditional of *Vouloir*.

E.g.: Would you come here, please?

Voudriez-vous venir ici, s'il vous plaît?

See **REQUEST**

(4) If "Would" expresses a repeated past action, use the imperfect of the relevant verb in French.

E.g.: We would always go to the beach on Sundays.

Nous allions toujours à la plage le dimanche.

See **IMPERFECT TENSE**

WOULD HAVE

"Would have" expresses the past tense of the conditional mood in English. The French equivalent is therefore the past tense of the conditional mood.

E.g.: I would have eaten (if I had been hungry).

J'aurais mangé (si j'avais eu faim).

See **SI CLAUSES**

See also **CONDITIONAL MOOD**

WRONG

(1) (Adverb) Meaning "Bad, wicked" = *Mal.*

E.g.: *C'est mal de mentir.*

It is wrong to lie.

(2) (Adjective) Meaning "Incorrect, mistake" = *Faux, fausse.*

E.g.: *Votre réponse est tout à fait fausse.*

Your answer is completely wrong.

(3) (Idiomatic expression) "To be wrong" (referring to a person) = *Avoir tort.*

E.g.: *Tu as tort de ne pas m'écouter.*

You are wrong not to listen to me.

See **AVOIR TORT**

Y

Y

(1) The pronoun *y* replaces the preposition "*à* + noun (a thing or an idea, never a person)."

E.g.: *Nous répondons à la lettre. → Nous y répondons.*

We answer the letter. → We answer it.

(2) The adverb *y* replaces the prepositions "*à, dans,* or *en* + a place."

E.g.: *Elle est à Paris. → Elle y est.*

She is in Paris. → She is there.

Ils sont dans la classe. → Ils y sont.

They are in the classroom. → They are there.

Il voyage en Italie. → Il y voyage.

He is traveling in Italy. → He is traveling there.

Y COMPRIS

(Idiomatic expression) = "Including."

This expression is invariable and is placed before the noun.

E.g.: *Il gagne 20.000 francs, y compris les droits d'auteur.*

He earns 20,000 francs, author's royalties included.

YEAR

(1) *An* (masculine) is used to express the unit of time.

E.g.: *Il a passé trois ans en Afrique.*   *Elle a dix-neuf ans.*
He spent three years in Africa.   She is nineteen (years old).

(2) *Année* (feminine) is used to express duration or to stress the length of time.

E.g.: *Au Kenya il fait chaud pendant toute l'année.*
In Kenya it is hot all year round.

Les années de guerre ont été pénibles pour tout le monde.
The war years were difficult for everybody.

NOTE:

The number of the year may be expressed in two ways:

(1) By using *Mille* (or the alternate form *Mil*).

E.g.: *Mil (Mille) sept cent quatre-vingt-neuf.*
Seventeen (hundred) eighty-nine.

(2) By stating the number of hundreds.

E.g.: *Dix-neuf cent quatre-vingt-quatre.*
Nineteen (hundred) eighty-four.

REMEMBER that the word *cent* must be stated in French.

YEARS OLD

See **AGE**

YET

(1) (Adverb) = *Déjà.*

E.g.: *Avez-vous déjà vu ce film?*
Have you seen this movie yet?

(2) "Not yet" = *Pas encore.*

E.g.: *Je n'ai pas encore vu ce film.*
I haven't seen this movie yet.

See **NE . . . PAS ENCORE**

YOU

(1) There are two ways of addressing a person:

(a) The informal *Tu* (second person singular) is used to address people one's own age or younger and members of one's family.

E.g.: *Pierre, tu travailles trop.*
Peter, you work too much.

(b) The formal *Vous* (second person plural, but used as a singular) is used for people one does not know and people who are older.

E.g.: *Monsieur, vous travaillez trop.*
Sir, you work too much.

(2) The plural form, used to address several persons, is *Vous*. It is the same whether addressing several people formallly or informally.

E.g.: *Pierre et Marie, vous travaillez trop!*
Peter and Mary, you work too much.

See **TU vs. VOUS**

SUMMARY TABLES

DEMONSTRATIVE ADJECTIVES
(See page 12)

Masc. sing.:	*ce* (*cet* before a vowel or unaspirated *h*)
Fem. sing.:	*cette*
Masc. and fem. plur.:	*ces*

INTERROGATIVE ADJECTIVES
(See page 14)

Masc. sing.:	*quel*
Fem. sing.:	*quelle*
Masc. plur.:	*quels*
Fem. plur.:	*quelles*

POSSESSIVE ADJECTIVES
(See page 16)

Referring to a masculine singular noun:	*mon*	*ton*	*son*	*notre*	*votre*	*leur*
Referring to a feminine singular noun:	*ma*	*ta*	*sa*	*notre*	*votre*	*leur*
Referring to a masculine or feminine plural noun:	*mes*	*tes*	*ses*	*nos*	*vos*	*leur*

PERSONAL PRONOUNS
(See page 178)

Subject:	*je*	*te*	*il, elle, on*	*nous*	*vous*	*ils, elles*
Reflexive:	*me*	*te*	*se*	*nous*	*vous*	*se*
Direct object:	*me (moi)*	*te (toi)*	*le, la*	*nous*	*vous*	*les*
Indirect object:	*me*	*te*	*lui, se*	*nous*	*vous*	*leur*
Object of preposition:	*moi*	*toi*	*lui, elle, soi*	*nous*	*vous*	*eux, elles*
Emphatic:	*moi*	*toi*	*lui, elle, soi*	*nous*	*vous*	*eux, elles*

DEMONSTRATIVE PRONOUNS
(See page 174)

	SINGULAR			PLURAL	
	Masc.	Fem.	Neut.	Masc.	Fem.
Simple forms:	celui	celle	ce	ceux	celles
Compound forms:	celui-ci	celle-ci	ceci	ceux-ci	celles
	celui-là	celle-là	cela (ça)	ceux-là	celles-là

INTERROGATIVE PRONOUNS
(See page 177)

	PERSONS	THINGS
Subject:	qui	qu'est-ce qui
	qui est-ce qui	
Direct object:	qui	que
	qui est-ce que	qu'est-ce que
Object of preposition:	qui	quoi
For choosing among options:	lequel, laquelle, lesquels, lesquelles	

POSSESSIVE PRONOUNS
(See page 178)

If the noun belongs to ONE OWNER:			
Masc. sing. noun:	le mien	le tien	le sien
Masc. plur. nouns:	les miens	les tiens	les siens
Fem. sing. noun:	la mienne	la tienne	la sienne
Fem. plur. nouns:	les miennes	les tiennes	les siennes

If the noun belongs to SEVERAL OWNERS:			
Masc. sing. noun:	le nôtre	le vôtre	le leur
Masc. or fem. plur. nouns:	les nôtres	les vôtres	les leurs
Fem. sing. noun:	la nôtre	la vôtre	la leur
Masc. or fem. plur. nouns:	les nôtres	les vôtres	les leurs

RELATIVE PRONOUNS
(See page 179)

SIMPLE FORMS:	PERSONS	THINGS
Subject:	*qui*	*qui*
Direct object:	*que (qu')*	*que (qu')*
Object of preposition:	*qui*	*quoi*

COMPOUND FORMS:

	SINGULAR		PLURAL	
	Masc.	**Fem.**	**Masc.**	**Fem.**
	lequel	*laquelle*	*lesquels*	*lesquelles*
With *de*	*duquel*	*de laquelle*	*desquels*	*desquelles*
With *à*	*auquel*	*à laquelle*	*auxquels*	*auxquelles*

SPECIAL FORM:

dont (= de qui, de quoi, duquel, de laquelle, desquels, desquelles)

ORDER OF DOUBLE OBJECT PRONOUNS
(See page 175)

BEFORE THE VERB (NORMAL POSITION):

me				
te	*le*	*lui*		
se	*la*	*leur*	*y*	*en*
nous	*les*			
vous				

AFTER THE VERB (WITH AN AFFIRMATIVE COMMAND):

	moi (m')		
le	*toi (t')*		
la	*lui*	*y*	*en*
les	*nous*		
	vous		
	leur		

CONJUNCTIONS
(See page 57)

+ SUBJUNCTIVE	+ INDICATIVE
à condition que	*après que*
à moins que	*aussitôt que*
afin que	*dès que*
avant que	*parce que*
bien que	*pendant que*
de crainte que	*peut-être que*
de peur que	*puisque*
de sorte que	*quand*
en attendant que	*tandis que*
jusqu'à ce que	
malgré que	
pour que	
pourvu que	
quoique	
sans que	

IMPERSONAL EXPRESSIONS
(See page 207)

+ SUBJUNCTIVE	+ INDICATIVE
Il est bon que	*Il est certain que*
Il est désirable que	*Il est clair que*
Il est (c'est) dommage que	*Il est évident que*
Il est important que	*Il est probable que*
Il est impossible que	*Il est sûr que*
Il est indispensable que	*Il est vrai que*
Il est juste que	*Il n'y a pas de doute que*
Il est nécessaire que	*Il paraît que*
Il est peu probable que	
Il est possible que	
Il est préférable que	
Il est regrettable que	
Il est temps que	
Il est urgent que	
Il est utile que	
Il faut que	
Il se peut que	
Il vaut mieux que	

PREPOSITIONS WITH PLACE NAMES
(See page 98)

To express "to" or "in":		Examples
en	+ *feminine* countries, continents, provinces	*en Allemagne* *en Asie* *en Normandie*
au(x)	+ *masculine* countries, provinces	*au Portugal* *au Languedoc* *aux États-Unis*
à	+ cities	*à Lyon*
To express "from" or "of":		**Examples**
de	+ *feminine* countries, continents, provinces	*de Chine* *d'Afrique* *de Normandie*
du, des	+ *masculine* countries	*du Canada* *des Pays-Bas*
de	+ cities	*de Paris*

THE MOST COMMON VERBS THAT TAKE À, DE, OR
NO PREPOSITION + INFINITIVE
(See page 171)

S'accoutumer à	S'ennuyer à	Passer (du temps) à
Achever de	Enseigner (à qqn) à	Penser à
Aider (qqn) à	Entendre	Permettre (à qqn) de
Aimer, aimer à, aimer mieux	S'entraîner à	Persuader (qqn) de
Aller	Entreprendre de	Se plaindre de
S'amuser à	Essayer de	Se plaire à
Apprendre (à qqn) à	Espérer	Préférer
S'arrêter de	S'étonner de	Se préparer à
Arriver à	Éviter de	Prier (qqn) de
Attendre de	S'excuser de	Promettre (à qqn) de
S'attendre à	Faire	Proposer de
Avertir (qqn) de	Falloir	Pouvoir
Avoir à	Féliciter (qqn) de	Punir (qqn) de
Blâmer (qqn) de	Finir de	Rappeler (à qqn) de
Cesser de	Se garder de	Refuser de
Chercher à	S'habituer à	Regarder
Choisir de	Hésiter à	Regretter de
Commander (à qqn) de	Interdire (à qqn) de	Remercier (qqn) de
Commencer à	S'intéresser à	Renoncer à
Compter	Inviter (qqn) à	Reprocher (à qqn) de
Conseiller (à qqn) de	Jouer à	Résoudre de
Consentir à	Jurer de	Se résoudre à
Consister à	Laisser	Réussir à
Continuer à	Manquer de	Risquer de
Décider de	Menacer de	Savoir
Se décider à	Mériter de	Sembler
Défendre (à qqn) de	Se souvenir de	Souffrir de
Demander (à qqn) de	Se mettre à	Supplier (qqn) de
Se dépêcher de	Négliger de	Supporter de
Désirer	Obliger (qqn) à	Tâcher de
Détester	Offrir de	Tenir à
Devoir	Ordonner (à qqn) de	Tenter de
Dire (à qqn) de	Oser	Valoir mieux
Écouter	Oublier de	Venir, venir de
Empêcher (qqn) de	Pardonner (à qqn) de	Voir
Encourager (qqn) à	Paraître	Vouloir
S'engager à	Parvenir à	

USEFUL CLASSROOM EXPRESSIONS

''How do you spell . . . ?''	= Comment épelle-t-on . . . ?
''How do you say . . . ?	= Comment dit-on . . . ?
''I don't understand.''	= Je ne comprends pas.
''Would you please explain?''	= Pouvez-vous expliquer, s'il vous plaît?
''Would you please repeat?''	= Pouvez-vous répéter, s'il vous plaît?
''Would you please translate?''	= Pouvez-vous traduire, s'il vous plaît?
''What does . . . mean?''	= Que veut dire . . . ?
''What is the word for . . . ?''	= Comment dit-on . . . ?